Learning Zulu

translation
TRANSNATION
SERIES EDITOR **EMILY APTER**

A list of titles in the series appears at the back of the book.

Learning Zulu

A SECRET HISTORY OF LANGUAGE IN SOUTH AFRICA

Mark Sanders

PRINCETON UNIVERSITY PRESS

PRINCETON AND OXFORD

Copyright © 2016 by Princeton University Press
Published by Princeton University Press, 41 William Street, Princeton, New Jersey 08540
In the United Kingdom: Princeton University Press, 6 Oxford Street, Woodstock, Oxfordshire OX20 1TR

press.princeton.edu
Cover image courtesy of PA Images.

Reprinted with the permission of Scribner, a Division of Simon & Schuster, Inc., from *Cry, the Beloved Country* by Alan Paton. Copyright © 1948 by Alan Paton. Copyright renewed © 1976 by Alan Paton. All rights reserved.

Reprinted by permission of The Random House Group Limited, from *Cry, the Beloved Country* by Alan Paton. Published by Jonathan Cape.

Scriptures taken from the Bible in isiZulu (Zulu) 1959/1997 © Bible Society of South Africa 1959, 1997. Used with permission. All rights reserved.

Excerpt from Sibusiso Nyembezi, *Mntanami! Mntanami!* in epigraph to chapter two used by permission of Pearson Marang (Pty) Limited.

All Rights Reserved

First paperback printing, 2019
Paperback ISBN 978-0-691-19146-1
Cloth ISBN 978-0-691-16756-5

Library of Congress Control Number: 2015939780

British Library Cataloging-in-Publication Data is available

This book has been composed in Minion Pro

Printed on acid-free paper. ∞

Printed in the United States of America

To my teachers

Contents

Introduction   1

Chapter 1   Learn More Zulu   14

Chapter 2   A Teacher's Novels   49

Chapter 3   *Ipi Tombi*   74

Chapter 4   100% Zulu Boy   96

Chapter 5   2008   115

Acknowledgments   145

Notes   147

Select Bibliography   183

Index   193

Introduction

Ngicela uxolo

I stand before the class, telling the students who I am, where I come from, and what brings me to the school. I notice as Mr. Nzuza, who is standing at the back of the classroom beside my desk, discreetly opens the book in which I have been taking notes. Although I am not exactly another pupil, he is the teacher and he has every right to examine my notes. He sees that I see him. I continue to speak. Maybe he wants me to have seen him—to be aware that he is watching, but also to know that he is curious to read what I have written. I cannot know whether this is what he intended. Yet my guess at it—which is already shaping the memory—leaves me with a twofold awareness: he is reading, and he is watching.

It is within the influence of this awareness that I embark on this book. I have to trust the reader. I have to trust that the one whom I picture as watching me as I write would like to think that he, or she, is reading something I wrote while he, or she, was not watching. If, for the reader whom I picture, to want this is to want the impossible, to imagine writing for such a reader, that is impossibility itself. Yet there is no writing without that step. Not for me, not with this book.

Our text is *Ngicela uxolo*, a play by Nkosinathi I. Ngwane,[1] an author I have never heard of. I am provided with a copy of the book on my first day. How uncanny that, only a few weeks before, I was reading an old radio play by D.B.Z. Ntuli with exactly the same title: *Ngicela uxolo* (I beg forgiveness). Like the puns that came to me as I took my first steps back into learning Zulu, as I worked with my teacher Eckson Khambule in New York City a few months before, the words *ngicela uxolo* had become a text for transference, a way toward finding myself in the language. "Finding myself"—it is easy to say, and to say, dismissively, of the one learning Zulu: he is finding himself, he is still finding himself. But there is more to it: in speaking a language, one appropriates the language, makes it one's own. One becomes a "self" by virtue of speaking that language—by assuming the position of "I." *Ngi-* . . . *ngicela* . . . *ngicela uxolo*.

The assumption of this position is, for me, not without inhibition. To speak is to bite one's tongue—such was the first coded sentence when, with Eckson, I began to play on words. To assume the position of speaking subject was to assume guilt, and to inflict punishment upon oneself. Although I have translated the expression *ngicela uxolo* as "I beg forgiveness," on its own the word *uxolo* can mean peace or calm. In uttering the plea *ngicela uxolo*, one takes up the position of speaking subject. One makes the language one's own as one speaks, but one also declares oneself guilty—of having committed a wrong, of having failed to do what was expected, of having, by some act or omission, broken the peace.

Mshazi—as Mr. Nzuza is usually called by the other teachers, who use his *isithakazelo*, or clan praise name—rouses his Grade 12 Zulu class, which, despite my rudimentary command of Zulu, I have been invited to attend. His powerful voice commands the entire classroom in a call and response in which the students answer his questions, and are expected to finish his sentences. Introducing the play, Mshazi utters a series of words, of which I catch only a few, but which includes the word *iphutha* (error, mistake, wrong), then *ucela* (you ask or beg). There is a pause, upon which the pupils conclude in one voice: *uxolo*. Will this imprecation keep following me, as if they were my first words, another version of speaking as biting my tongue? Of course, *ngicela uxolo* is probably not the first sentence that one utters when one learns a new language; Mr. Fani Ntombela, a senior teacher, puts forward *ngilambile* and *ngomile*—I am hungry, I am thirsty—as likelier candidates. One learns the sentence *ngicela uxolo* later, perhaps too late, long after one has found reason to utter it by stating a hunger and a thirst that, because they are in excess of sheer need, are experienced as greed, as a taking away from others.

It is April 2008, and I have come to Jozini to learn Zulu. You reach Jozini by driving up the side of a mountain. Down to the left lies the vast Jozini Dam. Formerly known as the Pongolapoort, the dam is one of South Africa's largest. The dam is a tranquil expanse of water cradled between the peaks of the Ubombo, fields of sugar cane stretching from its shores into the fever trees and scrub. Having reached the high point of the drive, you descend along the narrow and winding road to reach the town center, which is built on the hillside south of the dam wall. To the north lies Ingwavuma, and the border with Swaziland is not far away. To the east stretch the plains of Makhathini and eventually the sandflats of Mhlabuyalingana, up to Kosi Bay and Manguzi on the Indian Ocean, and Mozambique.

Eckson has helped to arrange my visit with Mr. N. H. Mkhwanazi, the principal of Sinethezekile Combined School, where Eckson taught before he came to Teachers College, Columbia University, for his Ph.D. When I reach the turn-off from the N2 highway, having driven through Mpumalanga from Johannesburg, I stop and call Mr. Mkhwanazi. I am to drive to the BP garage, where Mr. Mthembu, his vice-principal, will meet me to show me the way to the principal's house, where I will be staying. I am introduced to Nokuthula, Mr. Mkhwanazi's wife, who is waiting for us. She greets me warmly and shows me to the spare room, where I unpack my things. Later, Mkhwanazi arrives, and Nokuthula serves us dinner at the table. It gets dark, and candles are produced; there has been no electricity for a week, not because of the load shedding that Louise and I have become used to in Johannesburg, but thanks to a damaged transformer. Being without electricity is clearly frustrating, especially for Nhlanhla, their adolescent son, who enjoys watching television. Spirits seem low as a result, and everyone is early to bed.

The following day I drive to the school, which lies on the plain down from the dam wall to the east. I am introduced to Mshazi, who takes me to his office, where I receive from him my books: *Ngicela uxolo*, and an A4 counter book, of the kind with the black cover and red ribbon down the spine that we used in high school. I write my name in the relevant space, and in the space below that I write "isiZulu." My Zulu book—the one that Mshazi will discreetly open when I rise from my desk to speak in front of the class. My Zulu book, but also his Zulu book, for it is the book that he has given me.

Mshazi takes me up to the Grade 12 classroom on the second floor. Worlds, seemingly distant, connect. The students have chalked on the door the words "Wits University," evidently reflecting their aspiration to study at the University of the Witwatersrand in Johannesburg.

A few weeks before, when, as I sat with Eve Mothibe (MaSimelane) reading Ntuli's radio play in her office at Wits, the sentence *ngicela uxolo* became a sign for what it would take for me to learn Zulu. I would be making reparation. This would mean overcoming an inhibition of learning arising, as I saw it, from unconscious fears of retribution for a wrong that I imagined myself as having once done, but did not consciously remember doing. In framing things in this way, I am appealing to Melanie Klein, whose psychoanalytic work with young children from the 1920s and '30s elaborated and revised the theories of Sigmund Freud. She shows how, if one's guilty feelings lead one to fear retribution, one can also behave destructively toward the object one seeks to repair and toward which one endeavors to "make good." Her word for reparation, in German, is *Wiedergutmachung*—literally, to make good again. The object toward which reparation is made, according to Klein's theory, is, in early life, the maternal part-object: the breast.[2] Tradition tells us—and this applies in Zulu too, in which one speaks of *ulimi lwebele* (language of the breast, or mother tongue)—that it is from the breast that one's language comes, as does mother's milk. The figure we call the father is, for Klein, secondary, deriving from the maternal object. His penis, as part-object, thus gains the phantasy attributes of the breast. Metonymically, *words* displace the breast and its derivative paternal part-object.[3] It is thus that *language* becomes the focal point for reparative as well as destructive tendencies. There is greed, and there is possessiveness. Some of the more complex of these tendencies are those that, in professing to make reparation—and appear thus to the one doing so—actually attack the damaged object over and over again. Such is the power of the unconscious. Melanie Klein calls this manic reparation, while her follower Hanna Segal terms it "mock reparation."⁴ Because feelings of persecution are still strong, and paranoia predominates, reparation cannot succeed. The object, in phantasy, cannot be appeased, and it continues to attack me. In classic paranoid style, I thus "defend" myself against it. When endeavors at reparation falter, learning comes to a halt. The dynamics of infancy—the time when one is learning one's first language—unconsciously repeat themselves in different forms in later life. And, I would maintain, they repeat themselves with a vengeance when one learns another language.

D.B.Z. Ntuli's *Ngicela uxolo* is about a man whose father appears at his door one cold and stormy night to ask his forgiveness for abandoning him and his mother forty years before. Ignoring the pleas of his wife, the man gives his father no chance to explain. Offered no roof over his head, the old man goes back into the night and freezes to death. Before departing, he leaves behind a letter explaining how he suffered ill health, even spending several years in a mental hospital. The letter also bequeaths to his son all his savings.⁵

The play touches a raw nerve. I would be turning forty in ten days. My biological father has never made himself known to me. I cannot help asking myself what I would do were he to appear at my doorstep.

Eve has asked me to make up sentences using words from *Ngicela uxolo* that are new. I am tongue-tied from the start and decide to tell her about the parallels I perceive between me and Malusi, the character in Ntuli's play. I do so in English after things become too complicated for me to explain in Zulu. Once I have told her, I begin to construct my Zulu sentences. They end up forming a narrative about my late adoptive father. How he enjoyed telling *izinganekwane* (my translation of *bobbemeises*, Yiddish for old wives' tales) about the circumstances of my birth; how, as a traveling salesman, *wayehamba izinkalo aphathwe amakhaza* (he would travel over hill and dale and suffer from the cold) in Cape country hotels; and how, when I was growing up, *wayenyamalala izinsuku ezine maviki onke, wayonga imali ukuze ngifunde eyunivesi* (he would disappear for four days every week and save money so that I could study at university). Quite a transposition. From Ntuli's Malusi to me. From the bad father to the good. From the bad son to the son who makes good—the name *uMalusi* ironically evokes the Good Shepherd. Something has happened. The unconscious employs the language newly being learned in order to work its way through and around inhibition. In this way, the repressed returns. At the time, it is something of an answer to the question: Why are you learning Zulu? Not a reason, but the coming clear of a convincing motivation.

I connect less readily with Nkosinathi Ngwane's play of the same name. First published in 2003, the world of his *Ngicela uxolo* is of the present day. Its Zulu is more difficult than Ntuli's; it is syntactically more complicated, with inflections of the verb *ukuba* (to be) and *ukuba khona* (to be present) in the negative, in the past tense, and in relative clauses—which a student of Zulu cannot simply look up in a dictionary or grammar, but must slowly absorb through frequent encounter in speech and print. I remember spending an entire Saturday laboriously reading twenty pages of the play at the Mkhwanazis', with MaGumede bringing me a cup of tea and a pear as a snack so that I would not have to get up and interrupt my reading.

In Mshazi's class, when the parts in the play are assigned for reading aloud, I am asked to read the stage directions. Attempting to approximate the change of tone from the characters' speech that reading stage directions would require in English, I come across as stilted. I sense the pupils—or "learners," as primary and secondary school students are now called in South Africa—listening for my pronunciation, especially for my articulation of the clicks that distinguish the four so-called Nguni languages from their neighbor tongues. When Mshazi tells a boy in the class that he needs to go home and *practice* reading aloud, I can only nod my head and tell myself the same thing.

My reading comprehension is better now, so perhaps I can discover why I did not connect. Ngwane's play is aimed at youth, and is outright didactic, even if it professes "not to preach to anybody." It is against witchcraft: "Kanti buhle yini ubuthakathi?" (Tell me, is witchcraft good?)[6] As a literary theme, the question of witchcraft is somewhat hackneyed. Ngwane breaks no new ground, and as a writer he has none of the economy of D.B.Z. Ntuli, whose radio play of the same title, in a mere fifteen minutes, sets the scene, stages the confrontation, and reaches its unsentimental denouement. If the greats of Zulu literature—B. W. Vilakazi, H.I.E. Dhlomo, R.R.R. Dhlomo, Sibusiso Nyembezi—and their celebrated successors—D.B.Z. Ntuli, C. T. Msimang, among others—have begun to make way for new authors in an effort at keeping up with the times, then it is a shame that such undistinguished writing has taken their place. Such was my impatient sentiment then. But what do I discover on a second reading?

Ngwane's play is set in the "developed countryside" (*emakhaya aphucekile*).[7] The place is Dududu, inland from Scottburgh on the South Coast, and about fifty kilometers from Durban. Although the setting and circumstances evoked by the play bring back memories of Amaqongqo, near Pietermaritzburg, where I went later in 2008 as part of a group of Fulbright scholars studying Zulu—the codes of hospitality; the robust religiosity; the migration of women to work in factories in nearby or distant towns; the ubiquitous signs advertising *amabhulokisi* or simply *ama-blocks*, the cinder blocks used to build houses—I still struggle to locate the core of this play. (Perhaps teachers like Mr. Nzuza did too, for, as far as I can see, the play was not prescribed again after 2008.) It is clear enough that, as the plot unfolds, witchcraft brings woe upon those who fall victim to it, as well as to those who practice it. Mkhwanazi, the thrifty wage earner with whom the play opens, is poisoned by medicines purchased from a well-known *inyanga* (healer or herbalist) and secretly given to him by his wife, MaBele, in an effort to help them have children. As a result, Mkhwanazi can no longer work, and his project of building a new house is unfulfilled. MaBele, having left Mkhwanazi and their newborn child to find factory work, is left with nothing in the end, and Mkhwanazi withholds from her the *uxolo* for which she pleads: "I don't know" (*angazi*).⁸ Two local *abathakathi* (wizards), MaMthethwa and Zulu, witness their own house burn down just as, beset by envy, they call down lightning on Mkhwanazi's new house. They are rescued, but because their charms have been discovered with them, they fear the reprisals common against suspected wizards and witches, and disappear from the community under the cover story (supported by the police and by the Reverend Mbambo, a local minister) that they perished in the conflagration and that their ashes are to be buried in the government cemetery. Their whereabouts are unclear—perhaps Swaziland, where Zulu has a brother—but they continue to appear in dreams to Zinhle, their estranged daughter who lives at her uncle's house in Umlazi, near Durban. They tell her that they are dead, having deserved to die for their deeds, and call upon her to ask forgiveness on their behalf from victims of their wizardry. This Zinhle does, while she prepares to write her matric examinations and plans marriage with the mysterious Sizwe, a lawyer, whom she suspects of having a hand in the fire that destroyed her parents' house. Although several characters in the play ask *uxolo* of one another, there appears to be no clear pattern except to affirm that asking and granting it do not come easily, although doing so is a good thing.

But perhaps there is another layer to Ngwane's play. I see that the Senior Certificate exam for 2008 asks: "Which character is the hero or heroine [*iqhawe*] of this play? Why do you think so? (6 points)."⁹ Although the play begins and ends with Mkhwanazi, who goes back to Thobe, the mother of his child Dumazile, in order to make a new beginning after his failed marriage to MaBele, my choice, and perhaps that of many Grade 12 students, would be Zinhle, who, like them, is readying herself for the end-of-year examinations that mark the completion of high school. Zinhle overcomes the misfortune of having *abathakathi* for parents, writes her matric, and is going to marry Sizwe, whom she loves even if she does not entirely trust. It is she who is the messenger of *uxolo* more generally, atoning one by one for her parents' crimes—but, at another level, she is also the bearer—and perhaps the beneficiary—of the crimes of infanticide to which her parents confess.¹⁰ According to the conventions of Ngwane's play, characters who are absent (but not necessarily dead) appear in dreams in order to deliver messages that they could not deliver in person. The dreams are a way of bringing characters on stage absent with reason, without contradicting the reason for their absence. As a dramatic convention, it is well worn. But psychoanalysis teaches us to *interpret* dreams beyond their manifest content.

When we begin to interpret Zinhle's dream we can see how she is the heroine of the play because she is the bearer of guilt: she has agreed to atone for a series of crimes of infanticide that she did not commit, but from which she, ultimately, has gained—education, a husband with prospects—by virtue of being an only child. As MaMthethwa explains in the dream, "[t]here were two brothers of yours as well as a sister whom we agreed to wipe from the earth because we pursue our unrighteous purposes." (*Wawunabafowenu ababili kanye nodadewenu esavumelana ukubasusa emhlabeni ngoba siqhuba izinhloso zethu zokungalungi.*)[11] If a dream is, as Freud wrote, the presentation of a wish fulfilled, then Zinhle's dream may be interpreted as a sign of murderous sibling rivalry—a wish, on her part, to be the only child (infanticide is the only sin to which MaMthethwa confesses in the dream), which is then displaced onto her parents. Projection is in play. When she apologizes for what her parents have done, she is actually apologizing on her own behalf. When Zulu, her father, appears to her in a dream in the final scene in which Zinhle is on stage, he counsels her not to hold a grudge against Sizwe—and the play itself ends with MaBele citing the story of Jesus and the woman taken in adultery: "He that is without sin among you, let him first cast a stone at her."[12] Zinhle is not free of guilty feelings—she is, after all, visited by nightmares, which her friend Velephi calls "this demon of dreams" (*leli dimoni lamaphupho*),[13] and seeks to drive away through prayer—inviting the thought that the challenges with which life will present her have only just begun, for the victim herself carries guilt.

This is something to which I can relate: the victim of the sins of the fathers—and mothers—who wrought a system in which learning Zulu was made difficult for me (let that be a metonymy for much else), I am also the beneficiary of that system, and guilty for what it wrought and continues to perpetrate in what Jacques Derrida, following Walter Benjamin, described as the reiteration of a founding violence.[14] I can make reparation by learning the language, but, at any time, I can also lapse into a paranoia in which I feel myself persecuted by the language itself—and, to be sure, by its speakers. The language becomes my persecutor and prosecutor for wrongs that, although I am an accomplice, because they are not mine, but those of a multitude dead, living, and unborn, I can never set right on my own. Zinhle in Ngwane's play, despite being the bearer of a name that declares her beautiful and good (*-hle*)—one of, or the last of, the beautiful and good girls (*zinhle*)—is in an analogous position in relation to her parents' *izinhloso zokungalungi* (unrighteous purposes). If I make reparation toward the language, it is on account of such a crime, which is inexpiable because it is not over with.

These thoughts, as they come to me on rereading Ngwane's play, are not as immediate (or as raw) as those that arose with Ntuli's radio play as their catalyst, when a dedicated teacher guided me, without my quite knowing and understanding what was going on, toward an owning to myself of a father's *ngicela uxolo*: No, me, "*mina* ngicela uxolo," *I* beg forgiveness; since I need to have this "peace" in order to learn the language that I am learning; I want you to leave me alone, already. It is through such unexpected events, which I take to involve an unconscious repetition of dynamics of reparation from early life, that I understand the secret history of language, and language learning, that I am writing about. Historical wrongs may be nameable, and will indeed be named in what follows, but it is through this repetition as experienced by the language learner that they gain their meaning.

A Secret History

The most recent inheritor of this secret history is the migrant, who, coming to South Africa from countries neighboring and farther abroad, learns Zulu out of economic necessity, and in response to the pull of community. Zulu, the first language of about 11.5 million South Africans, living mostly in the provinces of KwaZulu-Natal, Mpumalanga, and Gauteng,[15] is also an important common language among black African people in the two latter provinces, the economic heartland of the country, to which many migrants gravitate. When, in May 2008, as in preceding years, some of those migrants were attacked, and some of those attacked were forced, under threat of violence, to pronounce shibboleths in Zulu, they may not have realized what history they were inheriting.

The fact that Zulu shibboleths were used suggests that, in South Africa, the signifier "Zulu" had come to have a unique and privileged status. For the xenophobes it functioned as a password, not only for identity as indexed to language—and this identity was no longer ethnic but national[16]—but also, and this was more important, for access to property and its rightful ownership: a house, a job, a shop, a plot of land on which to build. In short, to be able to speak Zulu entitled the speaker to the prerogatives of residency and citizenship.

The privilege of "Zulu" can be traced back to its elevation, dating from colonial times, into a sign for being African scarcely rivaled by any other name for an African language or people, and struggles, lasting more than a century and a half, for possession and control of that sign. In Europe and North America,[17] the symbolic power of "Zulu" has its beginnings with the defeat of the Redcoats by Cetshwayo's army at Isandlwana in 1879, whereas in South Africa it also comes from the figuring of the Zulu as quintessential African enemy by Afrikaner nationalists, who consecrated a national holiday to the defeat of Dingane by the Boers at Blood River in 1838. One could add to this the consolidation—through the migrant labor system that brought African men from all over the subcontinent to the mines of the Witwatersrand—of a Zulu ethnic identity beyond Zululand and Natal.[18] One could also mention the Zulu cultural nationalism that took political shape in the KwaZulu Bantustan, under the leadership of Mangosuthu Buthelezi, and the attempt, subsequently, by Inkatha and the Inkatha Freedom Party to identify black South African political interests with Zulu interests.[19] Although the attempt failed, this unique and unprecedented example in South Africa of black ethnic-nationalist mobilization reinforced, at least for whites, over a century of assimilation of being Zulu and being African in colonial and apartheid literature and popular culture, from the novels of H. Rider Haggard in the 1880s and '90s, to the theatrical spectacle of *Ipi Tombi* in the 1970s. The fact that colonial- and apartheid-era elevation of "Zulu" involved intensive white appropriation and translation means that when I refer to the Zulu language in English I do not use the word "isiZulu," which an increasing number of English speakers in South Africa prefer to do because it is the name of the language in Zulu. Similarly, in contexts in which the Zulu word *isiZulu* refers not only to the language but also to Zulu ways,[20] I usually place the Zulu word in brackets.

Running concurrently with the readily observable identification of "Zulu" with being African is a history of language learning. For a white South African of my generation to learn Zulu is not simply to learn an African language, but rather, because of the privilege of Zulu for which I have provided a brief genealogy, to learn *the* African language. Learning it has perhaps, for some, been a way of becoming African. One could certainly write interesting books entitled "Learning Xhosa," or "Learning Sotho," but those would be rather different books. Perhaps "Learning Afrikaans" would, albeit in other ways, set the stakes as high.[21] But this history of learning Zulu, despite its significance, remains a secret history, in the sense that it has not been recorded before, save in fragmentary form. Whereas the more- and less-alienating effects on Africans of colonial language teaching have been well attested, accounts of which are justly canonical,[22] the meaning of learning an African language, for colonials of European descent and their descendants,[23] or by those of Indian ancestry,[24] has scarcely been explored.

What *Learning Zulu* shows is that when missionaries in mid-nineteenth-century Natal, the most famous being Bishop J. W. Colenso, standardized the Zulu language by writing grammars and compiling dictionaries, they also made Zulu—in its "pure" or correct form—a yardstick for being good, both morally and politically. For them, learning Zulu thus became reparative, a method for Europeans to make good the ill they and their kind had done in Africa and to Africans, and to forestall its repetition. In the process, they, as well as their African converts, stigmatized the pidgin known to them as Kitchen Kafir (and later as Fanagalo) and broken forms of Zulu spoken in the workplace, along with their speakers. Even the producers of the practical manuals in Kitchen Kafir and Fanagalo that appeared later, although admitting the pidgin as a necessity, are apt to decry it as a "wretched . . . jargon."[25]

This way of seeing and of evaluating—which may well have resonated with older African attitudes in which social status was linked to dialect[26]—was taken up by some of the Zulu intellectuals who succeeded the missionaries and surfaces in the didactic commentaries and language textbooks they authored. This is where my own experience of learning Zulu, in which transference and repetition come to the fore, becomes a provocation to the secret history and a lens for exposing and scrutinizing the "hidden matters and motives" that, ever since Procopius of Byzantium published his *Secret History* in the fifth century, have defined the genre, distinguishing it from ordinary historical chronicle.[27] Because, in our time, psychoanalysis is the method par excellence for gaining an inkling of hidden human motives, it is what I employ to identify and describe what I call the psychopolitics of language. My inhibition in learning Zulu, which I have begun to describe, brings to light two interlocking trends that, working at different levels, both involve reparation and its attendant complications—first, at a psychical level, an unconscious repetition of dynamics of early life, which can affect the learning of other languages more generally; second, a politics of language learning that has, for more than 150 years, made learning an African language (specifically Zulu) a making-good for historical wrong. *Learning Zulu* shows that this psychopolitical nexus, which presents a different face depending on the context, is by no means unique to the author. If, to some readers, my use of psychoanalysis might from time to time sound hyperbolic, that is deliberate. I write in the mode of the familiar essay, and psychoanalysis works as a brake on the authority of the "confessional" or "personal," of the truth claims of the stories I tell myself about myself. At the same time, although psychoanalysis allows a definite pattern to be discerned in my wish to learn Zulu, which I go on to discover among learners of the language more generally, the sheer contingency of some of the events narrated in turn challenges the final say of psychoanalysis as a theoretical framework.

When the non-native speaker enters the schoolroom built by missionaries and the Zulu teachers who take up their project—the classroom at Sinethezekile, by contrast, was built for a different purpose, meaning that I was out of place—it is with the assumption that, as the pupil learns the language, he will undertake reparation, "making good" in at least a symbolic sense. If he uses the language manuals of Sibusiso Nyembezi, who was also a celebrated novelist in Zulu, then the pupil will have to give up Fanagalo. What he receives in return for careful study of Nyembezi's *Learn More Zulu* is entry into a humble, mostly rural world in which the effects of apartheid are subtly registered through understatement. He also has an opportunity to see himself differently, perhaps even to *be* different. What might then ensue is a curiosity about one's teacher: Who is he? What are his motives? There are no definitive answers to such questions, although the suspicion, when one reads Nyembezi's novels, is that his professed linguistic purism may stem from conflicts between the generations, especially between Zulu fathers and sons. But the teacher remains more than devoted to the pupil, and generous in his corrections. This is especially true when Nyembezi translates Alan Paton's *Cry, the Beloved Country* into Zulu as *Lafa elihle kakhulu* and must translate its Zulu-language-learning scenes from English into Zulu. Close analysis of Paton's novel shows that a wrong lesson is being taught to a small white boy. This Nyembezi silently corrects. What also emerges from these scenes of instruction is that, for the young white learner as imagined by the adult author, a paranoid fear is associated with learning the language, which revolves around not knowing it, or not knowing it well enough. At another level, this is linked, in phantasy, to the primal scene, in which the parents do things that the young child does not understand, and may also believe they deliberately keep secret from him or her. In the genealogy that I explore, language learning includes powerful feelings of jealousy and possessiveness, as well as feelings of guilt that arise from the aggression acted out, in phantasy, in response to those feelings.

You might ask: Isn't this infantile? As much is readily acknowledged when, remembering my role as a young boy in a junior-school production of the 1970s musical *Ipi Tombi*, I recall my puerile investment in "Zulu" as a phallic signifier. Although a great box-office success, *Ipi Tombi* drew criticism for being a hodgepodge of African song and dance reckless in its disregard for the integrity of its sources. Like Fanagalo, it seemed destructive, even as it professed to celebrate African performance. Viewing it retrospectively, I connect this destructiveness to an ambivalence toward the feminine condensed in the name of the show, which is usually translated as "Where Are the Girls?" or "Where Is the Girl?" I also contrast *Ipi Tombi* with the achievements of Johnny Clegg, who, famous for his mastery of Zulu music and dance, became known as the "white Zulu."

Pervasive symbolic over-investment in "Zulu," and its heavy identification with masculinity, has reciprocal effects on native speakers. These effects reached a pitch with the trial of Jacob Zuma, who became president of South Africa in 2009, for rape in 2006, and with the confident assertion, by those taking sides for as well as against him, of "Zulu" as a unitary signifier of African maleness. But a little more investigation—meaning a consideration, as far as possible, of the original Zulu of Zuma's testimony—shows that when he testified at trial to his state of mind, he alluded to his boyhood training in Zulu ways (*isiZulu*). The complainant in the trial, by contrast, testified to her choice not to follow Zulu or black African ways in the adjudication of the matter. There was thus, if one knew where to look, a fissure in the name "Zulu" between men and women, and between generations. There was, above all, contrary to the assumption that "Zulu" ways were immutable and compulsory, the hint that male as well as female conduct—like language—is learned, and can thus also be learned differently. Zulu has an expression, *umuntu ufunda aze afe*, a person learns until he or she dies; or, you are never too old to learn.

The parallel emerging in my mind between my learning Zulu, and one learning it as his or her mother tongue, led me to the larger question: What would it mean to generalize the idea of learning? This question seemed urgent in the shadow of the violence of 2008 and its death-dealing shibboleths. Although the white learner was no longer the central protagonist of the secret history of language learning that I was writing, perhaps his or her trajectory could be a guide to the psychopolitics of language involved. If migrants were reading the Zulu-language newspapers that I was reading, instead of the grossly xenophobic *Daily Sun*,[28] what would they have discovered? They would have found a struggle, by turns super-erudite and satirical, over what the eminent Zulu writer and public intellectual O.E.H.M. Nxumalo called "refined Zulu."[29] In this struggle of words, in which rights to settle, to work, and to trade are never far from the center, the actual learner of Zulu surfaces mainly at the margins—where she can be bitterly ridiculed, or, alternately, made fun of through mimicry. It is as if the endeavors of such learners had always been at issue, but also always a secret, if indeed an open one. I began to see that if the migrant, in a perverse sense, by dint of the shibboleths she is forced to produce, was being perceived as a learner, then in a sense any of the protagonists involved, including the native speaker, could be thought of as a learner.

If, by demanding a saying of the shibboleth, the xenophobe seemed at first to declare to the migrant *I have it, you do not, so you must go*, then perhaps there was a subtext, indicative of fears of dispossession, that, save for the conclusion, was precisely the reverse: *You have everything, I have nothing, so you must go*. This all-or-nothing idea is what theorists of relative deprivation seem to point to when they explain xenophobic violence.[30] Linguistic purism is, to be sure, not the same as the shibboleth. But I see enough of a connection between them to wonder whether a generalization of the idea of learning might not help to loosen zero-sum notions of property, proprietorship, and appropriation that, as much as they laid claim to exclusive possession of a language, betrayed fear of its total loss through theft by others—the *amakwerekwere*, the ones said not to "frame to pronounce it right."[31] "Because there is no natural property of language," Derrida reasons in *Monolingualism of the Other*, playing on different senses of *propriété* in French, where it can mean selfhood or something one owns, "language gives rise only to appropriative madness, to jealousy without appropriation."[32] When channeled into nationalism, Derrida argues, the political consequences of this "appropriative madness" can be violent. The events of 2008 seemed to confirm this. In that year some appealed to the past in order to show that migration and diaspora are as much part of Zulu history as stable settlement. Could a generalized idea of learning, likewise, be a condition of possibility for a different hospitality? Never quite having arrived, always underway—is that not what learning is?

One would surely wish to answer in the affirmative. Yet, a learner of a language—any language—always follows a pattern of making mistakes and accepting correction. This is perhaps why—although as I drew more actual Zulu words into my mouth, loosening my investment in the *name* of the language, and thereby lessening the feelings of guilt and paranoia that stemmed as much from my own background as from a history I shared with others—the words *ngicela uxolo*, and the way in which Mshazi explained them to the class, continue to resonate: *uma wenza iphutha* (when you make a mistake), I imagine he must have said, perhaps adding a phrase about remorse, *ucela uxolo* (you ask forgiveness). In receiving help, from him and from others, to correct the errors of my tongue, in being given a chance to make good, have I not been granted something like forgiveness? If learning a language is a highly regulated instantiation of the shibboleth—since the native speaker determines what is correct—it is also a perpetual process of reparation, of undoing of error.

To correct a learner of one's language is laborious, and it takes time. It also takes trust. The necessary time, but above all the trust, was generously given by Mshazi, and by the other teachers I got to know at Sinethezekile, just as by Eckson Khambule in New York City, Eve Mothibe in Johannesburg, and Audrey Mbeje in Pietermaritzburg. It is, first of all, to them, my teachers, that I confide this book.

CHAPTER 1

Learn More Zulu

> The ordinary white man in South Africa, who speaks good Zulu, is inclined to laugh at Kitchen-Kafir; but good Zulu-speaking white men are becoming scarcer every year, and those who are left are every day being brought more into contact with natives who do not understand their Zulu, but who do understand Kitchen-Kafir.
>
> A European landing in South Africa must take some years to learn to speak Zulu fluently. The average European picks up sufficient Kitchen-Kafir for his immediate wants and ceases to trouble about Zulu; and when he tries anything higher the result is generally incorrect.
>
> —B. G. Lloyd, *Kitchen-Kafir Grammar & Vocabulary*, 6th ed. (1944)

THE COLENSO LEGACY

Go back in history and you will see how much depends on the distinction between Zulu and Kitchen Kafir—or Fanagalo, as it was called later. Having placed "understand[ing] one another" second only to the will to "'solving the problem' of how to live together in peace and comfort," Harriette Colenso writes in her preface to the 1905 edition of John William Colenso's *Zulu-English Dictionary*:

> I believe that a fine language like the Zulu is a valuable possession for the country, and that the debasing of it into an ungrammatical mixed lingo, only half understood on either side, which is now going on, is a positive evil; not merely a measure of the harm done to the Native by contact with Europeans as he experiences it, but also a cause contributing to that harm. I therefore hold that those of us who realise this are bound to do what we can to present the language rightly, and believing that among many worthy efforts to that end my Father's is by far the most accurate, I may not acquiesce in its being set aside.
>
> Hybrid words must, of course, arise wherever two or more vigorous races begin to live and to work together (has not the English tongue been so built up?), and I have recognised this need by appending to the dictionary proper a list of

some of these words now in common use by Natives in Natal. But "kitchen kafir" proper is another thing. I quote a choice but by no means exaggerated specimen given recently in the *Natal Mercury*:

"Imagine anyone telling you: 'No, he good looking here you they call themselves I it cries.' . . . . And yet this is a verbal translation of *Ayi muhle le, wena ayibiza mina kukala?* which, interpreted, is supposed to mean: 'It is not well that you did not call me first,' or 'why the devil didn't you call me at once.'"

Or the following: "Hamba down to lo spring and tarter manzie and cadan stir up the bottom and if you don't make plenty checher I will bularler your scope with this here bit of kuney" [Go down to the spring and take water and don't stir up the bottom and if you don't hurry I will murder your head with this piece of wood].[1]

For Harriette Colenso, whose preface combines high moral seriousness with the persiflage that nearly always attends mention of Fanagalo, "Kitchen Kafir" is a "positive evil," because it does not achieve the goal of facilitating understanding between Africans and Europeans. The example that she provides from the *Natal Mercury* illustrates this by showing how a speaker of Zulu with no knowledge of the pidgin might make sense of a sentence in it. Although the sentence is meaningful in Fanagalo, when the sentence is heard as if it were in Zulu, the result is sheer gibberish. When Harriette Colenso explains that "Kitchen Kafir" is "not merely a measure of the harm done to the Native by contact with Europeans as he experiences it, but also a cause contributing to that harm," she formulates a project for the European, who, having caused harm through language, can also undo that harm through language. This project she takes up from J. W. Colenso, who, as Church of England Bishop of Natal from 1855 until his death in 1883, made it his business to refine, correct, and amplify existing grammars and dictionaries in Zulu.

Bishop Colenso's vision extended beyond the typical wish of a missionary to win converts. Wanting to found a "Kafir Harrow," which would nurture a literate Christian Zulu elite, Colenso recruited the sons of Natal chiefs and headmen to his school at Ekukhanyeni (Place of Light) just outside Pietermaritzburg.[2] Given the Zulu name Sobantu (Father of the People) by Africans when he arrived in Natal as Bishop,[3] Colenso proved unpopular with the white settlers. He was declared a heretic and excommunicated by the Church in South Africa when, after years of research prompted by a question from William Ngidi, his interpreter and language teacher, he published *The Pentateuch and Book of Joshua Critically Examined* (1862-63), which questioned the Bible as literal truth.[4] After mounting a series of legal challenges, Colenso succeeded in retaining his office as bishop. But Ekukhanyeni closed in 1861, "the boys . . . sent home" because of rumors of an impending attack by the Zulu prince, Cetshwayo, and Ekukhanyeni never re-opened again.[5]

Like Theophilus Shepstone, with whom he broke after the Secretary for Native Affairs led the armed suppression of the Hlubi under Langalibalele in 1873, Colenso sought to influence and transform relations between Natal's black and white populations—albeit in a different direction, from a different office, and using different methods. Shepstone is best known as the father of indirect rule—or the "Shepstone system"—which is commonly seen as a forerunner of the governing of Africans through customary law administered by chiefs during the segregation and apartheid eras.[6] As Colenso's guide on his first visit to Natal in 1854, Shepstone had won the newcomer's support for his most ambitious, albeit unrealized, scheme for indirect rule: a "Black Kingdom" south of Natal under Shepstone as "supreme Chief."[7] Colenso had favorably compared Shepstone to Brooke of Borneo. And Shepstone had helped persuade Ngoza and other notables to send their sons to Ekukhanyeni.[8] But Colenso's views changed, and so did his opinion of Shepstone.

The trial of Langalibalele demonstrated to Colenso how, having learned Xhosa growing up on the Cape Frontier,[9] and speaking Zulu fluently, Shepstone employed his command of the language to manipulate, mislead, and intimidate. After friction over the registration of guns, Langalibalele had been summoned to Pietermaritzburg by Shepstone, but failed to appear. Shepstone's messenger, Mahoyiza, accused Langalibalele of insulting him by stripping him bare; he had been asked to remove his coat and jacket so that he could be searched for weapons by the Hlubi, who feared that he had come to assassinate their chief. Emboldened after having presided over the installation of Cetshwayo as Zulu king in August 1873,[10] Shepstone, who did not know then that Mahoyiza had lied, treated this as an act of defiance, and proceeded to take the actions that led to the eventual dispersal of the Hlubi tribe.[11] Mahoyiza repeated his account in court. After Colenso asked Magema Fuze to approach Hlubi and other witnesses, Mahoyiza's perjury was exposed, although nothing was done to change the judgment or to mitigate Langalibalele's sentence of banishment for life. Until these events, Shepstone had managed to exert tight control over official communications between Africans and Europeans in Natal. This had required not only an insulation of Zulu and English-speaking publics from each another, but also a bifurcation of language in its oral and written forms. Colenso's intervention at the trial of Langalibalele exposed Shepstone's double dealing, ending the monopoly that he had held over the transmission of African views by virtue of his command of Zulu.[12]

Harriette Colenso followed in her father's footsteps politically by aligning herself with the Zulu monarchy, first Cetshwayo, and then Dinuzulu, whose legal defense she organized at both of his trials, and whose tireless advocate she was with the British government and before the British public. Further details of J. W. Colenso's remarkable career—and those of his children, Harriette Emily, Francis Edward, Frances Ellen, and Agnes Mary, and of the influence of Magema Fuze and his fellow Ekukhanyeni converts—may be found in the excellent studies of Jeff Guy and other scholars.[13]

For the secret history that I am writing, it is sufficient to observe that J. W. Colenso, through his work as a linguist, sowed the seeds for a motivation to learn—and to teach—Zulu that has lost none of its power because it is the motivation to make good, and to stand for what is right. This is no small turn; when Colenso first visited Natal, American Board missionary and linguist, the Reverend Lewis Grout, was referring to Zulu when he declared that "he would not have his little girl learn one word of that filthy language, on any account, if he could help it."[14] Colenso, of course, did not impose such a prohibition on his daughters. From his scattered remarks about learning the language, we can tell that he wasted no opportunity for improving his own command of it. Journeying by ox wagon in 1859 to ask King Mpande if he could build a mission in Zululand, Colenso found himself drawn to his companions—whom he refers to by their first names: William, who had come because Colenso wanted an interpreter and they were working on the grammar and dictionary,[15] Jojo, the driver, and the youthful Ndiyane and Magema: "The chatter of so many tongues a little interferes with one's more serious thoughts; but it is pleasant to hear them so cheerful, and one can get help in respect of the language by sitting close by, within reach of their conversation, instead of the little wagon-chamber being removed to a greater distance."[16] Colenso elsewhere lauded the fact that William Ngidi, who "still spoke the [i]siZulu of the Zulu kingdom. . . . 'spoke it with great correctness, in the pure Zulu dialect, and would immediately point out a deviation from it, just as an educated Englishman would detect a provincialism.'"[17] Ngidi's distinctions must have helped the Bishop to delimit his celebrated grammar and dictionary, in the elaboration of which his teacher was closely involved.[18] The *Zulu-English Dictionary*, first published in 1861, expressly excludes certain dialects.[19] By the turn of the twentieth century, for many educated Africans in Natal, this linguistic standardization,[20] and its attendant orthography,[21] was a *fait accompli*. By the 1850s, "speaking 'proper Zulu'" had become "not only the absolute benchmark of missionary identity, but also an ideal for ordinary colonists," whose settlement missionaries saw as promoting conversion among Zulus.[22] By the time that Harriette Colenso prefaces her father's dictionary in 1905, "those of us who realise" what harm is being done when Zulu is spoken badly and "are bound to do what we can to present the language rightly," include the Africans who addressed letters to newspapers defending the standard language and orthography that they had learned and embraced.[23] Like the latter, who, in so doing, "influenced Zulu politics,"[24] Harriette Colenso was prepared to generalize the ideal of "speaking 'proper Zulu'" beyond the missionary project.

The circumstances of the breach between Colenso and Shepstone suggest that the Bishop's eldest daughter could not have been naïve about what could be accomplished by having a command of Zulu.[25] We know from a letter written by her mother after her husband died that "her power in the way of colloquial Zulu was beyond her father's after all these years."[26] This had meant that, in the defense of Langalibalele, "[m]uch of the hard work fell on Harriette. . . . [S]he interviewed African witnesses, transcribed the evidence, wrote letters and petitions for her father."[27] The part that she played in these events would have shown her that, just as literacy and English would make Africans better informed, a more widely spread knowledge of Zulu among Europeans might allow greater "understanding" by counteracting the misrepresentations of those with a stranglehold over Zulu-English communications, as well as a sanctioned ignorance that is, as I have experienced firsthand, pervasive to this day. Although not a sufficient condition, since not all are of like will, knowledge of the language was a necessary one—the straw without which no bricks could be made[28]—and, for that reason, it attained an immense symbolic significance.

Assuming that the will exists, in order for the European to make good the harm done to the African through language, Zulu must be learned, and it must be learned, if circumstances dictate, in place of Kitchen Kafir. Although an appendix to the *Dictionary* newly supplies commonly used loan words that have entered Zulu from Kitchen Kafir (or *isiPiki*, meaning "speak"), the latter is said to be a "mixed lingo, like pigeon English, i.e., without grammar."[29] But Kitchen Kafir is "ungrammatical" only because it does not follow *Zulu*'s rules of formation. To speak well is to speak grammatically. Zulu is grammatical; to speak Zulu is therefore to speak well. Implied but not stated, this flawed syllogism prescribes a method for making good through speaking Zulu that, enduring for a long time, will never be separable from politics—although these politics will not always be the same politics.

Certain traits nonetheless remain constant, as when the pidgin is bound up with archetypal hierarchies of labor. There, violence lies near the surface, as Harriette Colenso's second, cruder, example shows; the speaker of Kitchen Kafir—more of a macaronic English with Zulu words—threatens to strike the head of the drawer of water with a piece of wood if she fails to make haste. If Kitchen Kafir tends to bring a chuckle, the joke is getting old. Although it is not without an air of election that the Europeans and Africans who are aware of the difference between the language and its pidgin make themselves the ones taking the lead in ending the violence of colonial relations,[30] the publication of a dictionary tells us that, by implication, if those who know are "bound to do what we can to present the language rightly," then the more who learn Zulu, the more will bind themselves to the practice of making good through speaking and writing well.

At certain moments, the trial of Langalibalele being one, the secret history intersects with recorded history, even if only with relatively little-known episodes. This may therefore be the time for a brief excursion into the type of chronological history that Procopius set aside for the history of "hidden matters and motives" that he wrote after a different plan.[31] The Byzantine author could assume that the eventual readers of his *Secret History* would be familiar with the events previously chronicled by him in his histories of the wars of Emperor Justinian against the Persians, Vandals, and Goths. With the secret history that I am writing, however, not every reader will possess a corresponding familiarity with events. Indeed, some readers may, when it is related, recognize more readily the secret history—for it is a history in which they have, all along, been actors. That has certainly been the case for me, having grown up in the Cape with tales of Wolraad Woltemade and Harry the Strandloper.

When it comes to "Zulu," questions are begged—many of them. It must have been colonial usage when J. W. Colenso wrote in 1854 that "[t]he natives of Natal are . . . commonly called by the general name of Zulus," although, "[s]trictly speaking, there are but a few within the Colony, who properly belong to the tribe of the Amazulu."[32] Yet historians nowadays tell us that "Zulu" as the generic cultural identity with which South Africans are familiar only coalesced for Africans themselves in the late nineteenth century, as labor migrants from Zululand and Natal sought to distinguish themselves from migrants from elsewhere, and may not have solidified until even later.[33] Reevaluating written as well as oral sources relating to the precolonial period, historians also show us that whereas older histories—the most influential being A. T Bryant's *Olden Times in Zululand and Natal* (1929)—place a fully formed Zulu Kingdom under Shaka at the center of the wars of devastation known as the *mfecane*, the consolidation of the Zulu polity in the 1820s was a reaction to expansionism and aggression by the neighboring Ndwandwe trading state, itself a reaction to the aggression of other polities.[34] Although the Zulu lineage group is certainly older, the Zulu, as a state formation that subjugated and incorporated groups of different lineages within a hierarchical system,[35] did not, strictly speaking, predate these events.

By the time that Colenso arrived in Natal, which, having briefly been the Boer Republic of Natalia, was annexed by the British between 1842 and 1845, the political and military system that Shaka had wrought some thirty or forty years before had passed its zenith.[36] Dingane, who had assassinated his half-brother Shaka in 1828, was defeated by the Voortrekkers at the battle of Ncome—or Blood River—in 1838, and, their territory much reduced, his successors, Mpande and Cetshwayo, were forced to compete and compromise not only with African centers of power, including factions among the Zulu, but also with the Boers and the British, whose geopolitical ambitions were growing in the region. The geographical boundary between Zululand and the "Colony," defined by the Thukela and Mzinyathi rivers, dating back to agreements reached between Dingane and the Trekkers, and Mpande and the British,[37] functioned politically and psychically in ways that influenced events in the region for a long time. When Colenso visited Mpande in 1859, he found that the King referred to Natal as *ngapetsheya* (on the other side),[38] and noted that Zulus referred to "Natal natives" as *amakafula*—a word that derives from "Kafir."[39] According to official surveys, there were sixty-five different tribes in Natal in 1837 and 102 in 1881. An 1854 survey classified these tribes into "aboriginal" and "refugee," meaning those that had fled Zulu domination. These tribes occupied "locations" on land allocated by the colonial government, to which they paid taxes, or lived on Crown land or white-owned lands.[40] They were, at least in principle, governed by customary law administered by hereditary chiefs, under the overlordship of the Lieutenant Governor of Natal and the Secretary of Native Affairs. Although some, such as the Qwabe, were understood to share cultural and social practices with Zulus, whereas others were not,[41] members of the former tribes did not necessarily align themselves politically with the Zulu Kingdom, and some even fought on the British side in the Zulu War.

Goaded by a Natal white settler population hungry for land and African labor, and fearful of the Zulu Kingdom that was its neighbor across the Thukela River, the British launched an invasion of Zululand in 1879. The defeat of Lord Chelmsford's army at Isandlwana, which would ensure for the Zulu a permanent place in colonial annals, was a pyrrhic one, for, after the war ended, Cetshwayo was captured and exiled, and the kingdom broken up into thirteen separate entities, purportedly representing tribal polities that existed before Shaka. After this settlement foundered, and Cetshwayo was restored in 1883, a civil war ensued, with the King's defeat and subsequent death effectively bringing to an end to the Zulu Kingdom's existence as a sovereign entity.[42]

Following a series of provocations and confrontations between the Usuthu, or Zulu royal house, and the colonial government,[43] Dinuzulu, Cetshwayo's son and successor, was arrested, tried, and exiled to the South Atlantic island of St. Helena in 1890.[44] In 1887 Zululand had been annexed as a Crown colony; in 1897 it was incorporated into the Natal Colony, and in 1910 into the Union of South Africa.[45] By this time, a major shift in political identity had taken place; Natal Africans, although living in various different chiefdoms, increasingly saw themselves as Zulus.[46] This helped to shape the conduct of the Natal chiefs who rose up in 1906 against the imposition of a poll tax, in what is usually referred to as the Bhambatha Rebellion.[47] The final significant uprising in the region against colonial subjugation and pressures toward proletarianization, this rebellion was brutally suppressed in 1906.[48] After being implicated in the events by the colonial government, Dinuzulu, who had been allowed to return from St. Helena in 1898,[49] was tried and exiled for a second time, this time to a farm in South Africa.[50]

Although the Zulu royal house enjoyed popular hegemony, the kings that succeeded Dinuzulu—Solomon kaDinuzulu[51] and Cyprian Bhekuzulu—could do little to alter the status quo. Yet, somewhat as Afrikaner nationalists did during the same period, Zulu cultural nationalists from among the mission-educated *kholwa* landowning class set themselves to work, founding Inkatha kaZulu in 1922 and, rallying around the king, cultivated the idea of a heroic Shakan past of which the Zulu of the present were the inheritors.[52] This ideology fostered ethnic unity, even in districts of Natal south of the Thukela that had not, historically, been under Zulu hegemony, and where, until the turn of the twentieth century, most Africans did not regard themselves as being Zulu in a political sense.[53] At the same time, liberal and radical politics began to gain a foothold among Zulus, with the formation of the South African Native National Congress (SANNC), which later became the African National Congress (ANC), and the Industrial and Commercial Workers' Union (ICU).[54] John Dube, before he became a Zulu nationalist, had been the SANNC's first president from 1912–17, and Albert Luthuli, chief of the Amakholwa people of Groutville until his dismissal by the government in 1952 for his support of the Defiance Campaign, was one of the most celebrated leaders of the ANC, winning the Nobel Peace Prize in 1960.

Despite ANC opposition led by Luthuli, in 1957 King Cyprian was drawn into the structures established under H. F. Verwoerd's Bantu Authorities Act.[55] The apartheid government's Bantustan policy was extended in the region by its proclamation in 1971 of the Zululand Territorial Authority, under the leadership of Mangosuthu Buthelezi.[56] This entity later became known as KwaZulu. In this dispensation, the king effectively became a figurehead.[57] The political power of Zulu nationalists grew in the region as Mangosuthu Buthelezi, with the initial blessing of the ANC, moved to revive Inkatha in 1975.[58] Buthelezi used Inkatha and his position as "homeland" leader to establish a significant regional power base. Although there were conflicts between him and Goodwill Zwelithini kaBhekuzulu, who had become king in 1968, the monarchy was also bolstered by the political structure of KwaZulu.

After 1990, with the unbanning of the ANC and other organizations, the armed conflict with Inkatha that ensued after the founding of the United Democratic Front (UDF) in 1983 escalated, and, in a virtual civil war between the two organizations in KwaZulu, Natal, and parts of the Transvaal, which sometimes involved state military and police "third force" elements, several thousand people were killed.[59] Although today KwaZulu-Natal, the province formed when KwaZulu and Natal were merged, is ruled by the ANC, the Inkatha Freedom Party is a spent force, and the monarchy depends on a stipend from the province, Zulu nationalists and monarchists continue to associate Zulu collective identity with the kingdom of Shaka, and the regional tourist industry uses "Zulu Kingdom" as a promotional brand. At the same time, national laws passed to affirm the authority of "traditional leaders" have allowed King Zwelithini to influence local politics.[60]

Whatever the fate of the kingdom and its rulers, it would be fair to say that "Zulu" has managed, over the course of nearly two hundred years, to achieve a status unrivalled in South Africa—and perhaps elsewhere—by any other name for an African language. This has, in part, been due to the fact that speakers of

Zulu outnumber any other linguistic community in the country, and Zulu has functioned as a lingua franca among Africans, especially on the Witwatersrand, but it is also because, historically, Zulu has been exemplary, for whites, of the "African." There has, to be sure, been in this the workings of chance, and this is where chronicle shades into secret history; when whites came up with the pidgin called Fanagalo, even if its earliest roots may have been in Kaffraria where whites learned Xhosa,[61] it was Zulu—and not Sotho or Tswana—that was its basis. And just as Isandlwana and Rider Haggard's Umslopogaas would capitalize on the name "Zulu" as warlike and loyal—a trait immortalized by Alan Paton—it was white appropriation that gave it its power and value relative to other African signifiers. All of that is taken for granted, just as questions are begged when the Zulu language is mentioned; since before a linguistic standardization embraced by Colenso and his successors, there was a Zulu royal house, a Zulu king, and a Zulu sphere of influence that changed over time in size and shape—but there had not yet emerged the linguistic hegemony that would make learning *Zulu* almost the automatic choice for the white person seeking to overcome the formidable obstacles to learning an African language.

Fanagalo

What are the obstacles? What stands in the way of learning Zulu, and thereby of making good? How is it that Fanagalo becomes a substitute for Zulu, and for other African languages? Different explanations may be given—linguistic, political, and psychopolitical. Ahistorical tautologies and fragments of outmoded scholarly models survive, tenaciously resisting critical revision, and they continue to constitute a certain common sense imbibed by any prospective learner.

What does the learner hear? I parody, but only slightly: Zulu is the language spoken by the Zulu people. Zulu is an Nguni language. The four Nguni languages are a subgroup of the Southern Bantu languages. If you look for a definition, these are the ones you will find. The one states the obvious: if you are a Zulu, Zulu is the language that you speak. Zulus speak Zulu. The other definition is taxonomical. As a language, Zulu is a member of a family of languages. The Nguni languages are said to be mutually intelligible. If you speak one, you can understand the others. They will be easy for you to learn. Thus, although Zulu is the language of the Zulus, it is also a language intelligible to others. It is a language that others, once they encounter it, and even before they encounter it, are learning. This goes for speakers of the rest of the Nguni languages—Xhosa, Swati, Ndebele—and also for those of the other Bantu languages—which are spoken from Cameroon to Kenya, and from Congo to South Africa, a ubiquity that for a long time has given historians a basis for conjecturing a vast east- and southward migration of what used to be called Negroid peoples.[62] This is because the Bantu languages all share a basic structure—namely the noun-class system, first brought to light for outsiders in 1659 by Giacinto Brusciotto, an Italian Capuchin priest, one of the "Angola Fathers," in his research on the Kongo language.[63]

Matters are otherwise if you do not speak another Nguni or another Bantu language. Zulu may well be a language always already being learned by others. But if the language you speak is not mutually intelligible with Zulu, is it in fact being learned by you?

Historically—or, said more accurately, when a certain historical alibi is put forward—the answer has been no. Speakers of English and Afrikaans—and Gujarati and Tamil—do not have the head start provided by mutual intelligibility and commonality of linguistic structure. Should they wish to learn the language of the Zulus—and this would apply to other Nguni and Bantu languages—all of these people would have to begin their studies from scratch.

Apparently the wish to learn has always existed. Close on the heels of the question, "Why are you learning Zulu?" one often receives the wistful confidence: "I have always wanted to learn Zulu, but . . . I once tried to learn Zulu, but . . ." Having received such confidences often, I believe that the wish to learn Zulu has, for as long as it has made its way into speech, been disavowed, a wall of "buts" erected against it. So few among the wishers have done anything to make their wish come true that, after witnessing the handwringing time and again, one begins to suspect the operation of a deeply rooted prohibition against the endeavor, or at least some powerful inhibition. One will point to apartheid and to apartheid education—but are they not rather the effects than the source of the prohibition? Before you know it, you get into deep and well-nigh unfathomable questions. There is a shrug of the shoulders, a knitting of the brow: the black languages, as some call them, they are just too hard.

But there have been circumstances—yes, certain circumstances—in which, notwithstanding any prohibition or inhibition, one has needed to avail oneself of an expedient (in times past, but even nowadays, though the remnant is acknowledged shamefully). Or else one will get nothing done. You know—at the mine, on the farm, down at the plant, over at the golf club. The name of that expedient is Fanagalo. Even in a 1920 *Miners' Companion in Zulu*, the tongue is considered "wretched," a "jargon" forced of necessity upon miner and mineworker alike.[64] Although they note the stigma of Kitchen Kafir, thereby elevating the learning of *Zulu*, manuals like this suspend further studies on practical grounds. They also relinquish, and perhaps even suppress, more generally, the prospect of making good through speaking to one another.

In the sphere of work, making trumps a making of reparation. For this reason, there was once no alternative to Fanagalo, explains the 1958 edition of J. D. Bold's *Dictionary, Grammar and Phrase-Book of Fanagalo (Kitchen Kafir): The Lingua Franca of Southern Africa as Spoken in the Union of South Africa, the Rhodesias, Portuguese East Africa, Nyasaland, Belgian Congo, Etc.*:

Fanagalo is a very much simplified form of Nguni (Zulu, Xhosa and related languages), with adaptations of modern terms from English and Dutch. It was probably evolved in the Eastern Cape and Natal, and later in Rhodesia, during contacts between European settlers and native tribes, and it developed on diamond diggings, gold mines and farms to meet the urgent need for a common language that could easily be acquired by Zulus, Xhosas, Swazis, Basutos, Bechuanas and Matabeles, and by the white men who employed them. These white men usually had no time to learn even one of the complicated and distinctive Bantu languages (each of which would have required several years of study to master). The raw native recruits, for their part, could not always keep pace with English and Dutch (later Afrikaans).[65]

On first looking into any Fanagalo phrase book, the learner of Zulu notices that Fanagalo places words from Zulu and other languages—though mainly Zulu—into a syntax approximating English. The noun-class system, which distinguishes the Bantu languages, and the consequent use of concords based on noun-class membership, is inoperative. Instead the language makes use of a limited number of Zulu absolute pronouns to replicate the way "I," "we," "you," "he," "she," "they," and "it" are used in English: *mina, tina, wena, yena*. The pidgin thereby reproduces the subject-verb-object structure of the basic English sentence. Among other typical features, the Zulu demonstrative pronoun *lo* is frequently used for definite and indefinite articles. Here are examples from the 1920 *Miners' Companion in Zulu*: "Ngifuna umuntu owazi ukusebenza nge Sipisane" becomes "Mina funa lo machine boy" (I want a machine boy), and "Angimfuni u lova" becomes "Mina hai tanda lo lova" (I don't want a loafer).[66]

Fanagalo is thus a language for the boss or—"the use of Fanagalo [having] spread . . . to domestic service and other spheres"[67]—for the boss-lady, in which to give instructions. As all South Africans know, or believe they know, it is in purpose identical to the language taught to Friday by Robinson Crusoe in order to make him more useful as a servant: "I . . . made it my Business to teach him every Thing, that was proper to make him useful, handy, and helpful; but especially to make him speak, and understand me when I spake."[68] And indeed the language did have to be *taught*. Although on the mines of the Witwatersrand knowledge of Fanagalo among speakers of Nguni languages would normally be taken for granted, newly recruited African mineworkers actually received basic instruction in Fanagalo: "They have to be taught a completely new language," states a 1951 Rand Mines document cited by David Brown.[69] With Fanagalo, as with the language Crusoe teaches Friday, we have an archetype of racist exploitation, and of a dehumanizing of blacks by whites—or, if Njabulo Ndebele's remarks about corporate English apply, by capitalism.[70] Fanagalo has, mainly for this reason, for some time supposedly been in the process of being phased out on the mines—its last significant remaining place of use,[71] and perennial source of Fanagalo dictionaries and phrase books. "Productivity and safety require every employee to avail himself of the opportunity of learning Fanakalo as rapidly as possible so as to be able to converse with other employees and to be able to give and receive instructions correctly." So runs the preface to the 1985 edition of the *Miners' Dictionary English—Fanakalo / Woordeboek vir Mynwerkers Afrikaans—Fanakalo*.[72]

Because Fanagalo is widely regarded as a demeaning substitute for one or other African language, to learn Zulu—if you are white or Indian or coloured—has required that one lay to rest the ghost of Fanagalo. I am speaking in historical terms. Biographically, this is not strictly true for me, having grown up in the Western Cape, where Fanagalo has never been in common use. But that hardly matters, since nobody in the country is untouched by the history made by distinguishing this language from its pidgin.

As one learning Zulu himself, I am therefore taken aback by something I come across in my research, about how missionaries in the early days of the Natal Colony may have had a hand at the inception of Fanagalo. I am reading the linguist Ralph Adendorff,[73] who draws on Rajend Mesthrie's important work to revise theses about Fanagalo's origins that have been in circulation for fifty years. One of the most tenacious of these theses comes from D. T. Cole, who in an article in 1953 in *African Studies* speculated that Fanagalo emerged among Indian indentured workers in Natal after 1860.[74] Another name in Zulu for Fanagalo was, after all, *isiKula* (Coolie language). But there is evidence for Fanagalo before 1860. The missionaries, or some of them, wished to learn Zulu as it was spoken by Zulus. Despite their pleas, however, their interlocutors inevitably supplied them with "foreigner-talk" typical of what linguists call contact situations. And, notwithstanding the grammatical studies that followed, notably those of Colenso and his immediate forerunners, evidence from the early years for the missionaries' command of Zulu is, to say the least, quite uneven. In fact, what passes for Zulu in some of their records looks to us nowadays much like Fanagalo.[75]

Some contemporary linguists explain features of pidgins and creoles by drawing an analogy between those features, and those that emerge in the process of an individual acquiring a second language. Working within that analogy, the linguist adds—and this cuts me to the quick—studies have shown that adults rarely learn a language beyond what is useful for the purpose at hand:

> It is unlikely that many of the missionaries emerged from their experience with the Zulu language as competent bilinguals. Research on second-language acquisition, particularly that of adults, cautions one very strongly against assuming this. Competence, for many missionaries, is likely rather to have fossilised at a point where it was clear to them that they commanded the respect of their interlocutors and were getting sufficient of their message across. Another way of putting this is that the missionaries' Zulu would have fossilised at the point where they felt that the language-learning effort exceeded its utility.[76]

Clamorous are the questions: What might my purpose be in learning the language? Why are you learning Zulu? At what stage will my particular purpose arrest my acquisition of the language? At what point is my Zulu, like that of the missionaries, likely to "fossilize?" I think back to those spring months of 2002 in Cambridge, Massachusetts, where, wanting to rekindle my Zulu studies, I took half a dozen lessons with Temple Mtembu, and he was puzzled by my obsession with absolute pronouns: *mina, thina, wena, yena*. Though I spoke not a word of it, Fanagalo must, inevitably, have been speaking through me. Yet can learning a language not be without a reason—or without reason? Or can it be in excess—or in deficit—of any definite reason? Reason or no reason, I find I cannot get around the findings of the experts. A nagging fear remains: How well do I know the language? Will I ever know it better than I do now? Why is it that I do not know it better than I do?

This question can be given a political answer—with specific reference to the politics of education. In addition to the obvious racial separation that made (and still makes) the white "farm boys" and girls who learned Zulu as children the proverbial exception,[77] and the inequality and discrimination that, for much of the twentieth century, ensured the subordination of African languages to the "official" languages of English and Afrikaans, one must also note the effect of a purism imposed on language learning in schools—beginning with English and Afrikaans—under the Bantu Education system as instituted by the National Party in 1953.[78] What painfully complicates matters is that a comparable purism is, as Harriette Colenso's preface shows, and the converts corroborate, as much a part of the Colenso legacy as the imperative to learn Zulu in order to make good.

When D. T. Cole, amid his speculations on the origins of Fanagalo, scoffed at the idea that Fanagalo was a Bantu language—as if that were the point—he entered into complicity with a linguistic ideology that, in his day, formed part of the larger ethnic-nationalist vision out of which N. P. van Wyk Louw's "liberal nationalism" and H. F. Verwoerd's Grand Apartheid would both spring. Cole, of the University of the Witwatersrand, whose colleague K. Hopkin-Jenkins had to his dismay just published a Fanagalo textbook called *Basic Bantu*, approvingly quotes his colleagues to the north, J. A. Engelbrecht and D. Ziervogel of the University of Pretoria, who wrote in the *Journal of Racial Affairs* of the South African Bureau of Racial Affairs (SABRA) that "The champions of Fanagalo still regard the Bantu as a hewer of wood and drawer of water, and not as a person with his own emotions, culture and traditions, thus he is to them merely *Wena boy, tshetshisa enza lo ti!* (You boy, hurry make the tea!). If this is to be our approach to the Native problem, it must remain a problem. If, on the contrary, our aim is to make the Bantu individual a good and independent fellow-countryman, we shall have to address him in something better than this jargon before he becomes convinced of our good intentions."[79] Engelbrecht and Ziervogel, it is interesting to note, foresee, as did Jacob Nhlapo in *Bantu Babel* (1944), a booklet published in Edward Roux's Sixpenny Library,[80] an eventual standardization of the Southern Bantu languages that would consolidate groups of related languages into a Standard Nguni and a Standard Sotho. After all, standardization had been taking place from the moment that the missionaries wrote their first dictionaries and grammars; J. W. Colenso is explicit about how his *Zulu-English Dictionary* "does not contain all the peculiarities of dialect which are heard among different tribes such as those which *tefula* or *tekeza* in their speech,"[81] and, acknowledging that *isiZulu* is a word coined by the missionaries, bases his choice of the dialect of the amaZulu as standard on political grounds: the "supremacy over the natives along the S. E. Coast of Africa, excepting, of course, those who have been living under British protection since Natal came under our Government in 1845," exercised by the amaZulu, from Shaka and Dingane to Mpande.[82] This was evidently consistent with earlier missionary endeavors to gain the allegiance of the Zulu court through the embrace of its dialect.[83]

Despite their advocacy of standardization, neither the Pretoria professors nor Nhlapo departs from the assumption that the resultant languages would, in structure, remain *Bantu* languages, an assumption challenged by the existence of Fanagalo, which has a structure similar to English. Like Harriette Colenso before them, Engelbrecht and Ziervogel maintained that language learning would promote better race relations and contribute to "solving the problem."[84] And, even if the subterfuge of the Zulu-speaking Shepstone is recorded in history, and all of us have heard of the racist who speaks fluent Xhosa,[85] who does not believe this? Race relations involve a wish to make good, and in Engelbrecht and Ziervogel it emerges in the wish to "make the Bantu individual a good and independent fellow countryman," and depends on "our good intentions." For the SABRA intellectuals, for whom they were writing, the races would, however, be separate; the anaphoric *eie* in "own emotions, culture and traditions" (*eie emosies, eie kultuur en eie agtergrond*) emphasizes their adherence to the notion of the *volkseie*—that which is proper to a *volk*—one of the governing concepts of the culturalist apartheid thinking that, as Aletta Norval has shown in detail, evolved after World War II as the tide of world opinion turned against scientific racism.[86] These men may thus have been products of their time, as official language policy, just as it introduced standards of correctness for Bantu languages, began to displace a quotidian acceptance of pidginization among whites, as evidenced by the market for Fanagalo phrase books (of which Bold's, published by the Central News Agency, went through five editions between 1951 and 1958).[87] Aside from fundamentally compromising the nexus between language learning and making good for historical wrong, apartheid education set standards for examination for languages taken as school subjects. Apart from inherent differences in linguistic structure between Bantu languages and English or Afrikaans, this might have contributed to the idea that learning Zulu was "difficult," a notion said to lie behind the woefully low high-school enrollments for Zulu as a second language still found in KwaZulu-Natal today.[88]

By the late 1950s, then, there was a spread into more general use of Fanagalo, a language widely considered to be demeaning and even dehumanizing. Writing in a tradition that, at least since the Zulu Orthography Conferences of 1905–1907, has associated a mutilation of language with colonial violence,[89] native speakers of Zulu are protective of their language, and defend it against Fanagalo. At the same time, opposing the acceptance of Fanagalo for reasons of its own, Bantu Education, and apartheid education more generally, have ensured a new and even more powerful politicization of linguistic standardization and purism through the notion of the *volkseie*, by using language as the basis of ethnic identity: Afrikaners speak Afrikaans, Xhosas speak Xhosa, and Zulus speak Zulu. Apartheid ideologues gave with one hand and took with the other. In return for definitively stigmatizing Fanagalo, even as a workplace expedient, and for restoring to Zulu (along with the other Bantu languages) its privilege as the medium through which there could be a making-good in race relations, they drew up the blueprint for an even more systematic repetition of the historic harm for which a making-good was supposedly required. These are the highly ambiguous circumstances in which the teacher of Zulu—and the student—find themselves in the heyday of apartheid. The classroom prepared by the missionaries and their successors has been redesigned and repurposed. Does the project of "making good" through speaking Zulu well survive? If so, how, and in what form?

I am not plotting a direct line—since apartheid and Bantu education constitute a distinct break—but it is remarkable that, more than sixty years after Harriette Colenso prefaced J. W. Colenso's *Zulu-English Dictionary*, the great Zulu writer Sibusiso Nyembezi (1919–2000) finds it unavoidable to confront the specter of Fanagalo when he addresses the reader of his language manual, *Learn More Zulu* (1970). He does this in Zulu, making fun of Fanagalo for the pupil, who, having mastered *Learn Zulu* (1957), is in on a joke that the uninstructed would not get: "Sifuna ukukhuluma isiZulu esihle. Asifuni ukuthi 'Fana Ka Lo.' Sifuna ukukhuluma njengoZulu."[90] The note from Nyembezi to the reader of *Learn More Zulu* does, of course, have an English translation beside it: "We want to speak good Zulu. We do not want to say 'Fana Ka Lo.' We want to speak like the Zulus."[91] For even the most diligent of his pupils might not grasp every word—and it contains an important message: now that you have begun, it is time to inform you, in case you have not noticed, that for us there is a difference between what you take to be our language—and indeed one still encounters people today, as I did in Pietermaritzburg, who say they speak Zulu when all they know is some Fanagalo—and the language that we speak. It is significant that Nyembezi writes, "We do not want to say 'Fana Ka Lo' "[92] instead of, "We do not want to *speak* Fanakalo." In the Zulu version of the note, the absence of a noun-class marker from "Fana Ka Lo" means that, grammatically, it is not a substantive, but rather quoted speech from another language. By separating the component words, but not translating them, the teacher is asking his pupil to grasp the fact that the name of the language itself derives from an imperative or instruction, the first word of which is elided, but which may be understood as either "khuluma" or—more fittingly—"yenza." "The appellation 'Fanagalo,'" writes J. D. Bold in his *Dictionary, Grammar and Phrase-Book of Fanagalo*, "probably derives from 'kuluma fana ga lo,' meaning to [*sic*] 'speak like this,' or 'enza fana ga lo' ('do it like this')."[93] For the reader of Nyembezi's *Learn More Zulu* there are no alibis. *Yenza* can also mean "make." Making good through learning a "good Zulu" also means owning up to a history of labor relations in which the imperative to make, and make thus, was strictly unilateral.

Having faced down the specter of Fanagalo, how does Nyembezi address the entrenched idea—which has regularly provided an alibi for Fanagalo—that Zulu is "difficult?" He tells his pupil that, if she wants to speak Zulu like a Zulu, work is necessary, every day: "Lokhu kudinga ukuba sisebenze. Kudinga ukuba sifunde ngokucophelela. Kudinga ukuba sifunde zonke izinsuku. Kudinga ukuba sikhulume isiZulu zonke izinsuku emakhaya nasemsebenzini." (This requires that we work. It requires that we study with great care. It requires that we study every day. It requires that we speak Zulu every day at home and at work.)[94] Although much is left unstated in *Learn More Zulu*, any South African reader recognizes that it is the workplace, with its racial hierarchies and gendered differentiations—"at home and at work"—that at once facilitates and complicates the "work" of language learning. But Nyembezi, despite alluding to the complications, never says that Zulu is in itself difficult. And, in fact, when he talks about writing in Zulu, he says it is easy, compared to writing in English. He lifts the burden of difficulty from his pupil's shoulders. Or rather, he shifts it—onto the will, the conscience, the heart. The difficulty lies not in the language per se but in making the commitment to speak it. Every day one must speak. It is by speaking that one commits oneself. Speaking Zulu is not merely utilitarian—in Nyembezi's scenario, it may happen *at* work, but it does not follow that it is *for* work. In contrast to the Fanagalo handbooks of Bold, Lloyd, and the others, and to the *Miners' Companion in Zulu*, Nyembezi's manual assumes nothing about the motives of the one making the commitment to speak. Nyembezi writes almost as if a commitment has already been made. His invitation is, except for the teacher's statement of what is required of the pupil, unconditional. It is perhaps when no conditions are set that something can happen and that something unexpected might take place. Is this the same as learning a language without a reason?

The teacher may be ready, but the student brings his or her own history. I acquired my copy of Nyembezi's *Learn More Zulu* at the South African Library in Cape Town—I think it was in 1998, or in 2000, the year that my father died. Nyembezi's book was among a pile of duplicate volumes being sold off by the library at an internet café that had just opened there. The price was only five Rand, less than one U.S. Dollar. Reading out the title as he rang it up, the man who took my money declared: "It's a very difficult language, isn't it." By then, having worked through some of *Learn Zulu* on my own, after having received a few lessons from Lynette Hlongwane at Columbia University, I knew that Zulu was no more difficult than any other language I had devoted time to learning. The price I was being asked to pay for learning Zulu, for learning more Zulu, was all of a sudden much higher than originally advertised. But I restrain myself and, inarticulate with anger that feels like righteous indignation, hold my peace.

When I encountered Aubrey Tearle on reading Ivan Vladislavić's extraordinary novel, *The Restless Supermarket* (2001), I recognized the one who took my money at the library as a type—the self-appointed adjudicator of correct and incorrect, good and bad, easy and difficult (which is to say good and bad), can and cannot, "thou shall" and "thou shalt not." Being white in South Africa boiled down to this shabby concentrate of inhibition—and perhaps, I told myself, it still does. It was pathetic, but it was also proof of the anal-sadistic arrogation of violent sovereign decision that had been a psychological condition of possibility for apartheid.[95] Providing an excuse for not learning an African language, it was sustaining apartheid well beyond its official demise.

I stand by my psychopolitical diagnosis. But I think that I see better now how my reaction was, in the Freudian sense, unconsciously "over-determined."[96] As I discovered when I struggled to converse in Zulu about D.B.Z. Ntuli's *Ngicela uxolo* at my lesson with Eve, the inhibition, which I attributed to the man in the library, and analyzed with such relentless clarity, was also my own. The inordinate anger that possessed me at being told that something for which I wished was "very difficult," and thus, as I heard it, too difficult for *me*, was Oedipal. Detecting a slight, I had, without having the words to express it, directed a murderous anger toward a salesman—which was what my late father did for a living—who was calling for a high price, as if demanding recompense. My memory, wavering between two dates, wants me to believe that this transaction took place in the year that my father died—and mourning is known to bring forth ambivalence, and thus projection arising from feelings of guilt.[97] Although invested with a different affective tone—not anger but contrition—and calling forth reparative instead of paranoid trends, then, in Eve's office, just as almost a decade before at the South African Library, my father was the one standing, in my phantasy, between me and the language that I wanted to learn. As if the linguistic, social, political, and educational barriers were not sufficiently formidable.

Again

I take up *Learn More Zulu* again. The idea is to make an analysis of the book. But before long I am using it to refresh my Zulu. Working through *Learn More Zulu* in sequence for the first time, I allow it to instruct me. From time to time this brings up a memory of the autumn, some three years before, when Eckson assigned me sections of the book for homework, and we read together from it. His infectious laughter and irreverent sense of humor would always make learning easy. There were the verbs of incomplete predication—some teachers just call them auxiliary verbs—verbs that need to be followed by other verbs in order to form a predicate: *-lokhu*, keep on doing, do persistently; *-hlala*, do from time to time, do habitually.[98] The latter is not to be confused with *hlala*, the commonly used intransitive verb, meaning to sit or to dwell.

Hlala is one of the first verbs that one learns in order to make conversation.[99] It is the same in Xhosa as it is in Zulu. My thoughts wander back in time to the first few weeks of Xhosa Intensive, a course at the University of Cape Town (UCT) designed for non-native speakers who have not studied Xhosa as a school subject. A group of students, most of us white, sits on the lawn next to the Arts Block with Professor Satyo. "Uhlalaphi?" It is my turn to introduce myself: "Ngihlala eObservatory" (I live in Observatory), or rather, as I say it, mimicking the way I imagine a black person pronouncing the name of the place: "Ngihlala eObzevatari." The Professor nods approvingly, perhaps satisfied by my attempt at the fricative *hl*, but I remember being the only one to have said Observatory in that way; mimicry can be mockery, and I am not certain that mine is free of the overtones of racist humor shared not so many years before by me and my schoolmates. Perhaps my sensitivity to the overtones is also why, terrified, I tend to avoid the language laboratory sessions at which I can hear my own voice coming back at me, in effect mimicking me—mocking me—mimicking, badly, what my ear hears of the native speaker as she draws the loan word into her language. No doubt this terror is reinforced by the language lab instructor—a young white man who must have gained fluency as a child growing up in the Eastern Cape—coming over my headphones to correct my flatter-than-flat intonation. Not only can I not claim the good fortune of his upbringing, I am also not far from being tone deaf.

But *-hlala*, as a verb of incomplete predication, brings new territory into view. Although I am familiar from my previous studies with the use of infixes standing for the objects of verbs, learning these verbs, which are also a feature of Xhosa, is a further step into the treasure house of Zulu syntax. For me it is, as Eckson likes to say, "a whole other terrain." It is terrain not covered in *Learn Zulu*, and, I believe, it does not even exist in Fanagalo. There are two separate sections in *Learn More Zulu* devoted to two different types of these verbs, with pages of examples. Eckson says that some of them are not used that much nowadays, but there are the important negatives *-soze*, *-zange*, and *-ngeke*.[100] "Lababafana *bangeke baphumelele* ekuhlolweni ngoba basebenza ngokunganaki." (These boys will never succeed in the examination because they work carelessly.)[101] Nota bene.

The verbs ringing in my head now as I write are not those of "never," but ones denoting repetition: *-phinde*, "to do again"; *-buye*, "and again."[102] *Ngiphinde ngifunde isiZulu*, I am learning Zulu again. Or I am reading Zulu again. Because the verb *funda* can mean to learn as well as to read, it allows a play on words. It is almost as if I say to myself, letting myself be influenced by the title of Nyembezi's book: I am learning more Zulu. That would be true—I certainly am learning more Zulu—but I am also learning Zulu again.

Will there always be this "again?" In my taking up of *Learn More Zulu*, in my taking up of Zulu? Was there ever a *first* time? Was I always already learning Zulu? This has to be a rhetorical question; somewhat like the non-native speaker I imagined in my musings on the Bantu languages, I will have been learning Zulu all of my life. Thanks to the mutual intelligibility of the two languages, to learn Xhosa is *also* to learn Zulu. Those sessions with Professor Satyo in the open air of the Cape Town summer were not the first time.

I remember one of those serious conversations that, in late boyhood, I would have with my mother. The memory brings up a visual image of the South African Broadcasting Corporation (SABC) building on the Sea Point beach front, with the bronze frieze of the signs of the zodiac gracing its façade. The building is adjacent to the high school I attended (the same one John Comaroff went to years before I did). We are walking past the SABC together, or maybe we are in the car, having been for an evening walk on the promenade. We are talking about life and death, and she, with the candor of somebody not driven into mystification by religion, agrees with me that there is no actual point to existing, no reason. It is during this same conversation that, as we move on to talk about how one can, in spite of the absence of a reason, choose to do something with one's life, she suggests—perhaps not entirely seriously—that one day I might become South Africa's ambassador to Transkei, the "homeland" that in 1976 received its "independence" from Pretoria; an event that, within our self-enclosed dyad, was at the time viewed as emancipatory. This was before I had heard the term Grand Apartheid, and Verwoerd was then, to me, just a face on an old postage stamp. I do not remember that in our conversation the need to learn Xhosa ever came up, but, let us imagine that Grand Apartheid succeeded, and that, by the time I was old enough, emissaries would still have been sent by Pretoria to Umtata, then, it would have followed, if I had sought to make this my career, that I would have had to learn Xhosa.

It would have been the first time—as far as I can remember—that a *reason* will or might have existed for me to have begun learning the language; deliberately, and not in the way that one acquires a mother tongue, or picks up a second or third language in early life. Will it have been with that sort of a career in mind—by then, it is true, an impossible career—that I sat with fellow students in a circle on the grass beside the Arts Block? Perhaps, and perhaps that is why, lacking any reason, I could not find it in me to persevere, when I wanted to go and study in the United States, and an upper second in English Honors for an essay on language policy was not going to get me there. "You could be a scholar of Mqhayi," Kelwyn Sole, my generous mentor in South African literature, kindly suggested, as he found me staring into space in the Arts Block corridor trying to decide. But what did I know then of S.E.K. Mqhayi? It was not enough of a reason for me, not for the unhappy twenty-two year old who could no longer bear to be in Cape Town.

But Xhosa Intensive was not the first time I was learning Zulu as I was learning Xhosa. All I can discover is a whole series of "again"—and repetition can have a maddening effect, as Kalahari Surfers demonstrated in "Reasonable Men," its pastiche in which the word "again" is repeated to punctuate repetitions of sentences from P. W. Botha's proclamation of a State of Emergency in 1985, and from a speech by the Chief of Police: "I call on all well-meaning and reasonable South Africans to join hands." "Movement will be restricted." "Again."[103] An Emergency would be proclaimed the following year, again. As I extend my series of "again" into the future—as I do with each stroke of my pen—I also take it back earlier and earlier, to a time when learning Xhosa—which was also learning Zulu—was without reason (and perhaps also not "reasonable"). Although as a child I was learning Xhosa from A., who looked after my sister and me as children—not much, to be sure, although it was not nothing: *ndakubetha* (note the pronominal infix -*ku*-)—there was no sense that I ought to be learning Xhosa because it was *her* language. There was nothing wrong with her English; when she asked me, years later, when I had already left home, why I was learning Xhosa at UCT I had no answer for her, realizing then that there had been an opportunity missed, rather a long time before. I might also have found out how the boy-mother dyad's phantasy of a diplomatic career for me in the Bantustans would have looked to somebody whose Herschel Hlubi community was, as I found out later, incorporated by fiat into Kaiser Matanzima's Transkei by the South African government—an act that also led to an exodus of Sotho people to QwaQwa, and Botshabelo near Bloemfontein.[104] This was what "independence" meant to people who came from there. It is painful for me to remember the ugly racist things that I would say to A.,—and, with a mortifying shame (although it should also be said that she gave as good as she got), I admit that the worst of these things were said when I was old enough to know better, or, put another way, old enough to know how much they could hurt her. But that "a long time before" of the missed opportunity was before I knew better, and before I knew enough to wound her with my words. Making reparation, I think it is for that before-time that I am learning Zulu, again; perhaps there is something from then that can be taken up again. Call it a life, if you will. And if life is without reason, then so is learning Zulu.

SECOND HAND

I am not the book's first owner, I remind myself, as I chart my history of attempts at learning Zulu in South Africa. Having owned this copy of *Learn More Zulu* closer to its date of publication, perhaps the previous owner will bring me nearer to its implied reader—the one who is advised by Nyembezi that it is not Fanagalo that will be learned from the book, but Zulu as spoken by Zulus.

Let us recall that in 1948 Shuter and Shooter, the most important publisher of Zulu language textbooks, had given its imprimatur to *Basic Bantu*, by K. Hopkin-Jenkins, a manual for whites in what its author dubs "Basic Bantu," the "dialect, the Native name for which is Fanakalo."[105] And, like *isiKula*—another name for Fanagalo, still current in the 1950s, that attributes the use of the pidgin to Indians, pejoratively referred to as *amaKula* (Coolies)—*Silunguboi*—language used by whites when speaking to the "boys"—suggests that it is not viewed by Zulus as their language.[106] This was the state of things when Nyembezi published *Learn Zulu* with Shooters in 1957, and joined the publishing house as an editor in 1960 after resigning in protest against Bantu Education from his lecturer's post at the University of Fort Hare.[107]

More and more I suspect that, as much as it means giving up one's claim to white supremacy and *baasskap*, and a violently adjudicative attitude, a giving up of Fanagalo by the white learner circa 1970 means relinquishing a familiar channel for white solidarity. D. T. Cole is correct to point to the crude racism in S. E. Aitken-Cade's *So! You Want to Learn the Language! An Amusing and Instructive Kitchen Kaffir Dictionary*, published in Salisbury in Southern Rhodesia in 1951: "BEAT, vb . . . *chaiya*. 'I'll beat you.' 'Mena chaiya wena.' If you are going to get any effect do it first and talk later."[108] But what is the purpose of the racism? And what is the purpose of the Fanagalo? In a headnote to his jocular little lexicon, Aitken-Cade writes that "K. K. stands for Kitchen Kaffir, a useful but incoherent language. The idea behind the dictionary is to provide the farmer with a vocabulary of Shona, but the author cannot agree that this will ensue."[109] When Cole quotes from Aitken-Cade, he elides the Shona words that precede those in K. K.: "BEAT, vb. very tr.—*rova, rowa*."[110] Is the joke not on the "farmer," who, although fancying himself the subject of this "very transitive" verb, might not have sufficient command of Shona to deliver his threat in that language? But with whom might this joke be shared?

Ralph Adendorff gives an example of some white South African immigrants to New Zealand who say things in Fanagalo in a video made for friends and family back home.[111] Fanagalo, Adendorff observes, appears to be a way for whites to bond. This, I believe, is also evident in *So! You Want to Learn the Language!*, even if the book professes to be about learning and wanting to learn a language. On the back cover of the booklet is an advertisement for Whitehead & Jack, Water Boring Specialists of Salisbury. In the form of a letter, the ad begins, "Zonke Shamwari gatina lapa Southern Rhodesia, Mena bala lo brief lapa gawena indaba zonke tina maboy lapa Whitehead and Jack tina funawena izwa lo indaba gatina. Tina funa wena na lo umfasi gawena na lo mombie gawena yena bona lo mugodi ga lo manzi ga lo mushi sterek." (To all of our friends here in Southern Rhodesia, I write this letter to you because all of us boys here at Whitehead and Jack we want you to hear our business proposition. We want you and your wife and your cattle to see the hole for the water that is really good.) The letter ends: "Goodiby, Mena boy gawena, Boss, [signed] R. K. Whitehead, for Jim Fish, Kero Whitehead & Jack." (Goodbye, I am your boy, Boss, [signed] R. K. Whitehead, for Jim Fish, care of Whitehead & Jack.) Addressed to a white farmer, who might need a borehole drilled in order to water his cattle and irrigate his tobacco, the letter presupposes that, although it is supposed to be the language in which the boss addresses his boy, the tongue of the brute who strikes first and threatens afterwards, the actual function here of the Shona-inflected Fanagalo—also called Chilapalapa in Rhodesia—is to foster cordial relations between whites. Whitehead plays the "boy" in order to drum up business for the firm. Similarly, years later, entertainer Wrex Tarr would have white audiences in stitches with his skits, which sold records for him called *Zonke Chilapalapa* and *Futi Chilapalapa*. Julie Frederikse, who registers black hatred of Chilapalapa, says that Tarr was a swimming pool salesman, and has a picture of him in *None but Ourselves* wearing a white safari suit with short pants and long socks.[112] Perhaps then it is the habits of white solidarity—my Sea Point classmates might remember some of the "Munt" jokes, racist exotica brought by the immigrant schoolboys from Rhodesia as their families fled the country in the late 1970s—as much as a white attitude toward Africans, that *Learn More Zulu* sets out to break.

My copy of *Learn More Zulu*'s first owner's name appears in cursive on the flyleaf: H. Eschen, or is it Th. Eschen? Close to Escher of the strange loops. The name, although it resonates uncannily with that of my teacher in New York, doesn't ring a bell. A few traces are left of Eschen's studies and concerns. The most revealing is a lined octavo page torn from a notebook with some cursive script; this now yellowing sheet serves as a bookmark to pages containing a reading exercise that begins: "Izindlela zesimanje zokulima azifani nakancane nezakudala." (Today's farming methods do not resemble in the slightest those of olden days.)[113] Was Eschen a farmer? Could Eschen have been a farmer of the sort imagined by Aitken-Cade, or the advertisement for Whitehead's boreholes? Probably not; one could open *Learn More Zulu* at random and find sentences and passages to do with cultivation and stock-raising.

Who was Eschen then? Unfolding the sheet of paper, I read, jotted down in English:

> Constitution
> 1960 Merger
> Structure
> 6 members of Circuit Council
> Dean, 1 Pastor, 4 laymen

Eschen's attentions are divided. Church matters compete with the Zulu lessons. I contact David Attwell, author of a splendid account of the Zulu poetry debate that took place in the late 1930s between B. W. Vilakazi and H.I.E. Dhlomo.[114]

From the nomenclature, David surmises, it is probably the Lutheran Church, adding that its various synods in Natal merged in 1960 against the wishes of the government.[115] Following the merger, which brought white and black congregations into a single structure, David wonders, might Eschen, as a pastor or layman, have seen a need to improve his Zulu?

On the outer folds of the sheet are some Zulu notes that Eschen made: "wonke umuntu" and "bonke abantu"—two ways of saying "everybody"—and what looks like "ihashi elisihlalo," perhaps meaning saddle-horse. (I don't recall this item of vocabulary being in *Learn More Zulu*, so was Eschen working with a teacher?) On the other outer fold, written twice, the second time partially underlined, perhaps in order to indicate cadence, is one of my favorite words: *ingxoxo*, a conversation, or a chat. There Eschen is, sitting with his teacher. Just the two of them—or is there a class? Eschen's mind is on the church while studying Zulu, and on Zulu when in church. Eschen, Escher. Were one to give the sheet of paper a twist and tape its ends together—I do not actually attempt it with this brittle leaf—the resultant Moebius strip would miraculously form a continuous plane out of what had been two sides. Study and its purpose would suddenly form an uninterrupted continuum. Would Eschen have wished for that as fervently as I?

I do not doubt it. Using David's clues to help me narrow down my investigations, I believe that I have identified my book's first owner. Hedwig Eschen, born in Germany in 1925, joined the Emmaus mission station in Natal in 1953, where she was given the task of working with the youth. In order to accomplish this, "Hedwig quickly had to learn how to speak Zulu from the black missionaries. She also studied through the University of South Africa (UNISA) and mastered the language through to Matric level." She was subsequently posted to Swaziland, and, "In 1974 the Berlin Missionary Society seconded her to the Bible Society of South Africa to help with the translation of the Bible into Swati." Being Nguni languages, Swati and Zulu are mutually intelligible. As she says, "Thanks to my knowledge of Zulu . . . I could easily master Swazi." Just as I was learning Zulu when I was learning Xhosa, Hedwig Eschen was learning Swati as she learned Zulu. After twenty years of collective labor, the Swati Bible translation appeared in 1996, and in that same year Eschen left Cape Town and returned to Germany.[116] I am guessing that, before she departed, she donated her books to the South African Library.

There are a few other notations here and there made by Eschen in *Learn More Zulu*. Some of them cross-reference sections in the Zulu grammars of Wanger and of Doke, which were first published in 1917 and 1927 respectively. This is the diligence that ultimately made Hedwig Eschen a Bible translator—and perhaps, by 1970, she had already finished her UNISA studies, and, as she evidently did, was "[teaching] missionaries from Germany, Sweden, and Norway to speak Zulu."[117] If her Zulu fossilized, then it did at quite an advanced stage. Some of her annotations occur deep in the book—for example, lesson 31, on verbs "indicat[ing] an Action or State which has not been going on hitherto" that use -*se*- as prefix or infix.[118] If I fasten onto repetition, Eschen remarks on the unprecedented. But she had in her hands a freshly printed first edition, whereas the same volume, for me, is a second-hand book from a different era with a faded cover.

But *Learn More Zulu* is still more than sound. At over 450 pages, excluding the key to the exercises, which takes it well over 500, when it was published it was easily the most comprehensive intermediate Zulu manual produced for non-native speakers, and may in fact still be. In an era when Doke's *Textbook of Zulu Grammar* remained in use as a school book—Njabulo Ndebele tells me that when he was in high school it was what they used for Zulu as a first language—it marked a distinct pedagogical advance. As with *Learn Zulu*, Nyembezi's primer, its points of grammar are illustrated with numerous examples. Sentences for reading and translation test the student on the grammar and new vocabulary introduced in each section. Nyembezi is systematic. As one moves through the book, the examples keep incorporating grammar and vocabulary from earlier sections. There are also, as in *Learn Zulu*, longer passages for reading, as well as clusters of proverbs—a staple of high-school examinations—accompanying most of the lessons. These are drawn from Nyembezi's *Zulu Proverbs*, which was originally his master's thesis at the University of the Witwatersrand.[119] In more recent intermediate and advanced textbooks, such as *IsiZulu soqobo*, sample texts are drawn from contemporary media and from literary works. In contrast, the longer passages for reading, with the exception of the Lord's Prayer and Psalms, all appear, like the sample sentences, to have been devised by Nyembezi himself to reinforce the grammar lessons; there are, in any case, no copyright acknowledgments that suggest otherwise. Without thinking, one asks oneself: Why did Nyembezi stop writing fiction after the publication of his wildly popular comic novel, *Inkinsela yaseMgungundlovu* (The Rich Man of Pietermaritzburg),[120] in 1961? But did he ever really stop? Even if they do not add up to a novel, or form a single continuous narrative, the fragments that Nyembezi composed for *Learn More Zulu* repeatedly bring his manual into the ambit of fiction. Like any work of fiction, *Learn More Zulu* reveals a world. It also invites the complicity of its reader.

World and Reader

What is the world of *Learn More Zulu* like? For most of its inhabitants, the world is rural. People travel to town, and to the big cities, to work. They also go into town to shop, to go to the cinema, or to appear in court. Some live in "locations," African townships that could be urban or rural. Much is revealed about their farming activities, as well as about home and family life, and the skills needed to build, sew, and cook. There is much concern among these people about education, health, and religion, so too about crime, and the workings of criminal justice. Less is said about sport and recreation, although occasionally people go away on holiday.

Their world is settled, orderly, even sedate. There are no great upheavals, certainly nothing of the magnitude of the great cattle killing of the Xhosa of 1854, an event known to history, Nyembezi informs us, as "The National Suicide of the Xhosa People."[121] There had supposedly been a "national suicide" of the Herero in German South West Africa in the decades following the 1904 genocide initiated by Von Trotha,[122] and the archaic explanatory model is being projected back. In the world of *Learn More Zulu*, there is poverty to be sure, and low pay. But some prosper, through honest hard work and good business sense, and not every employer pays a bad wage. Although some people are dishonest and cheat, their tricks never bring about the sort of crisis caused by Ndebenkulu, the confidence man in *The Rich Man of Pietermaritzburg*.

Already I am writing as if, from the outset, the world of *Learn More Zulu* is a Zulu world like Nyanyadu in *The Rich Man of Pietermaritzburg*. But that would be to pass over something uncanny that strikes one as soon as one reads the book in order—as I am doing for the first time now that I read it again. For at least the first fifty pages, there are no conclusive signs that any of the subjects in Nyembezi's book are Zulus, or even that one is in South Africa. Until we meet a certain Khumalo, when proper names are used, which is infrequently, all are English, and it is more than one hundred pages into the book before an actual place name—almost predictably, eGoli (Johannesburg)—is mentioned.[123] It takes more than fifty pages for racial difference to be explicitly registered—*umlungu* (whiteman)—and for the existence of apartheid—*ilokishi* (location, or African township)—to be hinted at.[124] It would take a pupil already quite advanced to recognize the hints of Fanagalo, and hence the possibility of it not being Zulu as it is spoken by Zulus, in the sentence: "Heyi wena! Ziphi izinkomo? Kanti ufuna ukusenga ngasikhathi sini wena namuhla?" (Hey wena! Where are the cows? Tell me, you want to milk at what time today?)[125] But the same pupil might have gathered that Zulu, just as it borrows extensively from Afrikaans and English, sometimes also loans words and phrases from Fanagalo. So is the sentence really evidence of racial difference?

The first intimation that the subject of a sentence might be a Zulu comes with the censure of a certain boy who accepts things that are given to him with one hand, which is disrespectful.[126] It is generally known that, among Zulus, as among Xhosa people, one receives and one gives with both hands. Even if one does not bring the edges of one's palms together, or cup one's hands, one grasps the right forearm or wrist with the left hand in order to give or to receive. This is also done sometimes when shaking hands. It is also generally recognized that this is not the way among whites, who think nothing of receiving or giving with one hand, and make no distinction between left and right when doing so. So, when receiving change in a shop, for example, a white customer might be handed her money with one hand, or she might notice that hand being supported by the left. The same thing might be noticed when the cashier receives payment. It can make a difference when the white person uses both hands to pay, and this is noticed, but it doesn't always make a difference.

But this "generally known" and "generally recognized" dynamic shows that *Learn More Zulu* assumes a complicity on the part of its implied reader, without which the book would be unbearably dry; when it is as fully assumed as the implied reader is able or prepared to, it allows the book to become an elaborate work of irony, or at least a great in-joke. This implication of the reader is, of course, already apparent in the prefatory remarks on Fanagalo in lesson 1, "Siqhuba izifundo zethu zesiZulu." (We move our Zulu lessons forward.)[127] Throughout *Learn More Zulu*, as in those remarks, the jokes are usually those in which the student is given leave by the teacher to laugh at himself as he is seen by the teacher, which is to say by Zulus—insofar as in lesson 1 the teacher professes to speak for Zulus more generally. Typically, however, it is the complicity made possible by a shared knowledge of social, political, and cultural context that provides the book's animating spirit. Because a great deal of this context is made available through elision, this requires a particularly attentive—and, let us admit, candid—reader.

For that reader, the enumeration of things considered polite among Zulus, but not observed by whites, might be redundant. Or it might not be. So, about 150 pages later, when Nyembezi lists "Certain Things about Respect as Practiced by Zulu People" (*Izinto ezithize ngenhlonipho yabantu bakwaZulu*), Nyembezi stipulates before anything else: "When you are given something you receive it with two hands; do not receive it with one hand. This differs in the custom of white people because they accept with a single hand."[128] It is hard to imagine that, having worked with a teacher through *Learn Zulu*, and having entered so far into *Learn More Zulu*, a process that would have taken at least a year or two, the student would not have received some hint about this. A private tutor might have accepted money, and any teacher some homework at least. And would a teacher not have used the example of the disrespectful boy[129] to at least remind her pupil—the quintessential receiver of gifts—of something he should, now that he is learning Zulu, be doing each time he accepts anything from his teacher? Even Eschen might have instructed her Norwegians thus, emphasizing the gratitude that, for Melanie Klein, is possible when one no longer envies the giver and her capacity to give. What actual teacher could have had the patience to wait so long? What flesh and blood teacher could have restrained himself from inviting his pupil to be in on the joke? Not Eckson, who, briefing me for my visit to Jozini, slyly asked me to turn to page 256 of *Learn More Zulu*. It is in this list of things too that the conventional Zulu gender and age hierarchies never contradicted by any of the book's examples are explicitly set out. But, then, thank heavens, he and I never worked through Nyembezi's book in sequence.

It is not necessarily a pleasure to be told the truth about how one is seen or heard. When Eckson and I listened to an episode of a radio drama together, in which a black actor was putting on the accent of a young white farmer speaking Zulu, I exclaimed: "That's not how I sound!" He assured me that, to him, I sounded just like the character in *Umhlaba kaJoji* on Ukhozi FM. Better to know than to labor under a delusion—and better to laugh at one's own deludedness than to ask others to take the delusion for reality. Perhaps David Brown is right to point to the salutary implications of parodic mimicry in "Fanagalo," the popular song Zoë Wicomb and Liz Gunner also remember hearing on Springbok Radio.[130] Before being recorded by the Petersen Brothers, an all-white band,[131] it was a hit in 1952 for the Woody Woodpeckers.[132] "Jim, shina lo shoes / Jim, pressa lo suit. . . . Fanagalo, Fanagalo / A Zulu boy will understand / Fanagalo, Fanagalo/ The magic word from Zululand," will thus first have been mimicry of a white master addressing his houseboy. *Silunguboi*, in other words, for the generic Jim.

And in those days there were still houseboys, just like the one who is the eponymous character in Donald Swanson's 1949 film *Jim Comes to Joburg*. And, indeed, one of *Learn More Zulu*'s most striking narrative vignettes is of a migrant worker recounting his experiences working as a houseboy in Johannesburg.[133] Like the book's opening remarks, it confides in the reader, opening a window onto how Zulus perceive whites, its frequent anticipatory negations—for instance, "Wayengangidlavuzi nje" (He wouldn't just scold me)[134]—telling the attentive reader that the teller knows that his interlocutor expects to hear predictable criticisms of the white employer (*umLungu*).

When *Learn More Zulu* speaks through elision, however, not all of its elisions are supplied in the actual pages of the book. The reader has to be implicated further than instruction alone would make possible. She has to bring her own knowledge, experience, and—above all—her candor.

As one reads on, the specifically Zulu (and black South African) character of *Learn More Zulu*'s world progressively grows; it is that which makes the relative blankness of the first one hundred pages stand out in uncanny relief.

Two Schools

Early in *Learn More Zulu*, there is a reading-comprehension exercise. Homework for Eschen, who has penciled "*Msombuluko*" (Monday) at the top.[135] The reading passage is about a meeting of parents and teachers concerning overcrowding at their school. This is a perennial problem in the rural heartland; in one of the classrooms at Sinethezekile, which had a student body of over 1,900 in 2008, I had to squeeze myself between the blackboard and the desks at the front in order to teach. They need to build, but there is no money: "The school inspector says that the government says there is no money. The school board also says it has no money. Even so it is necessary that there be building."[136] Stylistically, the passage is interesting, suggesting a clamor of voices stressing the urgency of action, much like chapter 12 of Paton's *Cry, the Beloved Country*. An appeal, made to the parents at large, takes the form of a series of second-person-plural imperatives: "Ngakhoke mina ngithi, bazali, sukumani. Linye kuphela ikhambi lokwelapha lesisimo. Yakhani nina isikole sabantwana benu. Yandisani lesisikole senu. Yakhani futhi nezinye izikole ezintsha. Lesisikhathi sethu sidinga imfundo. Ukungafundi kuzobalimaza abantwana bethu. Ngisho njalo mina." (Therefore I say, parents, stand up. There is only one remedy for this situation. You build your children's school. Expand your school. Also build new schools. This time of ours needs education. Not learning will hurt our children. I say so.)[137] The school—as a place of learning—is a highly invested site. Because it is where children go, it represents the future. Is there any place in the world where the school is not invested with the hopes—and therefore also the fears—of the parental generation? In *Learn More Zulu*, the implied reader of which is more mature than for *Learn Zulu*, which contains reading exercises like "My Cat" and "Our Dog,"[138] the school (or this school) is also a reminder of the value being placed on learning—and on learning Zulu—and of what obstacles are encountered for learning in general.

The implied reader is put in the place of the parent—being addressed at the meeting with an appeal for money, even for help to build. An implication in loco parentis, a gentle invitation into complicity. The final question in the reading comprehension is not actually a question, but an exhortation: "Shono (yisho) indlela yokuhlangabezana nalesisimo." (Say a / the way of meeting this situation.)[139] An invitation to composition. I would love to have seen Eschen's composition, or her students'. But there is no explicit sign in the passage that this is a Zulu school, or even a black school. Even the vocabulary is as unmarked as can be. Although the verb *biza* (to call, or to summon) is used, the noun *umhlangano* (meeting) is used rather than *imbizo* (meeting called by a chief or other authority). "Njalo nje, kukhon' imbizo," sings celebrated maskandi Phuzekhemisi in the 1990s, "sokhokhela . . . emakhosini, esikoleni." (All the time, there is *imbizo* . . . we are going to pay . . . at the chiefs', at the school.)[140] He speaks for those who have had enough of having to pay—to chiefs, to be sure, but also to their local school governing bodies. The charge or suspicion of misappropriation is never far away; even in *Learn More Zulu* there is at least one example of somebody unwilling to pay dues to an organization unless it is clear what will be done with the money.[141] *Inkohlakalo* (corruption) and *ukukhwabanisa* (embezzlement) are among the first new words that Eckson teaches me as we discuss current affairs. I would add *umkhonyovu*, not a word found in older dictionaries, but commonly used nowadays to refer to fraud. The latter, along with *ukukhwabanisa*, is what is often suspected of school boards and local government—anybody raising funds for any public project, really—by many people. I doubt, though, that the implied reader of *Learn More Zulu* is being encouraged by Nyembezi to go as far as this—imagine Eschen writing, in answer to question eight: Get rid of corrupt school boards! No, the implication is different in *Learn More Zulu*. Although there is irony, there is not necessarily cynicism.

What Nyembezi appears to be looking for is comprehension of a need that is genuine—it bears all the hallmarks of the era's protest writing—and, once that comprehension has been won, and the reader is himself doing the homework of finding a remedy, then another, rather different, tableau may be presented to him: "Lapha kulendawo yakithi sinenhlanhla enkulu. Kukhona isikole esikhulu semisebenzi yezandla yezinhlobo ngezinhlobo." (Here in this place of ours we have great fortune. There is a big school for manual trades of several different kinds.)[142] And not only a school, but houses, a huge hospital, and so forth. Have they been built by the community? There are, to be sure, school buildings that have been put up by the pupils at the trade school,[143] but construction on this scale, and the organization and planning it presupposes, could only have been undertaken by the government. We have before us, in other words, an example of "separate development." Yet, in contrast to the passage in which funds are being solicited from the parents because the government has no money, the government is not mentioned.

Eckson and I read the passage together: a proud parent is showing a visitor around, and they approach the school to meet the host's son, who is just getting out of school, where he is learning carpentry. The exercise introduces the locative demonstrative copulatives such as *naso*, *nazi*, and *nabo*, some of which, being unobvious in their relationship to their noun-class markers, take time for the non-native speaker to pick up and to use correctly; one has a choice between rote learning and the cumulative contextual exposure that will teach you, sooner or later, for instance, that *nangu* is what goes with *umuntu* or uKhumalo, and *nansi* with *imali*. But, as one of the proverbs just before the reading goes: "Ithemba kalibulali." (Hope does not kill.) Eckson is even ready to challenge the applicability, in this day and age, of the proverb "Umlungu angathunga isicoco," said by Nyembezi to be "descriptive of something that can never happen." I believe that Nyembezi himself might have thought it possible that a "whiteman may sew on a headring"—although, in truth, it is probably a long time since *anybody* sewed on a headring.

The reader is called upon to fill in the elisions: hospital, trade school, magistrate's court, hence government, hence separate development. In *Learn More Zulu* the pattern of elision reaches the highest echelons. Parliament in Cape Town is where representatives make laws for the whole country,[144] but nothing is said to indicate that, if black people from Natal are represented, they are, as I learned back in high school, represented indirectly—by white senators;[145] that it is whites who make the laws for the country. This contrasts with how Nyembezi makes this explicit in his translation of Alan Paton's *Cry, the Beloved Country*, *Lafa elihle kakhulu* (1957): "Phela uyazi ukuthi kukhona abelungu abamela abantu ePalamende." (You know that there are whites who represent blacks in Parliament.)[146] The blankness of Nyembezi's civics lesson in *Learn More Zulu* makes me weep—but what would it have done to *him*, as he wrote it? He did, after all, appeal to UNISA's 1974 graduating class to "speak up" despite "distrust[ing] even friends."[147] And after Bantustan structures were extended into urban areas, in July 1979 Nyembezi, then "a member of the Central Committee of *Inkatha*, resigned from Dr Koornhof's Regional Committee for the Durban-Pietermaritzburg area on the grounds that his participation ... was in conflict with his rejection of apartheid."[148] The splendors of separate development shown to the visitor—"Naso-ke isibhedlela" (There is the hospital); "Nazi izindlu abafundela kuzo, nansiya indlu abadlela kuyo, naziya abalala kuzo" (Here are the buildings in which they study, over there is the building where they eat, and over there are the ones where they sleep)[149]—are hardly darkened by the presence of convicts laboring in the gardens of the magistrate's court (even today you will see this sort of thing, as I did when I went to the Bramley police station to report damage to my car for the insurance claim). "Sengathi zitshala izimbali" (It looks like they are planting flowers). In *The Scarlet Letter*, Nathaniel Hawthorne called the jailhouse the black flower of civilization. Of what are Nyembezi's flowers? What we might call the structural conditions of possibility for separate development are not mentioned, or at least not on this guided tour. For that we have to page even more deeply into the book, in order to acknowledge that Nyembezi has by no means forgotten them, and is far from concealing their violence from view. Forced removals are alluded to—once—when a man describes how, after the government took his land, he moved his homestead to the foot of the Drakensberg.[150] And the pass laws are acknowledged in a single grammatical example, in which an employer or official asks people who have come to ask him to attend to their passes to wait until he finishes what he is doing.[151]

More powerful than the full-scale critique that began to appear in the protest poetry of around the same time, these single mentions (*hapax legomena*, as it were) reveal not only the existence of a system, but also of a strong tendency of that system to suppress critical discourse about itself; no, not even critical discourse, even the mere mention of aspects of it widely known, experienced, and considered to be unjust. Nietzsche wrote that "einmal ist keinmal," but the power of this rhetoric of singular mention must be registered. If patterns are typically established through repetition, here the pattern is evoked, in its elision, by the singular instance. For these two examples, there is no "again." Skip either one, and you miss it. *Ubandlululo*, the standard word in Zulu for apartheid, means discrimination. Forced removals and the carrying of passes were not measures imposed on whites. These two examples might take the reader's mind back to a much earlier reading passage—on the dipping of cattle, mandated by the government, but resented by some.[152] Historically, the reduction of herds, which is the context for *The Rich Man of Pietermaritzburg*, surely ranks as the greater oppression, but dipping was also resisted.[153] Picking up these signs depends on how much context the reader brings. Looking at them, one may speak, sociologically—short of state censorship, which was extremely strict at the time—of the pressures and strictures of self-censorship on an author and publisher writing for the school market. And one would have Professor Nyembezi on one's side. But that is only part of the story, and it should not prevent us from seeking out the rest. More interesting than the habitual lament about the schoolbook market's stultifying effects, and than the associated dynamics of protest and (self-)censorship, is what this elision and occasional mention means for the lesson (or lessons) being taught by *Learn More Zulu*.

Who Is Your Teacher?

Nyembezi's manual teaches one a great deal of Zulu, which it teaches very well, but it also teaches one a reading position: "Lencwadi, *Learn More Zulu*, sizoyifunda ngokucophelela okukhulu"—"This book, *Learn More Zulu*, we shall study with great care," Nyembezi translates.[154] But he could just as well have written: *read* with great care. Gayatri Chakravorty Spivak—dear and esteemed teacher—links reading position to a non-coercive rearranging of desires,[155] and, in learning a reading position from Sibusiso Nyembezi, there is also such a rearranging. Bonds of white solidarity are being displaced. But for that to happen the reader has to be diligent, as Nyembezi says right at the beginning: "Kudinga ukuba sifunde ngokucophelela." (It is necessary that we read with great care.)[156] We know from her life's work that Hedwig Eschen took these words to heart.

The energy of *Learn More Zulu* begins to flag after the reading exercise on pages 291–93, as section upon section is added on the structure of verbs, with page upon page of accompanying exercises. Although these sections add important information, it is information with which a good teacher could provide a motivated intermediate student in two or three lessons. It does not require the twenty-odd lessons and 150 pages that Nyembezi devotes to it; not surprisingly, the only things that Eckson asks me to look at from these sections are a couple of dialogues.[157] It is in these pages that the *hapax legomena* of forced removals and pass laws are buried. Good luck finding them, Mister School Inspector! There are, even so, a couple of remarkable passages for reading. First, there is a little ghost story that reminds me of D.B.Z. Ntuli's radio play *Isipho sikaKhisimuzi* (The Christmas Present).[158] There is also another vignette that I shall look at later in more detail; it occurs right at the end, just before a lesson on Zulu numbers and the sections of practical vocabulary (doctor's office, farm, building site, church), and after about fifty pages, for the duration of which, atypically, there occur no reading passages whatsoever.

But, beyond what he so skillfully teaches you, through his saying and his not saying, *who* is one's teacher? Is this not what the pupil—or at least a certain sort of a pupil—would really like to know? In Standard Four, I would ride my bike to the Mouille Point beachfront, where it was said that my beloved teacher had his flat, and circle about, hoping to glimpse him at home. But I never did see him, and I was left to wonder whether he ever noticed me on those besotted afternoons. Although he shared a great deal with us, including his holiday snaps when we learned about Holland and Britain in Geography, and also took the four of us with the most Good News Notes to see *Zulu Dawn* as our reward, I cannot say I ever got to know him. It was right, somehow. But every beloved teacher has his or her quirks, his preoccupations beyond the lesson, and Nyembezi is not an exception.

Throughout *Learn More Zulu* one discovers examples in which the subject of a sentence or passage condemns idleness and censures those who beg or borrow money without working. "It surprises me how these people earn a living because they do not work. Perhaps they live by begging. This is the very last time I give them food or money because I see that they want to sponge on other people."[159] A passage for reading has somebody delivering a stern lecture to a worker being fired for laziness and dishonesty.[160] Yet another example brands the poor as thieves: "Poor people who are not accustomed to working, who like merely to sit, are a nuisance because they steal."[161] Industry, thrift, and sobriety are, on the other hand, applauded.[162] The typical stance of a conservative, one might say—of the proud petit-bourgeois *umnumzane* of some of the grammatical examples, whose house has a study (*isitadi*) with shelves of books.[163] And one would surely not be off the mark.

But perhaps there is something else in play too. The great unstated fact of *Learn More Zulu* is the grinding poverty in which most Zulus live. "I should mention," Nyembezi himself emphasizes in a lecture on Zulu literature at the University of Natal in 1961, "that books cost money and the poverty of the people discourages them from using money to buy books instead of buying the bare necessities of life.... The homes are small and crowded and there is poor lighting which makes it difficult to read in the evening."[164] In 1971, the poverty datum line for an African family of six in Durban was estimated at 69.75 Rand, then about one hundred U.S. Dollars, but in 1969/70, according to research done by Lawrence Schlemmer, 60% lived below the poverty line: "He maintained that this depth of poverty probably represented relative luxury compared with conditions in many of the rural African areas in Natal and remarked: 'Ultimately all of us will have to pay dearly for this neglect of human needs.'"[165] I resort to South African Institute of Race Relations statistics and the accompanying commentary because I, like many a humanist scholar, struggle to find an idiom for poverty. Even Nyembezi's plain words sound like an understatement. Zulu has sayings and expressions: "ikati lilala eziko" (the cat sleeps on the hearth); "ukudla imbuya ngothi" (to eat wild spinach with a stick). The former is in *Learn More Zulu*,[166] and, as Eckson tells me, one will hear people use expressions such as "ukuxosha ikati eziko" (to drive the cat from the hearth), or somebody might say "ngiyasebenza ukuze ikati lingacambalali eziko" (I am working so that the cat will no longer recline on the hearth). These expressions relate to a shortage of food—no, to starvation—and the poverty and suffering associated with it. Might Nyembezi's quirk of berating the beggar and the jobless relate to this pervasive poverty, in that those petitioning figures represent to him his own impoverishment, or the prospect thereof? Nyembezi would not actually have had to have been poor himself, or to have struggled to feed his family, but only to have feared this happening. On this reading, a phantasy of deprivation gnaws holes in a fabric of compassion—*ubuntu* does not go unmentioned[167]—that will otherwise carefully have been woven, cared for, and repaired when necessary. It is no accident, in this light, that Nyembezi's most celebrated novel, *The Rich Man of Pietermaritzburg*, represents the prospect of total material loss, which is also the loss of personal and social substance. It is perhaps not surprising that the one perpetrating this total loss—the one who almost takes everything away—is a stranger (*umfokazi*), whose intentions will have been harder to gauge than somebody from the community. What is more curious is that for the threat that the stranger represents to the *umuzi* to be neutralized, the possibility of his having any genuine relation to Zuluness has to be ruled out. Perhaps I am over-reading, but is there not a direct line running from this work of exclusion—another meaning of *ubandlululo*—to the linguistic purism that prefaces *Learn More Zulu*? If I am to learn Zulu as it is spoken by Zulus, then I am entertaining complicity; this is not merely in a critical self-irony and a massive repudiation, by telling elision, of apartheid policy and white solidarity—but, in another irony and also a complicity—in the ruling out of the stranger. Remember how Tiyo Soga asked his readers to distinguish between travelers and beggars.[168] The implied reader of *Learn More Zulu* may be the English-speaking white who knows some Fanagalo, and who may have picked up Shooters' *Basic Bantu*, but the ones who depend on Fanagalo are the Indians who work side by side with Zulus in the sugar cane plantations, and the migrant workers from Mozambique and elsewhere. But they abide beyond the purview of the book. Although the ability to speak African languages is said to exist among whites[169]—and an example refers to Indians—Mozambican and other migrants from outside the borders of the republic are, to my recollection, never mentioned. When other countries are identified, which is infrequently, it is only England and America. No African country is ever named. If one is being taught a reading position, then it is not that of the non-Zulu migrant. One can allow the jolt of coming-to-know-how-one-is-seen-or-heard to turn into narcissism. I have to remind myself that when I set out to learn Zulu, it was with a view to being able to understand it in all of its registers, formal and colloquial (I was sick of listening to Zola rap without understanding any of the words). I am unlikely to reach that goal, since keeping pace with the evolution of colloquialism and pidginization is a full-time occupation, even for a linguist, and it requires residence, especially when the available dictionaries are at least half a century old. But if I do make any progress toward that goal, *Learn More Zulu*, despite its ambiguous implication of the reader, will have been a most expert and generous companion and guide.

Such a historical burden may be too heavy to impose on one's teacher, who, if he is worth his salt, will maintain a reserve that will allow no pupil of his to know where he actually stands. Nyembezi, who, according to an obituary, first stood in front of a class at the age of eighteen,[170] is such a teacher. And the voice of the nervous petit-bourgeois looking out at the world from the window of his study is only one of the voices in his book; "I almost collapsed," another example goes, "when I heard the painful and enervating news that our teacher was dead. I do not know where we shall again get one like him in teaching and goodness. This teacher had sympathy for the poor."[171] In his examples, Nyembezi assumes a multiplicity of personae, as one needs to do if one wants to hold the attention of the student or reader. But perhaps the most intriguing of his personae is the one that he takes on in the final reading passage of the book—in the passage that, a decade after his last novel, appears to mark his final exit from the stage of fictional prose writing. Unlike the ghost story, though, it is not marked as fiction. But how else does one classify a text in which one suspects that everything that is being said is being said, not by the author, but by a persona who is an invention of the author? Once there are different levels of narration, and we are in the realm of focalization, there is the potential for irony, and, as Mieke Bal instructs us when she analyzes suspense,[172] even for dramatic irony. The opinions expressed are, as it were, not necessarily those of the author. One thinks of Señor C's "Strong Opinions," all too easily attributed by some early reviewers of *Diary of a Bad Year* to J. M. Coetzee. But, every week, on a Wednesday in *Isolezwe*, the Zulu daily newspaper, we have an example closer to home—namely, the persona(e) of Volovolo Memela, first among them the Chief of the People of The Point. More than any of the other texts in *Learn More Zulu*, this final one—with the customary imperative "Funda" as its heading, but also with its own title "Ukujikijelana ngamatshe"—has an air of irony. Ending with an exhortation or peroration, its structure is that of a letter to the editor, which is a structure similar to some of Volovolo's columns: addressing a matter of common concern, but, in "Ngeso likaVolovolo" at least, doing so as parody. On the face of it, the text is *against* the "game" played by children—which is by no means a game: "umdlalo wabantwana ongesiwo neze umdlalo ngoba unengozi kuphela"—of throwing stones at one another. It is dangerous, people can get hurt: the players, of course, but also passersby: "By missing its mark a stone is now going to strike those people who are not involved in this business of throwing at each other."[173] These are, for all intents and purposes, the last words of the book. The irony, if there is irony, would be that the persona of the letter condemns stone throwing in order to draw attention to something else, which the implied author wants the reader to notice without his referring to it directly. I read it as a feint. When the youth rose up in the 1970s, stone throwing, which had already played its part in earlier episodes of political resistance, and was, if we credit Bloke Modisane, something of a "game" for boys,[174] was a defining feature; there is the terrifying documentary footage used by *Truth Commission Special Report* of a boy in school uniform shot in the abdomen or side, a stone clasped in his hand. Can this text of Nyembezi be the fearful prediction of the middle-aged educator, who, despite deploring the "game," acknowledges the advent of historical change, thanks to which his generation, although no longer at the vanguard, will be exposed to danger and the heartbreak of seeing a child die? When, with his dying breath, the eponymous old man in the great Triestine writer Italo Svevo's novella *The Nice Old Man and the Pretty Girl* (1929) answers the question, "What does youth owe to age?", he writes "several times the word: Nothing."[175] If, by contrast, the conservative's answer to the same question would be "*Everything, Everything,*" is it certain that this is the answer that Nyembezi would have given?

CHAPTER 2

A Teacher's Novels

> Lapha phandle nezigcwelegcwele zabafana zingamjikijela nanga-
> matshe zimlimaze.
> –*Mntanami! Mntanami!*[1]

The questions with which I left *Learn More Zulu* lead me back to Sibusiso Nyembezi's novels. I am tracking the teacher when, a little voice tells me, I should be paying attention to his lessons. But perhaps that is what happens once you get to a certain stage of learning a language. The learning curve flattens out, the wheels spin, and before you know it you are in transference. On the other hand, could this not also be an instance of something unexpected happening? Just as in *Learn More Zulu* the white language-learner finds him- or herself in an unanticipated reading position, from which vantage the South African scene appears subtly changed, can it not be that what Nyembezi tells us about the struggle over patrimony between fathers and sons leads us toward more profound inklings as to why he should staunchly defend Zulu against the depredations of outsiders?

My wager is that it does: bear with me as I depart from the scene of language learning in order to explain how. I leave for the time being the privileged space of the teacher-pupil dyad, and set out for where I will be outside of the scene, looking in. In addressing matters from before I was born, I stand on less firm ground than when I read a book from 1970. "Before I was born" may mean, in phantasy, before the son comes to harass the parental pair, but it may also mean that when the affairs of those years are imagined, jealousy comes into play more intensely because the pair is, so to say, inaccessible, and phantasy even more powerfully shapes what one discovers.

This is what is productive about the transference, and it is also its risk. What I find out about Nyembezi's fathers and sons may be unverifiable, except insofar as it coincides with lineaments of the transference. Once again, there is an "other hand"—is there not also the chance that Nyembezi's own strictures upon the outsider are transferential, or counter-transferential—an outcome of the more intimate familial struggles playing out in the books he wrote before I was born?

Think back to *The Rich Man of Pietermaritzburg* (1961) and the answer it gives: the father's generation is humbled, as the torch is passed to the son and his age-mates, who are better educated and more adept at switching between codes of country and town, and at negotiating rival cattle and cash economies.[2] In the end, though, you ask, does the know-how of both generations not bow before another system of assembling and organizing information? In Nyembezi's novel, this system is represented by the police detectives who, because they have eyes everywhere—or, at least, elsewhere—can link the stranger who calls himself Ndebenkulu to cases of fraud that have occurred in other places. Even if Nyanyadu's people have had their suspicions, only the police are capable of bringing forth the eyewitness who will make it possible for Ndebenkulu to be *identified* as the notorious confidence man also known as Mlomo. Although the male youth of Nyanyadu are instrumental in exposing his artifices, and they confirm their elders' suspicions that Ndebenkulu cannot be who he says he is because no such name as his exists among Zulus, it is the police who identify him because they can produce his record. Despite the testing of his Zuluness, and the power of laughter to undo the "Esquire" (*isikwaya*) his calling card claims him to be, both generations are, in the book's final denouement, ultimately in the hands of forces better placed to assemble intelligence and to act upon it. This capacity is the familiar hallmark of the modern state.

Although complicated by the incursion of the police, the resolution in *The Rich Man of Pietermaritzburg* still provides one side of an answer: the future— our future—is in the hands of our children. Yet, a decade or so later, in *Learn More Zulu*, because of what is literally in the hands of the children, it may be preferable for it not to be. There is thus an ambivalence toward the son—the boy who throws stones with his friends might get hurt because the adult who has been struck by a stray stone could get angry.[3] When one goes back a decade before *The Rich Man of Pietermaritzburg* and reads Nyembezi's first novel, *Mntanami! Mntanami!* (My Child! My Child!) (1950), one finds this ambivalence played out in the most violent of ways.

Mntanami! Mntanami! is the story of one Jabulani Dlamini, from Mnambithi, District of Ladysmith, in the Natal Midlands. Thrifty rather than prosperous, his parents are upstanding people, envied in the community, who believe in the value of education and send all three of their children to school. Dlamini is strict with his children and does not spare the rod, whereas MaNtuli, his wife, shows none of his harshness. Jabulani, the eldest of Dlamini's two sons, falls in with bad company. He takes up smoking at an early age and plays truant; then he and two of his friends are caught stealing money from registered letters they sign for dishonestly at the local post office. Jabulani does not go to jail, nor does he return to regular school attendance. His father gives him a choice: go to school, or leave my house. Believing himself to be hated by his parents and teachers, one day, without telling a soul, he takes the train to Johannesburg, where nobody knows him, and where he vaguely imagines finding work and starting a new life. There he receives the help of the brothers James and Jack, who, unbeknown to him at first, are criminals. Living at their house in Sophiatown, and having nowhere else to turn because he has no pass, he is initiated into their gang and helps them carry out burglaries in the white suburbs. He enjoys the swagger and material advantages of the gangster's life. One day, however, he is ordered by the shadowy head of the gang to carry out the killing of a young boy, whose body parts are purchased by a shebeen owner as good luck charms. Sensationalist South African newspaper headlines from when I grew up would have called this a "muti killing." Under the pressure of guilt, and under the influence of Alice, his pious girlfriend, as well as the stern Reverend Maphelu of Sophiatown, he confesses his crime to the police, informing on the others. Because of his youth, and his admission of guilt, his life is spared and he is sent to a reformatory, where he is to serve a five-year sentence.

It is impossible not to read *Mntanami! Mntanami!* in the light—or in the shadow—of Alan Paton's *Cry, the Beloved Country*, which appeared two years before it. In Paton's classic 1948 novel, the young Absalom Kumalo, having migrated to Johannesburg, where he turns from honest work to crime, murders Arthur Jarvis, a well known race-relations advocate, after Absalom and two accomplices break into Jarvis's suburban house. By an extraordinary coincidence, both Absalom and Arthur hail from the same place in rural Natal, near Ixopo, which is also in the Midlands. The story thus becomes about how their respective fathers, the Reverend Stephen Kumalo and James Jarvis, distanced by the quasi-feudal racial hierarchies of the colonial countryside, come to terms with each other, lending mutual support in their grief (Absalom will hang for his crime). It is, in the Christian terms that inform the story, a fable of redemption through suffering and sacrifice. The novel's backdrop, however, is the increasing politicization of urban Africans following World War II, and the hopelessness of "tribal" existence on dwindling and overworked rural reserve lands. A strongly positive value is nevertheless attached to a rustic paternalism. It is in this fictive domain, no less than in the "country" rhapsodized in the novel, that the Zulu language becomes a medium of reconciliation, even communion, between the races. Old Jarvis is respected by the Reverend Kumalo because of his mastery of Zulu, and the Jarvis grandson embodies hope for his boyish efforts at learning from the Reverend the language that his father before him was able to speak.

In contrast to *Cry, the Beloved Country*, where there are two fathers and two sons, as well as two grandsons, the moral business of *Mntanami! Mntanami!* is transacted in a relatively tight economy between father and son. As Nyembezi's story unfolds, however, paternal substitutions, both symbolic and characterological, take place. The parable of the Prodigal Son is heard by Jabulani in a sermon, making a deep impression on him, and Dlamini is, at a crucial turn in the story, displaced as father—by the Reverend Maphelu, whose sermon it is, and who speaks in loco parentis, as well as in the name of God the Father.[4] Such substitution is consistent with a polemical point made by the narrator, who deplores the fact that nowadays one hears a father up in arms when another responsible adult disciplines his child for some misdeed: "Akusilo isiko labantu lelo." (It is not the custom of black people, that.)[5]

Paternal protest is thus generalized—or generationalized. Sons are killing their fathers. Because of his son's misdeeds, Dlamini's hair turns prematurely gray then completely white, and MaNtuli frequently weeps, as paternal fears become parental ones. But more pronounced than those parricidal fears is the reaction of the father to them. Even if *Mntanami! Mntanami!* conveys the thrill of Johannesburg and the libidinal pleasures of criminality—a dimension absent from Paton's portrait of Absalom Kumalo, whose sexuality is reproductive but not declaredly allied to pleasure—and does so in a Zulu in touch with the patois of the Golden City, the novel is relentless in its punishment of its protagonist. As a boy, Jabulani is scolded without surcease and mercilessly beaten by his father. Even the sentence of corporal punishment with a light cane handed down by the magistrate for his juvenile thieving has nothing on what his father doles out with his sjambok.

Mntanami! Mntanami! can, however, be heard to speak with more than one voice. The title of the novel itself suggests this bivocality or equivocality, opening the possibility of a change of tone with its repetition of the vocative: *My Child! My Child!*—which is how Daniel Kunene translates the title, and almost certainly how I would have. Along with the standard tonal shift within the single word, there is the possibility in the word's repetition of further changes, depending on the speaker's idiolect and on the pragmatics of the utterance. The iteration might have a different tone. Could there not, somewhere along this spectrum of possible tonal change, reside an ambivalence toward the child, and specifically the son?

Much in the novel would suggest that this is the case. To the possibility of a difference in iteration, we can add a division of roles. When the words *Mntanami! Mntanami!* are uttered in the novel, they are uttered by MaNtuli, whether she is actually speaking, or whether Jabulani is imagining the words being spoken by her.[6] The words are thus marked by the maternal relation. Could a father even utter the words *Mntanami! Mntanami!*? Technically, yes, of course. But when a title is given to this book of fathers and sons, it is the mother's words of distress that supply it. Associated with her forbearance, which contrasts her with Dlamini, they announce a distribution of the parental law between father and mother. When Jabulani, beset by guilt, pictures his parents, this is what we read: "Omfica ngaleso sikhathi wayengathi unesifo senhliziyo, kanti phinde isifo sisemphefumlweni. Uma kungaqhamukanga yena lomfana, abone abazali bakhe bemi bembhekile, amehlo abo egcwele izinyembezi, bembethe izingubo zosizi, ezwe sengathi bathi, 'Hawu Jabulani, Hawu Jabulani.'

Kubuye kuvele unina eyedwa, ezihlathini zakhe kugeleza izinyembezi, emile ethi, 'Mntanami! Mntanami!' Lapho uJabulani ambhoze ubuso bakhe ngezandla efihla lento ayibonayo emehlweni akhe, abibitheke njengomntwana." (The one who found him at that time could have said that he had a sickness of the heart, but never, it was rather a sickness in the soul. When he—the boy—did not appear, he saw his parents standing and looking at him, their eyes filled with tears, wearing clothes of mourning, and he heard as if they were saying: "Hawu Jabulani, Hawu Jabulani." Once again his mother appeared alone, on her cheeks rippled tears, and was standing saying, "Mntanami! Mntanami!" When Jabulani covered his face with his hands, hiding this thing that he was seeing in his eyes, his face puckered like a child about to cry.)[7] First both his parents appear, and speak. Another time, his mother stands before him by herself and utters the words that give the novel its title. One needs to tread carefully here. I would not say that this distribution of roles simply effects a split in parental or even paternal authority, an expression by the mother of a love for the son that the father cannot express. The mother who weeps because she suffers can also always be read as an object of parricidal violence—that of the son, to be sure, but perhaps also of the father. There is an important basic ambiguity in this passage. Although the figures who appear and speak are ostensibly Jabulani's father and mother, the third-person pronoun in "abazali bakhe" (his parents) and the use of "unina" (his mother) make it possible for the figures to be read as the murdered boy's mother and father. That the figures are dressed in mourning reinforces this sense, generating a doubling identification where Jabulani is being mourned as the dead son—by "his parents"—in place of the boy he has killed. The passage does not definitively identify the parents as being Jabulani's. Thus, as other passages tell us, Jabulani, in being beset by guilt, is also beset by the paranoid fear that he is dead to his parents—or, in its more concentrated form, that they want to kill him.

As I pause to ponder this, I look more closely at the book I am reading. Like my copy of *Learn More Zulu*, my copy of *Mntanami! Mntanami!* bears the traces of a previous reader. This reader was, as I am, evidently learning Zulu. There are check marks against paragraphs, some with dates, written in the South African fashion (day-month-year), from the autumn of 1996. Sometimes there are labels for episodes, summarizing a given scene in English. I am reading a scanned copy of the 1950 Afrikaanse Pers-Boekhandel (APB) edition borrowed through interlibrary loan from the University of Wisconsin—could these marginal inscriptions have been made by a student of Professor Kunene, whose fine translation of the novel has just been published? The notations are mostly quite ordinary, paraphrases like the ones that I myself routinely make—for example, "The boy's leg in the pond"[8]—but on one occasion there is a telling misinterpretation, when we read "Mwelase = Brave" below the passage where Mwelase, the boss of the gang, cuts open the boy's body with his knife, ripping out his liver and gall bladder.[9] For the learner, this is an understandable error, for in Zulu *isibindi* (liver) also means courage, a sense not entirely unassimilable to English, in which a coward may be said to be "lily-livered." Unlike Hedwig Eschen, the learner who made these annotations is probably a relative beginner.

For the murdered boy's remains to be laid to rest, his missing leg and liver have first to be recovered from under the shebeen owner's bed: a making-good-again that could just as well apply to Jabulani, whose body has been cut by the cane and flayed by the sjambok. When Jabulani imagines that his parents and teachers hate him, Nyembezi is showing us how the guilty son is engaging in paranoid projection: "Lomfana wayelingisa iningi lezingane eziye zicabange ukuthi abazali bazo bayazizonda." (This boy took after most children, who sometimes think that their parents hate them.)[10] I notice that the corresponding passage is not in Kunene's translation, which is evidently of a later edition from which it and other passages to which I am drawn have been excised—most notably, the entire twelfth chapter, in which the narrator comments directly on the times, tracing social ills to the advent of whites and subsequent African adoption of white ways.[11] Kunene says nothing about which edition he has translated. Are the differences traces of censorship? Was Nyembezi asked to remove certain of his narrator's more pointed comments? Whatever the case, in the 1950 edition, we have the phantasy: I have harmed my parents—*because I hate them*: this is the repressed ingredient—and therefore they hate me.

But can this paranoid projection not itself be the expression of the ambivalence of the father toward the son, who will bring disgrace on his name and consume his cattle through the fines he would have to pay to get his son out of jail?[12] If so, it is the father who fears the son, and his son's generation. It will not study, and it will not work. And, when Jabulani goes to Joburg, the world is turned upside down: study becomes "study" and work becomes "work," euphemisms in the Sophiatown chapters for learning and pursuit of criminal behavior.[13] Just as with the "game" of stone throwing that is not a game at the end of *Learn More Zulu*, if read without irony, should these antitypes gain ground and rule over their types, then all is lost. It is against this scenario that the fathers take up arms against their sons, allying themselves with the teachers. The most strident of the narrative's commenting voices, in the chapter absent from the edition translated by Kunene, deplores a decline in respect for parental authority.[14] It even finds white law too lenient.[15] The Reverend Maphelu, acting in loco parentis, offers the strongest complaint: "Thina asiselutho." (We are nothing now.)[16] Thus, as in *Cry, the Beloved Country*, a paranoid fear of being killed by the son appears to govern the narrative, or at least energizes significant parts of it. Having narrated the crime of parricide—in displaced form: Absalom's killing of Arthur Jarvis—Paton's novel ends by putting the son to death. The father assumes the place of the rivalrous brother, fearing usurpation and deprivation of substance, and this leads to filicidal violence. The same occurs with the Reverend Kumalo, who hates his brother John, and takes the place of Absalom as father to his son's lover's child. In Nyembezi's narrative, however, the deprivation of substance feared in the early chapters is progressively forgotten as a "motive" (except, in passing, when Alice tells Jabulani how her father refused to pay for her to go to school because "akakwazi ukufundisa into okuzothi kusa ibizocelwa ngabafokazi. Akanayo imali yokufundisela abafokazi." (He cannot educate a thing that one day would be asked for in marriage by strangers. He does not have money to educate for strangers.)[17] When it lets speak the Reverend Maphelu, the novel more narrowly frames the national problem as disobedience to paternal authority.

In contrast to *Cry, the Beloved Country*, in *Mntanami! Mntanami!* the symbolic killing of the son is not deferred and does not await the imprimatur of judicial sentencing—as Jabulani carries out Mwelase's orders, the deed that later brings before him the vision of the dead boy and, ambiguously, "his parents." Incidentally, in another clue that the book's impulses lean heavily toward a symbolic killing of the son, in Nyembezi's narrative, the killing of a white homeowner surprised during a robbery is, in retrospect, imagined by Jabulani as a more acceptable deed than his killing of the boy.[18] Yet, unlike in *Cry, the Beloved Country*, the plot, although also relying on the decision of a white judge, leads to clemency—a sojourn for Jabulani in a reformatory: Diepkloof, perhaps? And, if one looks it up, the word *iphelu* means turncoat or betrayer: Maphelu, the Reverend Turncoat? The novel gives its final words to the mother—MaNtuli for certain now—who weeps: "Hhawu! Umntanami! Umntanami!" (Hhawu! You are my child! You are my child!)[19] Nyembezi disseminates his own patronym, displacing singular proper name with pluralized ordinary noun, dissolving, as it were, the name of the father in the tears running down MaNtuli's cheeks: "Amehlo akhe aselokhu agcwala izinyembezi." (Her eyes are now always full of tears.)[20]

If the novel does not allow its fathers to speak without being challenged, nor does it lay the blame for the crime—Jabulani's killing of the boy as displaced filicide—entirely at the door of the family. This is where the novel becomes political, in surprisingly overt ways, compared to the language manual Nyembezi published twenty years later. Its agonizing about the youth and about crime remind one, of course, of Paton. But whereas Paton and his Zulu cardboard cutouts tell us that "the tribe is broken" until it sounds like a stuck record, Nyembezi's Natal in *Mntanami! Mntanami!* is not exactly "tribal." The narrator of the novel says that the pass laws are to blame. If you do not have a pass you cannot legally work in Johannesburg, and if you cannot work then you must "work." It is not the son and his generation that have produced this antitype. Rather it is the system. Seeking to control labor, it produces unemployment and tempts the unemployed into crime, with Jabulani being no exception.[21] In *Learn More Zulu* the topic of stone throwing raised by the concerned citizen may be a red herring: the offended father could be sympathizing with the son, who could get hurt, and in turn hurt him—in politics as much as in a game that he and his age-mates play. But the father's sympathies remain obscure. All we have is a sign of possible subterfuge. In *Mntanami! Mntanami!,* stone throwing serves as a pretext to bring the unsuspecting Jabulani indoors where he will not be observed by others as associating with the brothers James and Jack: "Lapha phandle nezigcwelegcwele zabafana zingamjikijela nangamatshe zimlimaze." (Here outside there are gangster boys who can even throw stones at him and injure him.)[22] If the struggle for substance between the generations has been suspended in the interest of a larger national political struggle, with fears of deprivation at the homestead set aside under the pressure of a more systemic shortage, then Nyembezi's father figures will be the last to declare an armistice, even if in practice one is clearly in effect. Even so, it remains to be decided whether the strictures at the beginning of *Learn More Zulu*, a purism that may relate to a deeply feared deprivation of patrimony, are in place only for the non-native learner of the language.

SOMETHING BRIGHT

In *Cry, the Beloved Country*, once the deed is done—the father killed and then the son—a "small white boy" makes his entrance on a horse.[23] The Jarvis son, or grandson, carries with him the legacy of violence that has cleared the stage of Arthur Jarvis and, in a few more pages, will clear it of Absalom Kumalo too. Like Zinhle in Nkosinathi Ngwane's play *Ngicela uxolo*, the boy is, in only a superficial sense, innocent of the murders. As Paton apostrophizes: "Cry, the beloved country, for the unborn child that is the inheritor of our fear."[24] There is no doubt that, for the novel, the young Jarvis is one of the inheritors, as much as is Absalom Kumalo's unborn child. In an excellent essay on Paton, Tony Morphet shows how that fear arises from unacknowledged feelings of guilt connected to a history of colonial dispossession.[25]

What then does the novel have "the small white boy" do? It has him learn Zulu. In Paton's novel, the ability of white people to speak Zulu is remarked upon, and it is prized. Late in the novel, Kumalo tells a friend that "It was the daughter of uSmith who said, she did not know, she did not care. She said it in English. And when uJarvis said it to me in Zulu, he said, she does not know. But uJarvis did not tell me that she said, she did not care. He kept it for himself."[26] Jarvis had asked the former employer of Kumalo's sister, whom the Reverend has traveled to Johannesburg to seek, whether she knew where she had gone. Having recalled for his friend exactly what Smith's daughter said in reply, Kumalo has called after him to add how Jarvis thought to spare his feelings. Because Kumalo knows what she actually said, he also knows that Jarvis left out of his interpretation words that would cause needless hurt. Of course, for the narrative to relate such an act of kindness does not require that there be two different languages. All it would require is that Jarvis believe that Kumalo has not heard what Smith's daughter has said. But Paton seems to want to convey to us that because good (white) people speak Zulu, being able (as a white person) to speak Zulu is good. Because Jarvis's thoughtfulness allows Kumalo to recollect the exchange between the two of them with a softening of his initial bitterness, (a white person's) speaking Zulu also has the capacity, figuratively speaking, to make good. This is taken for granted, I think, when B. G. Lloyd writes in the preface to his *Kitchen-Kafir Grammar and Vocabulary*, that "good Zulu-speaking white men are becoming scarcer every year."[27] Nyembezi himself appears to subscribe to the same linguistic common sense, and to share Lloyd's view of the good white man's exceptionality. In *Ubudoda abukhulelwa* (Old beyond His Years) (1953), Nyembezi's second novel, Magistrate Jones is lauded because "IsiZulu siphuma ngamakhala. Akakhulumi yena into kafana ka lo. Yena uthi 'ngithi,' hayi 'mina tshela.'" (His Zulu is excellent. He does not speak the Fana Ka Lo thing. He says, "I say," not "me tell.")[28] But because Paton's novel shifts the decision between what is Zulu and what is not to the level of the narrative's own language, especially in part 3 of the novel, which is focalized mainly through the Reverend Kumalo, when Nyembezi sets about translating *Cry, the Beloved Country*, the reparation undertaken—what Klein calls making-good (*Wiedergutmachung*)—needs to be both of the non-native speaker learning the language, and, thereby demanding even more of the translator's art, of the language itself. If the former must speak a good Zulu, the latter must be rendered as to obey basic criteria of verisimilitude.

As is made clear by the use of the Zulu noun-class marker in "uJarvis" and "uSmith" in the dialogue just quoted, *Cry, the Beloved Country* represents, in English, the speech, thoughts, and perceptions of characters who speak Zulu. Instead of using Zulu, Paton often makes use of linguistic "transfer," a kind of direct translation. The fruits of this labor of representation, sometimes of a remarkable stiltedness, are easy to ridicule, and leave themselves open to impious parody: *Jarvis*: "Is it heavy?" *Kumalo*: "It is very heavy, unnumzana"; *Jarvis*: "Go well, umfundisi." *Kumalo*: "Stay well, umnumzana."[29] The result is off-key in the target language; one might say "Go well," although it is old-fashioned, but "Stay well" is less true to standard South African English than, say, "Keep well." And what about "heavy," apparently a transfer by Paton of *-nzima*? You decide.

I know that some of my friends will invoke Walter Benjamin and say that the source language should leave its traces on the target language. That is all very well, when what is being translated is *actually* the source language. Here, however, it is not. Rather, as J. M. Coetzee observes in *White Writing*, it is a "phantom Zulu" that Paton asks us to imagine as being spoken by these two characters.[30] When considered logically, this phantom Zulu, even if it can be imagined by the reader to correspond to Zulu as it is actually spoken, or to some putative "Bible Zulu" perhaps, only exists as a stylistic effect of Paton's off-key English. As Coetzee observes, why not simply write "serious," for this would be idiomatic, and, one might add, an accurate "translation" of the word *-nzima* as used in such an exchange? The reason, Coetzee tells us, is that, through this linguistic "transfer," Paton is using archaism and other stylistic means in order to foster the notion that Zulus—or certain Zulus—are of a bygone epoch, simpler and innocent of the depredations of modernity. So, when Paton's Zulus encounter the city, and tell each other about work on the mines, they resort to a picturesque figurative language that implies that Zulu is deficient in words for common terms used by miners:

> —That is the rock out of the mines, umfundisi. The gold has been taken out of it.
> —How does the rock come out?
> —We go down and dig it out, umfundisi. And when it is hard to dig, we go away, and the white men blow it out with the fire-sticks. Then we come back and clear it away; we load it on to the trucks, and it goes up in a cage, up a long chimney so long that I cannot say it for you.[31]

A certain infantilization is taking place, as an adult speaker struggles like a child to find the words to relate what he has experienced. The lack of proper English words figures a lack of words in Zulu. But, as Coetzee points out, Zulu has the word *umgodi* for "mine shaft" and the loanword *udalimede* for "dynamite," so why use "fire-sticks" and "chimney?" "Go away" and "come back" are also signs of how Paton figures a "Zulu [that] lacks words for the concepts" in question.[32] "So long that I cannot say it for you" is different; the romantic sublime, which we encounter from the first sentences of the novel—"hills . . . lovely beyond any singing of it"[33]—has been imported wholesale to serve as an organizing frame for the countryman's speechlessness in the face of urban industrial modernity.

Like all great teachers, J. M. Coetzee opens the door for his student. In the light of Coetzee's critique, I propose that one may perceive a symbolic injury to have been done to the language—as in the case of Fanagalo, which the African worker is expected to speak because the boss or the missus will have trouble understanding his Zulu (or Sotho or Tsonga or Nyanja), and maintains that the worker will not understand *isiLungu* unless it is *isiLungubhoyi*—the "magic word from Zululand." One sees this in Nyembezi's *Ubudoda abukhulelwa*, when the character Mpisi answers the scolding of his white employer in language *she* can understand: "Mina kade khona sonke s'khath misis." (I was here all the time, missus.) The missus, however, is unrelenting: "Wena maningi lazy, Jim. Zotshela loBas kosha wena. Mina bona wena hayifuna sebenza." (You very lazy, Jim. Will tell the baas to fire you. I see you don't like to work.)[34] But in Paton's novel, the mutilation of the language is subtler, for, within the world of the fiction, everybody who speaks Zulu, white and black, is supposed to be speaking a good Zulu. One cannot simply say: "She says 'Fana Ka Lo' whereas he speaks a proper Zulu." The trouble is not that Paton's "Zulu" is like Fanagalo or some broken version of the language but rather that, in certain of its features, it is unlike any Zulu known to exist outside the pages of his novel.

What, then, is somebody who translates *Cry, the Beloved Country* into Zulu to do? There are several conceivable strategies. One may take Paton at his word—or accept his linguistic fiction—and assume that there is Zulu behind his English—that the phantom walks and talks. In this case, one would simply restore the Zulu that lies "behind" the English. This is easy in cases where the putative Zulu "original" is obvious. *Jarvis*: "Hamba kahle Mfundisi." *Khumalo*: "Sala kahle Mnumzane." This is what Nyembezi does.[35] Or, which is less easy to accomplish, one may find a Zulu that, in its own idiom, expresses the archaism and infantilism that Paton's transliteration and transfer achieve stylistically in English. This would expose some of Paton's (or the book's) more questionable assumptions about Zulus. A third way of proceeding is essentially to rewrite Paton's book so that all of its dialogue and voice consciousness is idiomatic in a Zulu contemporary with the translation.

When Nyembezi translates Paton's novel as *Lafa elihle kakhulu* (It dies the very beautiful land; or, more idiomatically: Things were better in the old days) (1957), he appears to do a little of all three. He restores the putative Zulu when he can. Although archaism is indiscernible, at least to me as an intermediate learner, he typically retains Paton's infantilizing picturesque in order to show the country bumpkin encountering the city for the first time. He even employs some of the same stylistic means in his own fiction. Description, sometimes involving catachresis, serves in place of common names for things. In *Mntanami! Mntanami!* we read how Jabulani marvels at the "umhlola wesitimela esigijima singenanhloko,"[36] an image virtually lifted from Paton: "Here is a white man's wonder, a train that has no engine."[37] We also read of Jabulani's encounter with traffic lights, "Ezinhlanganweni zemigwaqo ahambe ebona lezindluluza zamehlo ezifike zibe bomvu zibe liphuzi, zibe luhlaza, angazazi ukuthi ngezani." (At the intersections of the streets he saw all the time these one-eyed things that become red, then yellow, then green, and he did not know what they were for.)[38] Jabulani again follows in Kumalo's footsteps, although the Reverend has, we are told, heard about how traffic lights work.[39] Nyembezi is thus not against this stylistic device in principle. But when he translates the conversation analyzed by Coetzee, Nyembezi changes some things:

> "Ehhene Mfundisi, ngamatshe aphuma khona emgodini, kodwa igolide selikhishiwe."
>
> "Aphuma kanjani la matshe?"
>
> "Siyehla siyokumba phansi Mfundisi. Uma kungambeki, abelungu balisakaze ngodalimede idwala. Sibuye-ke sizolisusa, sililayishe ezingolovaneni, lenyuka ngekheshe. Ikheshe lenyuka ngoshimela onobude engingenakubulinganisa."[40]
>
> ("Yes, Mfundisi, it is the rocks that come out there from the shaft, but the gold is already extracted."
>
> "How do the rocks come out?"

"We descend to dig below, Mfundisi. When it is not possible to dig, the whites blast the rock with dynamite [*udalimede*]. We return [*sibuye-ke*] to remove it, and we load it into the cocopans, and it rises by means of a cage. The cage rises through a chimney [*ushimela*] of a length that I cannot even estimate.")

In Nyembezi's translation, "fire-sticks" become *udalimede*, as Coetzee would have predicted. But "chimney" is rendered as *ushimela* (a variant of *ushimula*?), instead of *umgodi* or *ishafu*. The elision of "go away," with which "come back" is paired in Paton, makes *sibuye-ke* less obtrusive as a simplification. But when Nyembezi writes that the mineshaft is "of a length that I cannot even estimate" then he is displacing ever so slightly Paton's romantic sublime, in which the *immeasurable* robs the observer of language—"I cannot say it for you"—as if it had no counterpart in Zulu idiom (in which one can certainly be speechless, say, with admiration or surprise), in order to find something that does. At work is thus an attempt to *repair*—where restoring is not possible because there is no Zulu "original" that, in context, would be idiomatic. Paton's "fire-sticks" and "so long that I cannot say it for you" appear for different reasons to fit into the category of lexical items in need of repair.

It is thus with great curiosity that I turn to Nyembezi's rendering in *Lafa elihle kakhulu* of two particular scenes in *Cry, the Beloved Country*. In these episodes the Jarvis boy is conversing with the Reverend Kumalo, whom he informs that he is learning Zulu, and who, in turn, is willing to help him along in his endeavors.

In the first of the two scenes, Paton has the boy making a mistake in Zulu, which the Reverend Kumalo gently corrects:

> [T]he small boy said to him, Why are you laughing? But the small boy was laughing also, he took no offense.
> —I am just laughing, inkosana.
> —Inkosana? That's little inkosi, isn't it?
> —It is little inkosi. Little master, it means.
> —Yes, I know. And what are you called? What do I call you?
> —Umfundisi.
> —I see. Imfundisi.
> —No. Umfundisi.
> —Umfundisi. What does it mean?
> —It means parson.
> —May I sit down, umfundisi? the small boy pronounced the word slowly. Is that right? he said.[41]

Pages could be written about this exchange. Kumalo deferentially addresses the boy as *inkosana*, which Eve tells me would be well translated as *kleinbaas* (the son of the baas). The deference of an old man to a child irks even more than Kumalo's general deference to whites, and which led writers of the *Drum* generation to dismiss him as an Uncle Tom. Perhaps the best evidence of this is the mockery of Paton by Lewis Nkosi and his friends in the shebeen scene in Lionel Rogosin's 1959 film, *Come Back, Africa*.

But what strikes me most painfully, as one who is himself learning Zulu, is Kumalo's correction of the boy's mistake. As in all good scenes of language learning, there is laughter: the laughter of the teacher, and the laughter of the pupil laughing at himself. The boy displays the eagerness of the learner, applying what he has already learned: "Inkosana? That's little inkosi, isn't it?" He has come across the use of the *-ana* suffix to indicate the diminutive—vide *Learn More Zulu*, lesson 5. Kumalo's reply is as much for the reader as for the boy, who "knows" that he is being addressed deferentially as "little master," and presumably knows, but does not want to address, the implications of being addressed as *kleinbaas* by the elderly parson.

It is the words that follow, however, that lead me into a maze as I follow the thread with which I am left as Paton's text unravels. First it takes me to a room with a blackboard where I can stand up in front of my class, pick up a piece of chalk, and explain to my students that in Zulu there is a noun-class system, and the small boy has made what is a common error for the second-language learner, placing a word in the wrong noun class by using the prefix *im-* instead of the prefix *um-*. The error is obvious to a native speaker, since in Zulu there is no such word as *imfundisi*. So Kumalo offers the boy a correction: "No. Umfundisi." By now any reader of *Cry, the Beloved Country* knows the meaning of this word, and the gloss is redundant, perhaps even for the boy. But he is at an age where relentless questioning, even when he knows the answer, could be a clue to an Oedipal repression of knowing that, as Klein showed in an early essay, inhibits learning rather than advancing it.

A memory intervenes: Eckson and I are at the Language Resource Center in the basement of Columbia's School of International and Public Affairs (SIPA), where we have our meetings. I am in the middle of writing down something that he has written on the whiteboard. I look up. What had been on the board has been erased. Eckson is grinning. One of the first things he learned when training to be a teacher was if you realize that you have written something on the board that is incorrect you erase it immediately.

One could go on, filling the blackboard with chalk marks. But one would have to admit, after a while, that one had reached a dead end. For another detail tells the intermediate reader that things do not add up. So, noticing that the thread of the unraveling text doubles back on itself, I turn around and—in my mind's eye—leave this classroom, striding down the hallway with my students behind me, until the thread leads us into another room, where a freshly wiped blackboard invites a new set of chalk strokes. Before I take up the chalk, I ask them to turn to the back of their books, where Paton has usefully provided an alphabetical "List of Words" that provides the American reader with definitions and pronunciation tips for Zulu and Afrikaans words used in the novel. Right at the end of the "List"—following the entry for "Zulu"—one reads the following: "In all cases where such words as 'umfundisi,' 'umnumzana,' are used as forms of address, the initial vowel is dropped. But I thought it wise to omit this complication."[42] Wise? The blood boils. Omit?—when what is omitted is superadded, using up valuable ink and square inches of paper—just think of the waste, given the millions of copies of this book in print!

Let the blood simmer now. Let us look more closely at the effect of Paton's "omission."

> —Umfundisi
> —I see. Imfundisi.
> —No. Umfundisi.

Verisimilitude would dictate that when the Reverend Kumalo says "Umfundisi," he should, as a speaker of Zulu, actually be saying "Mfundisi." As Paton has told us, in the vocative the first vowel of the noun-class marker is elided (there are, of course, exceptions, in praise poetry, for example, and for some appellations that contain an honorific followed by a name, but this exchange does not fall into either of these categories). To the learner's ear, "Mfundisi" can easily be heard as "imfundisi." And "imfundisi" is surely close enough in sound to the vocative for the native speaker simply to let it pass. But we are not in the realm of the verisimilar. We are inside of Paton's textuality, and it is unraveling before our eyes. That textuality, which has produced pages and pages of "Umfundisi" as its rendition of the vocative, is what dictates the Reverend's correction. It is hopeless for him to do otherwise, since, being himself an artifact of Paton's pen, he is saying "Umfundisi" as if it were the most natural thing in the world. This is quite different from a beginner's over-generalization, such as is found in Colenso's *Ten Weeks in Natal: A Journal of a First Tour of Visitation among the Colonists and Zulu Kafirs of Natal* (1855). When the Bishop tells us how Natal whites mistakenly drop the prefix "u-" when referring to Ngoza, he doesn't seem to know that the prefix is dropped in the vocative when, having lost his way one night, he tries to speak Zulu himself: "*umFana! umFana!*—Young man! young man!"[43] A few years later, Colenso's grammar makes the distinction.[44] Reading Colenso, one also comes alive to the import of Paton's decision to use the name "Tixo" when Zulus refer to God (pronounced "Teeko"): "I rejected the Zulu word for the Great Spirit as too long and difficult."[45] If the singular name of god is substitutable, then so is any name. When Colenso visits Natal in 1854, he finds that the missionaries, having worked among the "British Kafirs," have introduced "uThixo" as the name of God—the name still used by speakers of Xhosa—when Zulus know "uMvelinqangi" and "uNkulunkulu."[46] He disapproves of this imposition, but also dislikes "uThixo"'s "odious click."[47] In *Lafa elihle kakhulu*, Nyembezi replaces "Tixo" with "uNkulunkulu." It is neither a long nor a difficult word.

One learns, and then one thinks that one knows. Is it possible, in all rigor, to speak or write without claiming to know, or even to know better? There have been times when I have, imagining I know more of the language than them, assumed toward my race-kin the air of superiority and election hardly different from what one discovers in Colenso and other missionaries of his era. *Learning Zulu* seeks to emphasize *learning*—and that means relinquishing the profession to better knowledge if it connotes moral superiority. One may attempt to make good, but finally one cannot make oneself good. That is in the hands of the other.

But one also *teaches*, and as a teacher must one not declare Paton's false vocative to be a scandal? At the very point where the boy is learning Zulu, he is being taught the wrong thing. I stand before my imaginary second blackboard, not yet having taken up the chalk, the slack thread of Paton's novel in a skein about my hand. What to do? What would Nyembezi have done? I take the chalk and write down on the board his rendering of the words. Most of the students know no Zulu, but maybe I can find a way of getting them see what he has done:

> "Nkosana? Lokho kusho iNkosi encane angithi?"
> "Yebo, iNkosi encane; umnumzane omncane."
> "Ngiyazi. Wena-ke ubizwa kanjani? Mina ngifanele ngithini?"
> "Mfundisi."
> "Ngiyabona Mfundisi. Kusho ukuthini lokho?"
> "Kusho umPristi."[48]
> ("Nkosana? That means little Lord I would think?"
> "Yes, little Lord; little master."
> "I know. And you, how are you addressed? What should I say?"
> "Mfundisi."
> "I see, Mfundisi. What does that mean?"
> "It means Priest.")

They nod their heads. They can see that Nyembezi has rendered "Mfundisi" in the vocative, correcting Paton's "omission." That is graphic. But they cannot read Zulu, so I have to explain to them that Nyembezi has also elided the little boy's mistake. There is no sentence that corresponds to the Reverend's "No. Umfundisi" to indicate that any mistake has been made, and, indeed, when the boy says "Ngiyabona Mfundisi" (I see, Mfundisi), he is perfectly correct. Nyembezi's Khumalo—in *Lafa elihle* the spelling of the name is changed—is not about to teach him a lesson that is incorrect.

Two important things flow from Nyembezi's translation of this scene. Unable to restore an "original" Zulu in a verisimilitude that would have produced Zulu vocatives with class-markers—think of an English-language text where all the vocatives for Kumalo / Khumalo are "The Reverend" instead of "Reverend"—he *repairs* the text so that the "original" is consistent with Zulu idiom. He thereby undoes the damage done by Paton. In so doing, he also eliminates the correction of the boy's mistake—for, unless Khumalo himself speaks Paton-Zulu and says "Umfundisi," there simply *is* no mistake for the boy to make. The boy is thus repaired along with the Reverend—the pupil along with the teacher, the son along with the father. In Part 3 of the novel, the bulk of which is focalized through Kumalo, this repair work involves extensive abridgment of Paton's text.

But because the mutilation has taken place *within* the phantom Zulu of the novel, as a result of Paton's decision on vocatives—and Paton-Zulu is the only Zulu that anybody speaks in *Cry, the Beloved Country*—it is not sufficient to repair, or make "good," the non-native speaker, who in *Mntanami! Mntanami!* or *Ubudoda abukhulelwa* might simply have been praised for speaking a proper Zulu instead of Fanagalo. The native speaker has also to be repaired. And Zulu itself has to be made Zulu again: a *Wieder-Zulumachung*? The Zulu that Nyembezi gives young Jarvis is good, even sophisticated, as his use of the enclitic ending in *wena-ke* suggests. But this making-good also exists only at the level of textuality. As Nyembezi's narrator tells us—which in this scene Paton's does not explicitly—the two of them converse in English: "Bathi ukuxoxaxoxa umfanyana ebuza amagama athile esiZulu. Phela babexoxa ngesiNgisi ngoba umfana lona wayengasazi isiZulu. UKhumalo wathi, 'Cha, Nkosana, usuzosifunda impela isiZulu.' Waphendula umfana wathi, 'Silula isiZulu.'" (They conversed for a while, the little boy asking some words for things in Zulu. Of course they spoke in English because the boy did not know Zulu. Khumalo said, "Indeed, Nkosana, now you are really going to learn Zulu." The boy replied, "Zulu is easy.")[49] Thus, even if the act of reparation is purely textual, in effect honoring the boy's putatively correct English in Zulu "translation," can we not nevertheless call it what Fredric Jameson has termed a "socially symbolic act?"

The second scene of language learning is also a scene of paranoid phantasy—since, as the narrator makes clear through what Kumalo says, the boy does not really understand Zulu. He enters the Reverend's house, and he enters the language. He gives up *possession* of his own language—albeit minimally, if he is actually speaking English. This is not experienced as a problem by him, but the Reverend's wife alerts us to the stakes involved. She fears that the boy will be able to overhear them; as he gains language, possession of what is held between them alone will be lost:

—When are you going back to Johannesburg, inkosana?
—When my grandfather comes back.
And Kumalo said to him in Zulu, When you go, something bright will go out of Ndotsheni.
—What are you saying, umfundisi?
But when Kumalo would have translated, the small boy cried out, No, don't tell me. Say it again in Zulu. So Kumalo said it again.

—That means when you are gone, said the small boy, and say the rest again.
—Something bright will go out of Ndotsheni, said Kumalo in Zulu.
—Something about Ndotsheni. But it's too hard for me. Say it in English, umfundisi.
—Something bright will go out of Ndotsheni, said Kumalo in English.
The small boy laughed with pleasure. I hear you, he said in Zulu.
And Kumalo clapped his hands in astonishment, and said, Au! Au! You speak Zulu, so that the small boy laughed with still greater pleasure, and Kumalo clapped his hands again, and made many exclamations. The door opened and his wife came in, and he said to the small boy, this is my wife, and he said to his wife in Zulu, this is the son of the man. The small boy stood up and made a bow to Kumalo's wife, and she stood and looked at him with fear and sorrow. But he said to her, You have a nice house here, and he laughed. She said to her husband in Zulu, I am overcome, I do not know what to say. And the small boy said in Zulu, I hear you, so that she took a step backwards in fear. But Kumalo said to her swiftly, He does not understand you, those are only words that he knows, and for the small boy he clapped his hands again in astonishment and said, Au! Au! But you speak Zulu. And the woman went backwards to the door, and opened it and shut it and was gone.[50]

In Paton, the scene is a projection of an Oedipal phantasy that the father and mother are doing things that are secret and that they are keeping from the child, going as far as to deceive it: "But Kumalo said to her swiftly, He does not understand you. " The dramatic detail that Kumalo's wife "took a step backwards" and "went backwards to the door" almost tells us that things are reversed, and need to be turned around in order to make sense. The mother's fear is actually the child's fear—but the child who fears is not the one actually in the scene. Rather he is the one who looks on, guiding the narrator and blocking out the positions and movements of the actors on stage. Kumalo's wife's fear is twofold: fear of the boy because he is the son of Jarvis, and—this is given greater emphasis—because he might understand Zulu. Both fears are analyzable as those of the onlooker: the son has murdered the father—Absalom Kumalo assumes the parricidal impulses of the boy—and he wants to have what the father and mother have.

In the phantasy, the child is jealous because it wants the mother and her breast to itself, and so it does destructive things. When Melanie Klein analyzes envy, following the classic distinction between jealousy and envy, she points out how the prodigious breast itself, rather than the infant's imagined rival for the breast, may be attacked in phantasy.[51] It is surely no accident that the baby-talk of Paton's Zulus first makes itself heard when they are discussing gold mining, the violent extraction of ore from the earth. I remember how the late Nick Visser, another of my teachers at UCT, became impatient when in a long essay I persisted in applying Althusserian ideology critique to a pair of novels about gold mining. Wasn't it obvious that Wilbur Smith's 1970 melodrama, *Gold*

Mine, was all about penis envy—that is, the white man's envy of the virile black man, embodied by the powerful mineworker Big King? The reading seemed to apply less readily to the emasculated Xuma in Peter Abrahams' *Mine Boy* (1946), making this politically committed novel less appealing to read. I now read Paton's classic in a similar vein as I was encouraged to read Smith, except that I have in the intervening years been reading Klein, who shows how in the beginning envy relates to the breast. Mining is getting inside of the mother, robbing her of good things; the "mine" is also the sign of jealous appropriation, as the voracious embrace of Soho Eckstein, the tycoon in William Kentridge's short 1991 film by that title, reminds us. The infant's destructiveness, in Klein, prompts guilt feelings and leads to efforts at reparation. In Paton's first language-learning scene, the Jarvis boy makes a mistake in Zulu. The mistake is "innocent," incidental to learning a proper Zulu—there is no hint that the boy has picked up Fanagalo—yet, when it is analyzed along with Nyembezi's translation, it shows an unlikely mistake and an *impossible* correction. It thus reveals a mistake that, made by Paton, is not at all innocent, and shows the destructiveness of his choice about how to render the vocative. What Coetzee calls a phantom Zulu is also a phantasy Zulu.

In this second scene, the boy *is* learning. He is making an effort to listen. In *Lafa elihle kakhulu*, he does not make a mistake that requires correction. As in his rendering of the previous scene, Nyembezi gives the boy a sophisticated Zulu, as if to render idiomatically the polite speech of the native English-speaker. In the corresponding scene in Paton's text, in contrast to the previous scene, changes in the language spoken by a character are clearly indicated. Nyembezi reproduces this, so that we can tell when the boy is saying something in Zulu and when he is not. Aside from when he simply utters Zulu words, there are two occasions where he says something in Zulu that appears to fit the context. When Kumalo—or Khumalo—explains to him what he has said, we have the following from the boy: "'Wo, sengiyezwa,' esho ngesiZulu." ("Wo, now I understand," saying it in Zulu.)[52] And then, after Khumalo's wife expresses her fear: "Wathi umfana, ngiyakuzwa, esho ngesiZulu." (The boy said, I understand it, saying it in Zulu.)[53] Two different statements, meaning roughly the same thing in context, translate what, in Paton, is rendered on both occasions as "I hear you."[54] This variation might indicate a greater suppleness to the boy's Zulu than Paton's Kumalo acknowledges—"only words that he knows"[55]—and that Nyembezi's Khumalo could be telling his wife a reassuring white lie when he says: "[H]hayi bo, akakuzwa. Wazi lokho kuphela." (Hhayi bo, he does not understand it. That is all he knows.)[56] The boy's Zulu could easily be better than one thinks. In other words, in the reparative act of making good, by lending him a better Zulu, there is still a fear that the narrator perceives and shows to be operative. The wife / mother still moves backwards from shock. This fear, even if it does lead to obvious damage to the body of the language, as in the first of the scenes, will lead to a kind of masquerade in which nobody is told the truth because the truth—whatever it is, but especially if it means acknowledging improvement, a making-good that enriches *him*, and thus, in phantasy's zero sum, impoverishes *me*—is too terrifying to contemplate.

A student who knows some Zulu puts up her hand and asks: Doesn't the verb *zwa* also mean to understand? Yes, it does indeed! (And, among other senses, it also means to feel, to be alive, and so forth). There could thus be a key ambiguity in the text: does the boy understand, or does he only hear? Paton uses the word "hear" in each instance, as if to convey the latter, but then he could also be employing one of his transliterations in order to suggest that the Zulus, being simple people, when they mean "understand" they say "hear," because they have no other words for "understand." This is another non sequitur—whether the language has only the one word or not (and Zulu certainly has more than one verb for "understand," as has French, in which *entendre* can generate similar ambiguity), when Zulus, or any other people, say "hear" they mean "hear," and when they say "understand," they mean "understand." Nyembezi's translation retains the single verb, *zwa*. A "restorative" translation. And it is clear from the context that, for Nyembezi, *zwa* means "understand." But here is where real ambiguity enters. How can Khumalo know—for certain, that is—whether the boy does or does not understand? It is clear that he has heard *something*, but *what* is it that he has understood from what he has heard? Even if her words were not understood perfectly, Khumalo's wife's shrinking back in fear would have been legible. Reading and understanding: I recall a discussion by Wittgenstein in the *Philosophical Investigations*, where the ability to "go on" is a sign that what has been read has been understood.[57] But the boy is not given leave to "go on." Rather he is cut off and muffled by Kumalo's / Khumalo's false praise—a manic reparation that stems from the fear pervading the household when the little stranger enters.

Whose fear is it, though? Surely that of the one who stands outside the scene, observing. The one we call "Paton." The variation in the boy's speech *in Zulu* suggests, however, that the phantasy of the jealous child looking in is not only that of "Paton," but, since he introduced the variation in the boy's diction, that of "Nyembezi" himself.

Something else strikes me as I read *Lafa elihle kakhulu*. In *Cry, the Beloved Country*, the boy who enters also "goes out." To be precise, as Kumalo tells him, repeating it for him in Zulu, and then in English when he cannot quite follow: "When you go, something bright will go out of Ndotsheni."[58] There is room for interpretation, for Kumalo might be saying that the "small . . . bright . . . boy,"[59] who is about to leave for Johannesburg, is the light that Ndotsheni will give to the world. This would be consistent with what Kumalo says about Arthur Jarvis after learning of his death, vaguely remembering him as "a small bright boy."[60] But he could also be saying that Ndotsheni will thereby be deprived of his light. When Nyembezi translates this exchange, he strongly favors the second interpretation, separating its metaphorics from Khumalo's memory of the father, whom he recalls as "umfanyana ophapheme" (an alert little boy).[61] What is more remarkable still is that, in order to make his translation, he plays on Paton's English, as if Paton had meant Kumalo to say that a light would "go out" in the sense of being extinguished. "Mhla uhambayo," he writes, "kuyofana nokucima kwenkanyezi eNdotsheni." (The day that you go, it will be like the extinguishing of a star at Ndotsheni.)[62] The verb *ukucima* (extinguish) does not have the sense of "going out" as in leaving. After *ukucima* there is no going anywhere: no leaving and no return. The words of Nyembezi's Khumalo suggest annihilation.[63] There is none of the sidereal periodicity that we find, say, in S.E.K. Mqhayi's poem, "The Prince of Britain" (1925): "The stars we count out years by, the years of our manhood." (*Yona nkwenkwezi yokubal' iminyaka,— / Iminyaka yobudoda, yobudoda!*)[64] In Nyembezi's rendering, the Jarvis boy's lessons come to naught, and he may as well have died along with his father.

Despite the mortal ambiguities one finds in Nyembezi's translation, there is an effort by him at making-good: of the boy's language, and thus by the boy himself. Klein tells us that when reparation has succeeded, paranoia has a chance to recede. But in Nyembezi's text, it is the boy's ability to vary his *Zulu* that makes Khumalo—and not his wife, who only hears the second of the boy's phrases—afraid enough to tell a lie. This fear—a projected fear of being deprived of one's language—is something that Khumalo appears to disavow, but he has already uttered the word *ukucima*, as if the one whom "Nyembezi" has made good, threatens to become, if not his better, perhaps then his rival. Is this outcome generalizable—to all the fears of a deprivation of substance, and their allied mutual fearful projection, of fathers and sons afraid of mutual annihilation that besets these Cold War books, which leads to the phantasy of the murder of the father and the murder of the son?

Learn Fanagalo?

If one concentrates on language and connects *Lafa elihle kakhulu* with *Learn More Zulu*, perhaps what we see is that a deal has been reached. The deal has been struck with the boy, but not exclusively with the "small white boy": You can be good, I will make you good, so long as you speak a proper Zulu: "Zulu as spoken by the Zulus." In *Lafa elihle kakhulu*, however, Nyembezi leaves out the cliché given to Kumalo by Paton—"You will be able to speak in the dark, and people will not know it is not a Zulu"[65]—instead having him say: "Usikhipha ngamakhala,"[66] which, literally meaning that he draws Zulu from his nostrils, is an expression commonly used when somebody speaks a language really well.

The first time I read *Cry, the Beloved Country*, I was already in my teens. Yet can I deny that my own learning of Zulu is in some way motivated by this possibility of being told that I am a good boy? There is, however, a catch: You will receive praise and you will be celebrated, so long as you conform in your speech to the law of the Father. Of course, once you reach a certain competence, then you may play, and even subvert, and analyze your teacher, but that is your own unauthorized Oedipal business. But what if, as a learner of the language, you never demonstrate conformity? From the examples I can find in Nyembezi, then it looks as if the dice are loaded against you. *Lafa elihle kakhulu* and *Learn More Zulu* entirely, or almost entirely, exclude non-standard forms of Zulu. Old Jarvis is a master of Zulu (*Sasiphuma ngamakhala phela*).⁶⁷ And Magistrate Jones in *Ubudoda abukhulelwa* is lauded for speaking Zulu—"Isizulu siphuma ngamakhala"—and for not speaking Fanagalo, which is what dishonest Indians speak when they address Zulus, and what whites use to scold their servants.⁶⁸

Mntanami! Mntanami!, however, does entertain non-standard forms of the language. The stone throwing at the close of *Learn More Zulu* can be read as a feint, like the pretext employed to bring Jabulani indoors in *Mntanami! Mntanami!* Similarly, one could read against the grain of that novel's association of patois and crime—disobeying the father—and hear another *voice*, which is also another *wish*: the voice of *jouissance* out of earshot of the father, where his law of language does not apply.

When Jabulani first arrives in Johannesburg, he is at sea because he does not understand Sotho or Afrikaans, which he hears spoken all about him.⁶⁹ In Sophiatown he hears young men address each other in Flaaitaal, or what today would be called Tsotsitaal, which Nyembezi represents by including a few terms of greeting and address such as "*Hheit*" and "*maan*."⁷⁰ We do not get a representation of Tsotsitaal in all of its plenitude, just the flavor, as we sometimes do in Modisane and other *Drum* writers: "*Heit bricade*."⁷¹ Flaaitaal words are glossed in footnotes, suggesting a definite foreignness of the talk in relation to the standard language of the text: "'Futhi uma ungasebenzi, bazokuthathela* iseksheni. . . .' *Uzoboshwa." ("Also if you don't work, they will take you off* to the section. . . . *You will be arrested.")⁷² The moment that distils Jabulani's situation as a newcomer also presents him as *infans*. James tells him:

> Umsebenzi ozowenza ufuna ukuba wazi izilimi zalapha eGoli, isiBhunu nesiSuthu. Akunandaba noba awuzikhulumi kahle. Uke ubezwe abelungu namaNdiya bethi, "fana ka lo" sebeqinise izintamo ukuba bekhuluma sona impela isiZulu uqobo? Umuntu uyezwa ukuthi bathini, kodwa abakhulumi sona isiZulu. Naweke kufuneka wazi-nje u "fana ka lo" wesiBhunu nesiSuthu. Uma ikhanda lakho lingesiyena usemende, uzosheshe ukufunde-nje lokho.⁷³

(The work that you will do requires that you know the languages of over here in eGoli, Afrikaans and Sotho. It makes no difference to anybody that you do not speak them well. Haven't you sometimes heard Whites and Indians saying "fana ka lo," swelling with pride to be speaking for real a genuine Zulu? A black person understands what they are saying, but they are not speaking Zulu. You too only need to know a "fana ka lo" of Afrikaans and Sotho. If your head is not made of cement, you will just learn it quickly.)

The syntax of James's admonition reminds one of Nyembezi instructing the reader of *Learn More Zulu*: "Kudinga ukuba . . ." (It is necessary that . . .).[74] The main difference, of course, is that James is encouraging his pupil to learn exactly the opposite of what one might imagine Nyembezi, were he instructing his reader in the learning of English or Sotho, to be recommending. But in eGoli work is "work," and other things are also topsy-turvy. Thus, although Natal whites and Indians are routinely mocked by native Zulu speakers for proudly believing that they speak Zulu when they actually speak Fanagalo, or derided for speaking Fanagalo at all,[75] in eGoli the Afrikaans or Sotho equivalent is all that Jabulani need learn: "You too only need to know a 'fana ka lo' of Afrikaans and Sotho." And, furthermore, "If your head is not made of cement, you will just learn it quickly." The tables are turned. If in Natal, although the whites and Indians are not speaking Zulu, a "black person understands what they are saying"—an ironic, complicitous countersignature to "the Zulu boy will understand," if ever there was one—it follows that in Johannesburg Afrikaans- and Sotho-speakers will understand broken versions of their languages. "You will just learn it quickly": Again an antitype, or partial antitype, since to learn is actually to "learn," since what is to be learned is a degraded form of the respective languages in question. Yet, this sliding into the antitype, or partial antitype, should not prevent us from seeing how James's words liberate Jabulani from the grip of a linguistic purism that, although it might apply at home, need not apply in the city.

Juxtaposed with the preface to *Learn More Zulu*, where it is emphasized that you have to speak every day, and work with care—even if writing Zulu is said to be easy—this emphasis on ease of learning is as remarkable as its tacit making-good of the bad example: the white or Indian Fanagalo speaker. There are thus other ways of making-good than having the non-native speaker learn a good Zulu, Sotho, or Afrikaans. The non-native speaker's attempts, whatever they amount to, can be accepted for what they are. Is this what is actually going on in *Lafa elihle*, when the little white boy is praised? I do not know, and, in any case, how could one possibly *know*? What nevertheless seems likely is that, in *Mntanami! Mntanami!* this liberation, like the other forms of freedom offered by crime, is being presented as a false one. The boy—or son—may "learn" Afrikaans or Sotho in the way that James proposes, but that will not have meant that he has learned those languages. If that applies to Indians and whites then, it must also apply to Jabulani. Within Nyembezi's worldview there is, in the end, no substitute for honest hard work. But it makes for boring reading to have a character like Vusumuzi Gumede in *Ubudoda abukhulelwa*, who, after receiving a beating from his father once, never steals again, is a diligent pupil and excellent sportsman, and dies having lived up to his name by reviving the house of Gumede by becoming a prosperous shopkeeper and owner of land. Any deviation from such a pattern of life, as celebrated in the biography of Vusi written by his friend Msezane in his study, gives rise to feelings of guilt: the superego tells one that nothing one has done is good enough, and this translates into "Everything I have done is bad."

Even so, it would be hard to believe that there is nothing in Nyembezi—or in his narrator—that revels in the excitement of the underworld. It is surely not the didacticism of Jabulani's guilt-beset conversion, but rather the vivid Sophiatown chapters, the gangsterism and the muti killing, that would draw today's readers to *Mntanami! Mntanami!* Who, other than the most diligent of scholars, would nowadays make it to the end of *Ubudoda abukhulelwa*? And it is not just because of the Sophiatown industry that swung into high gear in the late 1980s, with the reissuing of banned works, the revival of films such as *Come Back, Africa*, and the printing of glossy books of photographs from *Drum*. Like most crime fiction, the middle chapters of *Mntanami! Mntanami!* allow the reader (and the writer) the frisson of criminal violence, of a sadism without guilt or punishment that the genre provisionally provides. It is no wonder that Geoffrey Cronjé, writing at almost the same time that Nyembezi left Johannesburg for the University of Fort Hare, wanted to ban pulp fiction coming from abroad, much of which was crime fiction in the form of cheap "pocket books," which "constitute a deliberate and outright exploitation of illicit sex relations, lust, sadism and perversion and are doing irreparable harm to the moral standards of this country." That the country in question is the United States hardly matters to Cronjé, who is quoting with approval the *Report of the New York State Joint Legislative Committee to Study the Publication of Comics* (1955). Cronjé also cites as "authoritative" Fredric Wertham's *Seduction of the Innocent* (1954), whose notoriously overblown condemnation of comics alerts us that the "moral standards" defended against the play of phantasy are censor's code for a law of fathers that is ubiquitous: "The contempt for law and police and the brutality of punishment in comic books is subconsciously translated by children into conflict with authority, and they develop a special indifference to it."[76]

If a sadism without remorse is secretly wished for by certain voices in Nyembezi's novel, then it would be a wish that is borne out historically. After 1958, when Sophiatown is razed, one (paternal) wish is fulfilled, and another (the son's) wish is crushed. The ambivalence linked to the place and to the father will, in some instances, be irreducible; Bloke Modisane's *Blame Me on History* begins with the words "[s]omething in me died, a piece of me died, with the dying of Sophiatown,"[77] and goes on to describe the death of Modisane's father in the gutters of Sophiatown. *Mntanami! Mntanami!*, with its dialogization of Zulu, is a crucial missing piece of the record we have of this terrible ambivalence—toward language, toward the youth—from before the state's deliberate destruction of the legendary place led to such a difficult mourning for those who survived: the fathers and sons whose struggles against each other were puny compared to the power of the state, but whose fight over patrimony appears to inform, in complicated and puzzling ways, the strictures imposed on outsiders who wish to learn Zulu.

When I say "strictures," I still have in mind Nyembezi's preface to *Learn More Zulu* and its gentle chiding of the white person who wishes to learn Zulu. I am also thinking of how, in Nyembezi's novels, as in Paton's most famous work, white people can be ennobled by speaking a proper Zulu, whereas the incorrigible lowness of Indians and Chinese is signaled by their speaking of Fanagalo. As Khumalo's response to his wife's fear in *Lafa elihle kakhulu* suggests, subscription to this hierarchy, which makes good those at its pinnacle, does not entirely allay the fear that a learner—especially the most avid learner—might be depriving one of something. In 2008, the African learner is met by shibboleths in the Zulu language, demanded by those who, in the name of being Zulu, jealously guard what they consider to be their *own*. But before those events come to be witnessed, the call to learn the language well and the willingness of the teacher to guide will be sorely tried by the destructive tendencies that came into effect, years before he reads *Cry, the Beloved Country*, when—I exaggerate, but not greatly—a certain "small white boy" answers his curtain call. If with his entrance on stage, identification takes the place of learning, so too will it when Jacob Zuma's supporters, demonstrating outside the court that tried him for rape in 2006, proclaim him "100% Zulu Boy," and themselves to be "100% JZ." Although others will point to the civil war of 1990–94 between the ANC and the Inkatha Freedom Party that killed several thousand people, Zuma's trial may have been the beginning of the end of "Zulu" as a master name—*the* African language to be learned if you were South African or wished to be South African—*the* language for phrasing ubuntu in public discourse[78]—riven as it became by sexual difference, misogyny, and hatred directed in speech and act toward homosexuals and foreigners. "Zulu," the ultimate letter in the NATO phonetic alphabet, the omega before the alpha in "ZA" and ".za," would slowly have to be worked out of each of its nexuses and textualizations. By 1985, as if no longer needed as a point of reference, as it had been in the Kitchen Kafir handbooks of Lloyd and Bold, Zulu had indeed fallen out of the *Miners' Dictionary English—Fanakalo / Woordeboek vir Mynwerkers Afrikaans—Fanakalo*; the manual, updated and revised over the years, that succeeded the 1920 *Miners' Companion in Zulu*—although its ghost remains in the adoption of the standard Zulu orthography for the word "Fanakalo." We need to remember that "Zulu" as the name of a language was an aftereffect; as Colenso wrote is his *First Steps in Zulu: Being an Elementary Grammar of the Zulu Language*: "Missionaries sometimes use the words *isiZulu*, *isiXosa*, &c., to express the language of the *amaZulu*, *amaXosa*, &c. It is convenient, of course, to employ such words: but they are not used by the natives themselves."[79] Detailing the differences between Zulu and dialects distinguished in terms of *tekeza* and *tefula*, he is clear that he was choosing one language to serve as the standard, a choice that became the basis for his inheritors' purism. Colenso's grammar was first published in 1859. Nowadays, as for more than a century, native speakers use the word *isiZulu* to refer to the language they speak. Just as there was a time when they did not refer to their languages as *isiZulu*, there is no reason why the epoch that produced "Zulu" as a fetish will not some day draw to a close, just as the "small boy" must loosen his investment in the name as he bears witness to a history of language that no longer has him at its center.

CHAPTER 3

Ipi Tombi

> Shosholoza, shosholoza!
> Kulezo 'ntaba
> Isitimela siphumela
> Wen' uyabaleka
> Shosholoza, shosholoza!

How to make a Zulu hut: take an old telephone directory—Yellow Pages or Residential—and, starting from the first page, fold the top right-hand corner over so that the top edge of the page meets the inner edge to form an isosceles triangle. Left-handed pupils may fold from the top left-hand corner of the second page. The outward side of the triangle forms the hut's sloping roof. The lower half of the page presents a straight outer edge. This is the wall of the hut. Fold each page in this fashion. When you are finished, carefully fold the phone book's covers in the same way and staple them together securely back to back. This forms a stable base for the hut once the book is stood on end. Ask each pupil to bring an old phone book from home. A group of Zulu huts makes for an eye-catching display in which the Sub-Standard A or B boy can take pride. Exhibited with other handwork, it brightens up the classroom for parent-teacher evenings.

Although I remember the finished product, making a Zulu hut was not something I could remember how to do. Traditions are sometimes lost. So I had to find a knowledgeable informant, and then I had to write myself a set of instructions so I would not forget next time around. But the song I can remember (see above): all I have done is to put the words in standard Zulu orthography. How did I come to this song? How did it come to me? How did a little boy growing up in the Cape come to be learning Zulu? That is what I am about to tell you.

In the classroom where we would run our fingertips down Miss F's back to keep her calm—a collective exercise for the greater good, in which I was less adept than others, my caresses not being calming enough—the lift-scheme mothers gather to make us up for *Ipi Tombi*, which has been chosen as the school play for 1975. Or maybe it was actually 1974, as the school magazine for

1975 has a report on a junior-school production of *Cinderella*,[1] whereas the 1974 magazine makes no mention of any play. Or perhaps it is because ours was one of the pirate productions of *Ipi Tombi* that proliferated. Family has intruded in the private, secret space of the schoolroom. The intrusion of family into the school—this is a theme on which I could enlarge: Two years later, at an evening P.T.A. meeting, my father writes on the blackboard: Big Brother Is Watching You. The inscription is still there the next day. I have no idea what it means, and my Standard One teacher has no idea why my father would have written it there. I am embarrassed. Some time later that day, it is erased. Was it I who was asked to erase it, as if I had been the culprit?

The mascara I allow. But I draw back at the lipstick; it smells and tastes like the kiss of a female relation—or perhaps that is why I shrink from such a kiss: girls wear lipstick, and I am not a girl. Tonight I am a boy, a Zulu boy. Chilly in my P.T. shorts, bare from the waist up, I clutch my cardboard assegai and wait for the curtain call. I do not remember the rest of my costume—maybe there was also a cardboard shield—although I am certain that we were not in blackface. There is a photograph of me, a little older, in Purim fancy dress: a red Indian, with grease-paint stripes across my ribcage, a headdress of seagull feathers. I wear fawn corduroy pants, with a tasseled strip from a box of upholstery offcuts sewn onto the sides. I shake my head at the photograph in *Tourner les mots* of a shirtless Jacques Derrida, up in a tree at age fifteen, bow and arrow in hand, "Profil de l'artefacteur en jeune singe"[2]—what is it about Jewish boys in the colonies? But to be a red Indian—of which the wish to be was immortally captured by Kafka—is it the same as being a Zulu boy? Provisionally, let me say "No," even if either character could be improvised by mothers' hands from similar materials. And those hands could even make a boy into a girl, if one is to credit what was said about *Cinderella*: "Finding and making costumes for boys and 'girls' of all shapes and sizes was not as difficult as it seemed at first because of the co-operation of the mothers."[3] As rehearsed, a drum roll from Mr. J. is the cue for our troupe of Zulu boys to ascend the stage. We line up at the very front, the lights in our eyes. Behind us the bigger boys play the leading parts, so we never see the show. Did we stamp our feet in dance? Probably, but what I remember is singing "Shosholoza," because I can remember the words (see above). If there were other songs we sang that night, I have forgotten them. Could it be a screen memory? I doubt it.

The Show

Ipi Tombi must have been chosen as our school play because of its huge success. After opening in Johannesburg in March 1974, where it ran for several years at the Brooke Theatre, *Ipi Tombi* went to London. Before becoming a fixture in the West End, it had been to Australia, and by the end of 1974 it had come with a second company to Cape Town, where it played at the Three Arts Theatre.[4] The original cast would perform in May 1975 at the Nico Malan Opera House.[5] That was where I saw *Ipi Tombi* with my mother and sister. Was A. with us? She might have come along, as she did to a screening of *E'Lollipop* at the school hall, since what brought people to *Ipi Tombi* was not simply the drumming and the dance and the chants of "Haya!," which are what I can remember, but another drama taking place offstage, in which all of us were the protagonists. In February 1975, the formerly segregated Nico Malan was allowed to open its doors to people of all races.[6] It was a crack in the edifice of apartheid, and whites, for their part, were curious to squeeze their way through.

After a tour of Israel and a run in Paris,[7] the show made its appearance at the National Theatre in Lagos, Nigeria in the lead-up to FESTAC '77. The claim by the Nigerian *Drum*, a South African-owned magazine, that the tour was a "demonstration of Nigeria's unequivocal stand against apartheid"[8] leaves us none the wiser as to how it eluded the boycott, particularly given the opposition voiced in the Nigerian media.[9] When Andrew Horn quotes a program for *Ipi Tombi* issued by Nigeria's Federal Ministry for Information, we are closer, I believe, to grasping how the petronaira-propelled Pan-Africanism of the Second World Black and African Festival of Arts and Culture could give it center stage: "The intellectual foundation of *Ipi-Tombi* is the conviction that indigenous African culture is one of the world's most valuable civilizations and that its dancing, its vivid clothes, its religions and beliefs and its absorption of the individual in the communal are things for the lack of which the world would be both duller and poorer. . . . The performance of *Ipi-Tombi* at the official opening of the National Theatre is a symbolic event reflecting Nigeria's dynamic response and responsibilities toward kindred brothers and sisters with common cultural roots and problems of African identity."[10] Although questions remain about the inclusion of *Ipi Tombi*, one can say that Nigeria's military rulers, as hosts of FESTAC, were broadly inclusive of almost anything African, rather than carefully discriminating.[11]

After the Nigerian interlude, *Ipi Tombi* returned to London.[12] By then, history had slowly begun to overtake it. The schoolchildren of Soweto had risen up in June 1976, and, with the advent of greater state repression also came a greater self-assertiveness influenced by Black Consciousness. The 1970s had seen the rise of black trade unions and an increase in strike action. Some members of the company who flew back to South Africa after the events of 1976 had had their passports confiscated on arrival, and a dispute over wages and working conditions had already flared up in May that year. Cast members protested that they were being "treated like slaves," and, in a formidable *coup de théatre*, a performance nearing its finale at Her Majesty's Theatre "was halted . . . when demonstrators in various parts of the theatre protested about pay and conditions for the cast. Some of the cast joined the protest, holding up a banner which said 'Ipi-Tombi cast victimised.'"[13] By the time *Ipi Tombi* came to New York in the frigid winter of 1977, it was a *cause célèbre*. Up to five hundred demonstrators from the Patrice Lumumba Coalition and other groups picketed the Harkness Theater in the snow, and the production folded after a few weeks, having failed to break even.[14] Aside from the question of wages and working conditions, the demonstrators accused the show of being a propaganda ploy by the South African government to promote the idea of "happy natives," whereas, as everybody who read the papers knew, people were being killed in the townships just for expressing their political views. Placards read, "Stop Ipi Tombi," "Remember the Children of Soweto," and "Apartheid's Genocidal Racist Exploitation Must Come to an End."[15] The rhetoric of the protests was a retort to the marquee slogan for the show: "Happiness is an African Musical called Ipi Tombi."[16] The company denied any government sponsorship, but it was observed that cast members were granted permission to travel abroad,[17] something not routinely granted to black South Africans at the time. This was partly to prevent political opponents from being heard, but also because granting a South African passport conferred South African citizenship, which went against Grand Apartheid and its goal, beginning with Transkei in 1976, of creating independent "national states" of which Africans would be citizens. Demonstrations also helped to close down *Ipi Tombi* at the Huntington Hartford Theater in Los Angeles in 1980.[18] A strike took place by cast members in Houston later the same year.[19] In the United States, only in Las Vegas, it would appear, was the production free of controversy, and a box-office success. Publicity materials from Las Vegas dating from 1980 and earlier make no mention of the New York pickets, eliding the New York engagement save for a single mention: "At this writing, Ipi Tombi is triumphantly encamped on Broadway, at the Harkness Theatre, where it opened on Wednesday evening, January 12, 1977."[20]

If baldly denying the protests seems like false advertising, the cultural boycott was a blunt instrument. Amid all of the critique about exploitation wages and white theft of black culture, there was something that did not translate. And that was the other drama unfolding inside the theaters in South Africa; actors in *Ipi Tombi* rejected the idea that the show was "connected with the government." Interviewed by the *New York Amsterdam News*, Matthew Bodibe insisted that: "Our entire cast is against apartheid. We know what it means to live under apartheid. The sister of one of our cast members, Lydia Monamodi, was blinded in the riots there. Ipi-Tombi . . . has helped change some of the laws in South Africa, where it was performed in all the major cities. It was the first time Black people played to white audiences in white theatres—and it also played to integrated audiences. It was the first Black show performed in the Nicomalan [sic] Theatre in Capetown [sic] and it played to an integrated audience in the opera house, where no Black had ever performed or sat in the audience."[21]

That what may have been most significant about the play for its South African audiences was overlooked by American protestors is perhaps not surprising: one can take a play overseas, but the theatre surrounding it will not travel. One can narrate all one wants about the political context, but in theatre mimesis will trump narration every time: unless one puts context on stage, as the London cast did with their banner, the demonstrators outside the door will command the attention of the audience. Incisive theatrical critiques were made by some who went to see the show, but their analyses were not what closed it down. A year later, out of work, members of the cast who had chosen to remain in New York were again interviewed by the *New York Amsterdam News*: "All we want to do is prove that we're not traitors or tools of the South African government."[22]

Most of these events took place in the months and years after our school play. And none of it appeared on our radar. Fathers with guns patrolled the school grounds in 1976, after the June "riots" spread to the Cape, but that was later, and before the boys from Rhodesia arrived. It could hardly have been clear to us, as it is safe to say now, that the integration of the opera house was *Ipi Tombi*'s chief claim to historical significance. But the history I am relating is not that history—it is a secret history. There is something that signifies for me about having been a Zulu boy in a play, despite one's later knowledge, and the sensation of politically progressive cringe that made one draw back from *Ipi Tombi*. Russell Vandenbroucke is correct that "[n]othing can justify *Ipi-Tombi*,"[23] but then so many things in the realm of art are without justification and without reason, without what N. P. van Wyk Louw called a *bestaansreg*, a right to exist.[24] But that does not mean that such things are without analyzable motivation. I would not say that what signifies is unaffected by the history and politics that came later—as early libidinal positions are inevitably modified through what Freud calls *Nachträglichkeit*, or deferred action[25]—but its effects have been felt over and over when learning Zulu has meant deliberately learning the language. If the words of the song appear, in their intelligibility, to indicate an entry into what Jacques Lacan called the Symbolic, then can one be sure that this is entirely so? Just as with the Hebrew songs we sang at Temple Israel in Portswood Road, the words of "Shosholoza" were repeated by us with only partial knowledge of their meaning. And elements of the song are themselves mimetic, the word "shosholoza" audible as onomatopoeic of the sound of a train. I am a train. And perhaps I played with a toy one when our mother, beside herself, took my sister and me as young children to the psychologist, David Evans, who, because he had his rooms at Wolraad Woltemade's house, remains a hero in my memory, an immovable object of positive transference.[26] In learning a language the mimetic is irreducible. This means that it is affected by what Lacan called the Imaginary: the dimension of identification,[27] where not only am I a boy learning Zulu, but I am a Zulu boy, as I will have been ever since I got ink on my fingers folding the pages of my telephone book into a house.

But what was *Ipi Tombi*? Haven't I told you already? If the show's historical significance were all that needed to be noted, then I have given you all that you need to know—and then some. But let us have a closer look. Reduced to its narrative skeleton, *Ipi Tombi* is a version of "Jim Comes to Joburg," by 1974 a terrible old cliché. Seeking his fortune in the Golden City, an African man leaves his rural home—in Tsomo, the Las Vegas program says, which is the name of an actual place in the Eastern Cape—only to return, having experienced the hardships of city life. As just about every theatre critic observes, this narrative is not distinctly realized by the music and dance numbers that comprise most of the action on stage. Most of the critics find themselves relying on the plot summary from the program: "this African import describes life in a tribal village, and tells the tale of a young man who joins that drift to the big city which has been the lot of rural folk world-wide in search of a better life. It tells of his experiences, disappointments and his ultimate return home, and provides a vehicle for the pulsating rhythm of African drums and the inexhaustible energy that is Africa."[28] In the production itself a narrator is employed—the young man looks back—whereas the expectation, typically, is that in a standard musical the songs, and usually also dialogue, contain the information needed to explain the action on stage. The show thus falls short of being the "musical" it is billed to be, and is perhaps more accurately viewed as a music and dance variety or revue—which is evidently what it was in the beginning—with elements of costume extravaganza. As the program states, it is a "vehicle" for African-style drumming and dance. Because of this it was easy for American critics to observe continuities between it and their own blackface minstrelsy of yesteryear—for instance "those Jungle Club revues that Harlem used to do in the 1920s, the closest American referent."[29] Its New York opponents were almost certainly alluding to this tradition when they pointed out how publicity for *Ipi Tombi* exploited "the race stereotype of the happy Darkie and the super sexual males and females as sexual animals."[30] It was thus easily viewed as simply a pretext for sexual titillation: "Sex is an obsession in this show, not as an aspect of touching, but as a nasty little sweetmeat. Tourist bait. . . . This says far more about the culture that concocted 'Ipi Tombi' than the culture it is supposed to celebrate. Naturally the show knocked 'em dead in Las Vegas."[31] No doubt this was also why the show knocked 'em dead in South Africa, where white audiences were, after years of being barred from this voyeuristic pleasure, suddenly given license to watch black performers in costumes that were as revealing as some of their dance moves were suggestive. Although I do not know for sure that the South African productions billed topless dancers, the program for the Las Vegas production, predictably, has photographs of female performers displaying their breasts. Show business is show business. What were we putting on show in our little production?

It has been a long time since I saw the show, so forgive me if I use the program and the *Original Cast Recording* (Gallo South Africa, 2002) to refresh my memory. In the program I have, *Ipi Tombi* is divided into two acts, separated by a twenty-minute intermission, with an overture and finale. Each of the acts is divided into four scenes. Scene one is "The Village of Tsomo," in which "[t]he women [are] busy about their duties, grinding corn, preparing food and drink for the return of their menfolk from the hunt." It is "tribal" African boilerplate, as in the opening shots of Donald Swanson's *Jim Comes to Joburg*. This is followed by "The Baptism," a dumb show "interpret[ing] the conflict" between Christian missionaries and "the influence of the witch-doctors." This scene drew criticism in South Africa for presenting "[t]he witch-doctor [as] the most feared and the most powerful person in the village"—he makes his entrance with distinctive special effects: a thunderclap and lightning flash. As was wryly noted by Mshengu, a theatre critic writing in *S'ketsh*,[32] both cast members interviewed denied that, for them, a "witch doctor" was a figure whom they feared.[33] This is followed by a brief scene with "Nadia: A Song of Hope," upon which the action moves to "Ê'Goli—The City of Gold." After the intermission, the performers return for "Sunday on a Mine," which is followed by "The Township Wedding." "A Workday on a Mine" rounds out the young man's stay in the city. Scene four, "The Warriors," explosively brings the action to a close.

Each of these scenes includes at least one song. If the song I remember from our junior-school production is in Zulu—or I remember it as having been in Zulu, which is the main thing—not all of the songs are. In fact, several are in Xhosa—or in English, with a line or two in Zulu or in Xhosa. This is the pattern in "Mama Tembu's Wedding," which was a recording hit before being incorporated in *Ipi Tombi*. The title song, "Ipi Tombi?," is entirely in English except for a few lines: "Haya! Haya! / Haya hho, ntombi yami! / Iphi intombi yami? Intombi yami." "The Warrior," the third major hit from *Ipi Tombi* and like the other two songs a success on the album *The Warrior* (1973) with Margaret Singana before the show coalesced, has, except for lines to which I will return, only a few words in Zulu: "Woza / Woza hho! . . . Iphi le ndoda?" And, on the *Original Cast Recording*, even "Shosholoza," sung in male-voice two-part harmony, gives way to several lines by female voices in English that identify it as a work song. Clearly I have been remembering selectively, a sign that my investment has always been in the name for a language, which may really be a displacement of the investment in being a Zulu boy—which is to say, in being a boy, which is to say: not a girl.

The songs in *Ipi Tombi* are, notoriously, credited to Bertha Egnos and her daughter, Gail Lakier: "Conceived, Devised and Produced by Bertha Egnos. Original Music by Bertha Egnos. Lyrics by Gail Lakier."[34] Why notoriously? Well, writes Mshengu: "almost all the songs and most of the dialogue, such as there is, are in Zulu, Xhosa and Sotho. Did they write this then? And did they write the *Xhosa Proposition*?"—a number made up of a series of words with clicks.[35] Some of the songs they are calling their own are "traditional," as is acknowledged with the *Original Cast Recording*. "Shosholoza" is an example. What is also said is that there was a failure to acknowledge that the content of the show was produced collaboratively and also includes material from an earlier play by Gibson Kente. Mshengu provides an inventory:

The truth is that almost all the songs and dance steps were contributed, devised and practiced by cast members. Pinise Saul brought *A la Qaba* (unfortunately from [Gibson] Kente's *Sikalo*) and other Xhosa songs. Martha Molefe contributed *Bayakhala emakhaya* and others. Leah Mabuza accounted for *Meme Mntanami*. And so on. The Bhaca Gumboot Dance was coached by an anonymous black man brought from some mine or other. Nowhere in the programme is this reflected. Only a few names (first names only) of individual performers. Our directors added some indifferent numbers and 'tidied up' the riches of Black music, and *Ipi Tombi* became 'their' musical.[36]

By the time the show gets to Las Vegas, "A la Qaba" and "Meme Mntanami" are no longer on the program. To point to white appropriation with little or no acknowledgment is one response. Notoriety also derives from the sense that song, music, and dance are being presented as authentically African—or at least received or marketed as such—when they are not. The two lines of response must diverge if, musically and choreographically, this is an adaptation, a pastiche of existing and newly composed material. As Russell Vandenbroucke observed, *Ipi Tombi* is best understood as an example of white culture: "*Ipi-Tombi* . . . is the latest in a series of musical plays from South Africa that are primarily designed for white audiences and use elements of black culture, especially legends, music and dance."[37] *New York Magazine* was not wrong to compare it to *Hiawatha*.[38] That it was produced with the collaboration of black people, contains African music and dance, and was enthusiastically consumed by black audiences[39] does not necessarily make it an African show. One might wish to point to hybridity, and that would be correct insofar as "white culture" is not purely white. But that would not make *Ipi Tombi* into an "African musical," unless the Africans one is talking about are white Africans. It is from them that the initiative stems, and among whom less than openly declared motives may be sought and discovered.

The Legend of Johnny Clegg

Standing in vivid contrast to the dubious successes of *Ipi Tombi* are the achievements of Johnny Clegg. Gaining worldwide fame in the 1980s as a pop singer blending rock with elements of Zulu music and performance, Clegg earned the French epithet "le Zoulou blanc" (The White Zulu, or The White Zulu Man)—a name that, as Louise and I discovered when we stopped for gas on a journey through Catalonia in the 1990s, had made its way beyond the borders of France.

Others have been called "white Zulus," perhaps most notoriously John Dunn, the nineteenth-century Natal hunter and trader who, like other white men trading at Port Natal in the early 1800s, took up Zulu ways and maintained a large polygamous household.[40] Dunn served for two decades as a chief under

Cetshwayo until turning against him.[41] When we first heard the epithet "le Zoulou blanc," we were not thinking of John Dunn. Johnny Clegg's being Zulu was, for us, an unalloyed good. The name, when we heard it in Catalonia—the man who spoke to us danced a few steps—nevertheless suggested to us that what seemed to matter most for a metropolitan public was Johnny Clegg's adeptness at mimicry, and his embodiment thereby of the sign of virile African manhood par excellence that is "Zulu." But anybody who has paid closer attention knows that Johnny Clegg's has been a far harder act to follow than that.[42] Because of the thoroughness and depth of his learning, he appears to have eluded the destructive tendencies that marred the endeavors of some of his less-able precursors. Yet even he had to come to terms with the secret history.

As much comes clear in a series of expansive interviews given by him between 1987 and 1991. To listen to Johnny Clegg speak is to hear a legend. One could say that the legend of Johnny Clegg is the secret history *in nuce*. In the beginning, there was a *secret*—and it was, for the fourteen-year-old Clegg, a thing of fascination. It was what drew him into Zulu dance and song in the late 1960s. Years later, he would remember how he was taken by his "first teacher," Charlie Mzila, who worked in Johannesburg as a janitor, to a dance competition in a courtyard at the Lady Dudley Hospital workers' hostel. He tells anthropologist David Coplan in a 1991 interview:

> While they were doing this, I had the feeling they knew something I didn't know; a very powerful sense of being outside a profound mystery. Not a mystery so much as a sacred knowledge being enacted. As I walked up, I could feel in the concrete the stamping of the feet, and the power of the humming.... I wanted to be able to do that, to know what they were feeling. And it was such a *foreign* movement. I felt as if I had been made privy to an important, significant behavior and a secret, as if I was being inducted into some kind of cult: you know, the young fourteen-year-old. Nobody, nobody knew that in the middle of Johannesburg in a courtyard, a traditional Bhaca war dance was being stamped out every Tuesday and Thursday night. There was a sense of being elected. This was serious shit.[43]

Details change in the retelling, but being outside—and then in on—a secret is at the core of the legend of Johnny Clegg. "Every adolescent possesses his secret garden where he loves to take refuge, and the hostel became that place for me," he tells Philippe Conrath.[44] "It was as if some very powerful disclosure was being made to me," he explains to *Rolling Stone*, "and I didn't understand it. And that freaked me out..... There was a secret locked in there. And then I knew that I had to know that secret."[45]

Without a father at home, the adolescent was looking for a mentor who would initiate him into the secret, knowledge of which would ensure his passage into manhood;[46] at the age of thirteen, declining to observe the rites of passage expected of him by his mother's family, he had refused to have a bar mitzvah.⁴⁷ The relation to the secret must, at some level, be seen as typical for the boy becoming a man: "you know, the young fourteen-year-old." Because Johnny Clegg tends to look back on his early life in ways that evoke psychoanalytic understanding—Philippe Conrath refers to the interviews in his book as Clegg's "biographical 'psychoanalysis' "⁴⁸—I do not think that it would be unjust to take my cue from him and say that, in general, the boy's relation to the secret may be interpreted as his jealous feeling of being excluded from the primal scene, "an important, significant behavior and a secret" shared by and kept from him by the parents.⁴⁹ So the phantasy runs. In our history, and Johnny Clegg's, the relation to the secret kept by "Zulu" is, however, distinctly marked. Remember the Jarvis boy from Alan Paton's *Cry, the Beloved Country*. He wants to learn Zulu from the Reverend Kumalo, yet for Paton the "bright boy" appears to represent a paranoid fear of not-knowing and not-understanding that is intolerable. Those few Zulu words are all he knows, the Reverend assures his wife. Johnny Clegg uses a vocabulary of not-knowing and not-understanding to capture his adolescent's response to the Bhaca dance: "I had the feeling they knew something I didn't know," he tells Coplan; "I didn't understand it," he tells *Rolling Stone*, "And that freaked me out."

Clegg himself maintains that "[t]he Zulu . . . have had a huge impact on the white psyche."⁵⁰ When it comes to the secret, then, things are powerfully overdetermined. For historical reasons, Zulu language and music will have been forbidden terrain for a white Johannesburg adolescent growing up in the late 1960s on the fringes of the middle class. The paranoia relating to the primal scene infuses and suffuses the historical, making Zulu and its music a no-go zone that must be traversed for the boy to become a man. So, the fourteen-year-old white boy, who is drawn to music—and whose mother, Muriel Pienaar, is a singer and works at a record company and is supportive of her son's endeavors—is so to say adopted by Charlie Mzila, who, symbolically speaking, completes the parental couple, but at the same time affords the boy access to the "mother," because he plays the guitar and teaches Johnny how. In symbolic terms, it is a perfect "reparation." The manhood attained by the boy turns out to be a Zulu manhood. "The Zulu gave me those masculine values which clearly somewhere I was needing."⁵¹ The boy's father, Dennis Clegg, is divorced by his mother when her son is six months old, and he only meets him when he is twenty-one.⁵² His stepfather, Dan Pienaar, from whom he inherits a fascination with Africa, and who treats him more like a brother and confidant than a father, deserts his family when Johnny is about twelve, meaning the loss of a father figure at a crucial age.⁵³ Johnny Clegg's own first marriage ends up on the rocks "because I had rejected the concept of [male] monogamy I think."⁵⁴ I cannot tell whether he means that this was because the Zulu manhood he gained does not impose monogamy on men; whether he is saying so or not, he may be read as following in the footsteps of the father. Whether he stays or goes, this father will, in the boy's phantasy, always be with the mother, even if it is not the same mother. (The actual life trajectory of the stepfather, who left Johnny's mother for another woman, taking their three-year-old daughter with them to Australia, is nearer in its lineaments to the phantasy than the life of the father, who evidently had to go because, not being Jewish, he was unacceptable to his wife's family.[55]) A father—or a father figure—is required who will let Johnny be like him. Or better, one who will give Johnny prizes for imitating him.

Do not suppose, however, that this process was a simple one. Although, as Sipho Mchunu remembers, Johnny Clegg was "this white guy trying to be like a Zulu,"[56] the boy speaks Fanagalo to begin with,[57] or "a very rough mixture of Zulu and Fanagalo and English."[58] He is an excellent mimic and sings Zulu songs without understanding what the words mean: "I found I was very good at mimicking exactly what was sung, but I never knew what was sung."[59] Up until then, give or take a few years of age, musical talent and training, knowledge of languages, social contact with black people whom he accords the same respect as he does his parents and age-mates—a result of having grown up in Rhodesia and Zambia, where he had "experienced being with blacks in school [and] had a lot of black friends"[60]—Johnny Clegg could almost have been me singing "Shosholoza." But his relation to "Zulu" never remained merely mimetic, as mine was at the age of seven. His mother called up the university when Johnny was fourteen and talked Raymond Mfeka into letting her son into his Zulu course.[61] If Johnny Clegg bears the secret history's trace, that history also fails fully to contain him. Perhaps that is what makes his story a legend.

But what unfolded from those tentative and audacious beginnings—I do not understand, and it freaks me out, but I go on—drew Clegg into the world of migrant workers' hostels, with its dance competitions, and eventually into one of the great collaborations in South African popular music when he and Sipho Mchunu, a talented Zulu guitarist, recorded their first single in 1976 and formed the band Juluka in 1979.[62] Clegg himself explains the epithet of "White Zulu" as defying the apartheid order—which dictated that certain cultural and linguistic identities be racially exclusive.[63] Zulus speak Zulu, and a Zulu is a black person. Clegg's contradiction of apartheid took place through dance and song; it was by going further than mere mimesis that he brought the official mutual exclusivity of being white and being Zulu to crisis. With Mchunu he developed the crossover of folk-rock and Zulu *maskanda* that became Juluka's signature style in its classic early albums: *Universal Men* (1979), *African Litany* (1981), and *Scatterlings* (1982). Although migrant workers were a significant part of the band's audience,[64] it was only in 1982 that an all-Zulu full-length album was released, *Ubuhle bemvelo* (Beauty of Nature); it included the duo's pre-Juluka 1977 hit, "Woza Friday."[65] A listenership developed at the same time among white university students, but the band soon came up against the restrictive purism of apartheid cultural policy: "Their songs were banned from the government's English [radio] station for having Zulu lyrics and from its Zulu station for having English lyrics."[66] And critics on the left accused Clegg, who had danced with his age regiment at King Zwelithini's wedding to a Swazi princess,[67] of being a "cryptotribalist romantic."[68] His response was to write lyrics for Juluka in English.[69] Despite these headwinds, Juluka forged on, earning acclaim abroad, especially in Europe. After Sipho Mchunu left the band in 1985, Clegg formed a new one called Savuka, which, although one sensed that the magic of the collaboration had passed, enjoyed even greater commercial success than Juluka. The fame in France that won for Clegg the epithet "le Zoulou blanc" dates from the Savuka years.[70]

The memory of the collaboration between Clegg and Mchunu, however, is what underwrites the legacy in South Africa, along with a recognition of Clegg's mastery of Zulu language, music, and dance. In a recent column in *Isolezwe*, Bhungani kaMzolo refers to Clegg as "a young man who was white but spoke Zulu." "It was a marvel indeed," Mzolo continues, "the matter of a white and a black person in those times, whereas apartheid did not allow that thing, namely that the races do things together. Today it is just that which made Sipho Mchunu and Johnny Clegg into idols for many black people. It made black people glad, this thing of a young man who was white performing the *indlamu* dance and danced in the style known as *ukugiya*, holding his shield as well as his fighting stick."[71] This sort of recognition may explain why in Pietermaritzburg, when Audrey Mbeje, who uses songs to such effect in her classroom, taught us Fulbright scholars the use of the subjunctive, she had us sing "Impi! Wo! Nans' impi yeza / Ubani obengathint' amabhubhesi?" (War! Wo! Here is war, it is coming / Who is going to be able to touch the lions?)—a battle cry heard all over the world as the lead song on Juluka's second album, *African Litany*.[72]

Not as well known as his achievements as a performer is that Johnny Clegg's learning of Zulu language and music became the basis for an academic career that, although coming to an end in 1982 when he became a full-time musician,[73] brought him significant recognition independent of his performance career. Although Clegg's writings from the early 1980s in anthropology and ethnomusicology are not easy to find, they are to this day cited by specialists in the field.[74] It was when he was a student at the University of the Witwatersrand that he met David Webster, the anthropologist and activist assassinated in 1989 by Ferdi Barnard, a member of the Civil Cooperation Bureau, a clandestine South African army hit squad responsible for several targeted political killings in the late 1980s.[75] Clegg was devastated by the murder of his teacher, mentor, and friend.[76] David Webster had done his fieldwork in what is today northern KwaZulu-Natal in the 1970s and '80s, among Thonga migrants. This I had known from reports about his death, which speculated that he might have stumbled upon covert state activities in the region, which is near the border with Mozambique.[77] But I would never have anticipated that, when I went to Jozini I would learn from Musa Mthembu, vice-principal at Sinethezekile school, that David Webster, who had stayed in their community at Kosi Bay, had bought him, then a teenager, a bed as a parting gift. I have never met Johnny

Clegg, and I never met David Webster, but Musa's memory of his generosity spins a thread that brings me closer both to the musician and his academic mentor. The latter was never satisfied that he knew enough. Others will quote Webster's anthropological writings, including his doctoral dissertation on the Chopi of Mozambique, recently published in Portuguese translation,[78] but I prefer to quote from his notebook, where in 1986, he wrote the simple words that resonate for me: "It is clear to me that my Zulu needs a ton of improvement. It must go very high on my list of priorities."[79]

Boys and Girls

To David Webster, Johnny Clegg must have been an example of what can be accomplished through learning a language well, just as he was to me and others who came of age listening and dancing to the music of Juluka and Savuka. The force of Clegg's example, and its continued affirmation in the Zulu opinion pages of today, may suggest—and what I am about to say will not sit easily with everybody—that to criticize *Ipi Tombi* for its *representation* of African culture is legitimate enough, but somehow misses the point. A show of its kind is not simply a representation of some thing but, because, when one is in a production or just dances or sings along, it involves an animation of limbs and vocal cords, it is also a "learning" through mimesis.

As much is apparent also in *Pagan Tapestry* (1940), the memoirs of Bertha Slosberg, which Loren Kruger kindly suggested I read, and which, standing out from the dominant masculine genealogy of identification, has its author jubilantly hear herself "singing like a Zulu girl."[80] A Lithuanian Jewish refugee, who came to South Africa as a teenager and freely owns to a "persecution complex" that she relates to her history,[81] Slosberg, working with the Mthethwa Lucky Stars and Darktown Strutters, produced, with mixed success, a series of African song and dance shows in the 1930s with titles like *An African Entertainment* and *Bantu Medley*. The pinnacle of Slosberg's theatre career is her role in producing "native dances" for *The Sun Never Sets*, a stage adaptation of *Sanders of the River*, at Drury Lane in 1938. In partnership with Makumalo Hlubi, a South African expatriate, she coaches a troupe of Londoners from Nigeria who were, she writes, reluctant at first to perform Zulu dance and song: "When they saw that I could simulate primitive movement and expression, they fell in with all suggestions in their own high-spirited way."[82] In order to become stage Africans, the Nigerians imitate the "Zulu girl" as she directs. Put on stage, "Zulu" is cut loose from Zulus, making it pointless to complain, at least in this instance, about a lack of authenticity.

Like the efforts of Slosberg, which were, in their time, linked to elite African efforts at "retraditionalization,"[83] *Ipi Tombi* is an episode in the secret history of learning Zulu that, with white learners at the forefront, begins with Fanagalo and reaches its high-cultural apogee with *Cry, the Beloved Country*. Zulu might be learned, and learned well, as Johnny Clegg showed us it can be—even if his first steps were in Fanagalo, and he began singing in Zulu without knowing what the words meant. Or, if it is not learned, Zulu might be put on, but at the same time also attacked and mutilated—and thus never, properly speaking, learned. If Fanagalo forces Zulu into an English mold, and Alan Paton's Zulu lesson includes a mistake that no speaker of Zulu would make, *Ipi Tombi* raises questions about motivation by assimilating Zulu, Xhosa, and Sotho as if there were no difference, leading, as Mshengu writes, to "countless and grotesque incongruities.... [T]hey go to Zululand and sing Zionist [Christian] songs in Xhosa. Blanketed Basotho sing *Bayakhala emakhaya* and *Jikelez' umzi weny' indoda*."[84] It is a hodgepodge, a symbol of a failure or obstinate incapacity to learn.

In making such observations, one can come across as a purist—and that is the critical risk, the risk of simply substituting severe anal differentiation for undiscriminating oral assimilation. Apartheid, at least in Geoffrey Cronjé, as J. M. Coetzee writes, was a counterattack against the latter (*rasse-mengelmoes*, race-mishmash),[85] and the urban milieu that might have made such crossing imaginable. And my old identification with "Zulu" is no doubt related to such dynamics—via apartheid ethnic differentiation, but surely also via the (regressive) anal tendencies of the seven-year-old latency boy. But is lumping not a legitimation of apartheid by reversal? Is, as Zoë Wicomb points out in her commentary on Coetzee's *Disgrace*,[86] interracial sex—I allude to *Ipi Tombi* as breaching the Immorality Act by displacement by playing before racially mixed houses—not a politically naïve overturning of apartheid? I would answer both questions in the affirmative, with the proviso that—in the persona of the Zulu boy—I am not to be seen as a disinterested party. That identification depends on a purism, and a certain purism depends on it, even if the condition of possibility for enacting that identification resides in hybridity: I am a Zulu boy, but only by virtue of having a part in *Ipi Tombi*, which is a mishmash. But if one cannot rigorously free hybridizations and pidginizations from psychical trends of an aggressive kind, then perhaps one can still see an attack for what it is—although that is not so easy when oral and anal are, thanks to regressive tendencies, not always well differentiated for the boy in his latency. One might still discern the manic-reparative at work, as the object is attacked from which, in phantasy, one fears retribution for an earlier wrong. If Slosberg's "persecution complex" is a clue to deeper motivations for her ease in making "Zulu" float so freely as a dramatic signifier, there may be other parallels to these dynamics in the history, for which documentation is scarce, of white women identifying as "Zulu girls."

Let us return to *Ipi Tombi*. Introducing the final scene, which the program entitles, "The Warriors," the young man narrates: "I returned home to find my people preparing for battle. A war over cattle—what does it matter? A cow, a loaf of bread, a kingdom? The blood still flows. Dear God, where is peace?"[87] The stage is set for a climactic battle. In this war over cattle—presumably cattle that have been stolen—no enemy is actually present. The program says that "[t]he dance movements depict [the warriors'] mode of attack, their boasting of their prowess, the dodging and feinting with their imaginary enemies . . ." The text leaves the ellipsis, keeping it unstated who might be imagined by the warriors to be their enemies. If "cattle" are a synecdoche for a stolen "kingdom," historically, there is really only one answer. "The blood still flows." The liner notes to the compact disc, published many years after the original production, state this explicitly: "A dramatic musical description of the now famous 'Battle of Blood River' between 10,000 Zulu Warriors, and a small party of Boer Settlers led by Andries Pretorius—the Boers defeated the Zulus."[88] The same notes say that "[t]he SABC banned airplay of the album [*The Warrior*, 1973] because the track, *The Warrior*, made reference to the Battle of Blood River."[89] If there is a reference to Blood River it is elliptical, however, with the lyrics running thus:

> A vulture flies
> The wind that cries
> The warrior dies
> At the battle of blood
> The scavengers wait
> Each man the bait
> Death his mate
> At the battle of blood.[90]

In each instance, the male vocals are oversung at the end of the line by the female so that, if the word "river" were to have been sung after "blood," it would not have been audible. The last verse of the song, sung by a female vocalist, corresponds to the narrator's doubts about violence:

> The fight's over
> And the battle's won
> The fight's over
> And the deed is done
> The fight's over
> But which side has won?
> The fight's over
> But has it just begun?[91]

On the original cast recording, alternating with these lines is a repeated sharp male-voice chant, which is in Zulu: "Ngigwaza ngomkhonto / Ngadla! / Ngigwaza ngomkhonto." (I stab with a spear / I have killed / I stab with a spear.)[92] Umkhonto weSizwe (Spear of the Nation), founded by Nelson Mandela and others as the armed wing of the ANC, carried out its first sabotage missions on December 16, 1961, the day commemorating the battle of Blood

River, and known among whites as Dingaan's Day.[93] The implication is clear: there will be retribution, the defeat of 1838 will be overturned.[94] For English colonials, a better example of Zulu martial prowess would be the battle of Isandlwana in 1879, in which the British were defeated by Cetshwayo's army; as I read in *Sawubona*, the South African Airways in-flight magazine, this event, for better or worse, remains the source of the Zulu-warrior stereotype exploited in the promotion of tourism in the "Zulu Kingdom" today: "The Zulu brand . . . rocketed to international prominence when the British army tried to justify and explain its annihilation at the hands of Zulu warriors."[95] But, despite the ensuing destruction of the Zulu Kingdom, because at Isandlwana the Zulus defeated the British, it retains none of the ambiguity that would make Zulus victims as well as victors.

It is not the threat of retribution that is censored but the guilty fear of it—which is also of violent penetration. It thus *is* an anti-apartheid play: not by being protest theatre, but by acting out a fearful phantasy of coupling. The capitalization of "Boer Settler" and "Zulu Warrior" in the liner notes indicates an apocalyptic clash of ideal types, one that will be repeated as, following the theft of their kingdom, "The Warriors" await their "imaginary enemies." In the narration, the young man who has returned evidently wishes to break the cycle of blood-letting, but mimesis in the form of martial dance and music overpowers his message of peace, just as the male voice in Zulu interrupts the questions asked in English by the female vocalist. The fear of retribution animating the colonial fetish of the Zulu warrior—who is also the sexual rival toward whom one has a masochistic relation—is what drives the finale. "How strange," W. S. Kaplan wrote in the *Argus* on first seeing the show, "that it is at the theatre that we hear the songs of our neighbours, and applaud their war dances that once struck terror into the hearts of our forefathers."[96] A castration-play, in other words. But it is the Zulus who were defeated, whose blood dyed the Ncome River red; when the London cast's protest banner read "Ipi-Tombi cast victimised," it showed that there was little doubt about who had been the victor, and who in the 1970s continued to be in a position to victimize. Isandlwana, on the other hand, would have told the London audience something else.

If, in psychoanalytic terms, battle involves a paranoid splitting that may be destructive—when coupling is violent—the wedding that is the other main set piece in act 2 is about a different kind of coupling, and is reparative. "Mama Tembu's Wedding" is an answer to the question, "Ipi tombi?" Somebody is coupling with "Mama," or the mother.[97] But there are other scenes that deserve analysis. Who is it, in "The Garbage Collectors," who has made Zulus absorb the waste matter of whites? An allegory at a number of levels; Bertha Egnos once told a journalist how the name for the show came from her Zulu cook, and how the original cast included "former nannies, school teachers, and there is even a court interpreter. Some were unemployed." Perhaps it would not be fair to say that Egnos liked to think of the actors as her servants, but there is little doubt that she thought of herself as the boss: "After all, we have been able to offer work and to pay them more than they have ever earned before. Isn't that better than being unemployed?"[98] I leave it to others to answer Egnos's rhetorical question and to analyze the manic-reparative undertone of "better than." There were, to judge from Matthew Bodibe's interview with the *New York Amsterdam News*, probably those who were inclined to see it her way.[99] And, certainly, once the cast learned the power of strike action, its members demanded as much as they could, materially. Yet, some critics were still uncomfortable that they were singing the "rubbish"—Mshengu's word for some of Bertha Egnos's songs—that had been put into their mouths by their boss. This is what Vandenbroucke has to say: "The singers, dancers, and drummers wear irrepressible smiles. Perhaps they really enjoy their work, or are embarrassed by their participation in it. Perhaps *Ipi-Tombi* is, simply, an opportunity to advance their careers. It is easy for actors to be unaware of a director's true intentions; the cast of *Ipi-Tombi* appears naively innocent of the merry villager impression it creates."[100] Or perhaps they were just acting well, Professor, complying with the terms of their contracts.

The circumstances of performance have a way of entering into the piece. Listen once more to "Fanagalo" by the Woody Woodpeckers. There is the chance that when they sing "Jim, shina lo shoes / Jim, pressa lo suit / Baas, hamba city world tonight / African jazz," that the Baas and his Missis might be listening to the song as it is being performed by "Jim"—say as part of African Jazz and Variety, the popular South African Institute of Race Relations show for which the song was first performed in 1952.[101] The slight shift of tone going into "hamba" suggests that it could be Jim who says that he is going to city world—or the City Hall—for African jazz. The houseboy, as in Swanson's *Jim Comes to Joburg*, can also moonlight as an entertainer. When the Petersen Brothers covered "Fanagalo" on their album *On Safari* in 1958, the hint at the venue of performance—occupied by Jim, as well as his Baas and Missis—is absent. The white trio changes the words, and all we get is flat white English intonation and a series of Fanagalo instructions. If they had wanted to, could the Petersens have found a way of signaling that they were doing a white parody of a black parody of a white attempt to mimic black speech? I wonder—in any case, "Jim" only speaks once, when taking up a theme from the original song, he declares "Missis hamba shaya golf / Me babysit."

On the other hand, it is not as if the artifice that the professor of drama misses in *Ipi Tombi* never becomes visible, and at the director's instruction at that; in Los Angeles, "[t]he singing [was] largely lipsynched, to a tape that [went] hiss and pop. Tacky."[102] The tackiness was registered from the first night that *Ipi Tombi* opened in Johannesburg, with Percy Baneshik in the *Star* making plentiful use of scare quotes: "If it weren't for the natural talent and exuberance of the performers, the word might be 'ersatz.' But these dancers and harmonisers, Black skins a-gleaming and white (with a lower-case 'w') teeth a-flashing, come triumphantly through the synthetic fibre 'sheepskin' leggings and machine-made 'savage' finery, to give an overwhelmingly vigorous African kick to the spectacle."[103] Things like this ought to have made *Ipi Tombi* a cult classic, like Ed Wood's 1959 film *Plan 9 from Outer Space*, in which an alien space ship is visibly suspended by a thread from somewhere at the top of the frame.

But perhaps the actors also sensed that there was something masochistic about the show, that the rubbish that they were taking in and letting out was the manic-reparative detritus of a deep-seated colonial fear of retributive punishment. Remember that Freud described the fetish, which is used to disavow castration, as an *Ersatz* (substitute).[104] Energized by unacknowledged white motives, *Ipi Tombi* is masochistic, even if white people never appear on stage, in contrast to the mimicry of the Woody Woodpeckers' "Fanagalo" or *Woza Albert!*'s clown-nosed Baas Kom: "Zuluboy!"[105] The elided term does not have to appear, since it is the operative one. Ours might have been the first ever performance by an all-white cast, but *Ipi Tombi* has always been a white play.

No more so than in its title. When the show hits the road, its title is *Ipi-Tombi*, with a hyphen, whether it is the road to Johannesburg, New York, or Las Vegas. Some people object: This is Fanagalo, a corruption of the correct Zulu or Xhosa—it should, Mshengu in *S'ketsh* is the first to write, be "Iph' intombi?"[106] Granted. But what is missed in the correction of the spelling of the show's name is what the phrase, in its most literal sense, actually means. The researcher is faced with a puzzling fact. Nearly everybody—from the show's promoters, to theatre critics eminent and not, to the most erudite of scholars—finds the need to gloss the title, but, let me say provisionally, *nobody glosses it correctly*. The phrase is said by Bertha Egnos, who says she got it from her Zulu cook, to mean "Where Are the Girls?"—and everybody else merrily follows the pied piper.[107] It is the gloss I remember receiving from my mother, who could hardly have sucked it out of her thumb.

But the phrase, even when put into standard Zulu or Xhosa orthography, does not mean "Where are the girls?" It means "Where is the girl?" *Intombi* (girl) is singular. Its plural would be *izintombi* in Zulu and *iintombi* in Xhosa. So, in Xhosa, might one be able to hear "Iphi intombi?" as including the plural *iintombi*? Yes, except nobody who speaks the language would hear any such thing, since there must be agreement between the noun-class markers of the plural noun and the interrogative adjective. In Xhosa the question, "Where are the girls?" would be "Ziphi iintombi?," and in Zulu it would be "Ziphi izintombi?" or, for speakers of Zulu who elide the *zi-* in plural nouns, something closer in sound to the Xhosa. The error in translation, and its nearly universal perpetuation, are all the more striking in that the show's title comes—as an allusion, but also chronologically—from the song "Ipi ntombi" (*Original Cast Recording*) (or "Ipi 'n tombia," glossed as "Young Girl" on *The Warrior* sound album in 1973). The refrain of that song, "Iphi intombi yami?" means "Where is my girl?" and the surrounding lyrics, sung by Margaret Singana and lipsynched by her successors, with a male vocalist taking up the refrain in the background, suggest a longing for a girl of one's own: "It"—presumably the question "Iphi intombi yami?"—"trembles in my mind / And on my lips / Down my spine / And across my hips.... It rises through my head / And hits my brain / It locks my soul / And what's to blame?"[108]

The title song is in the singular, but the show proffers "girls" in the plural. How to explain this? What's to blame? Here is one account: "Those of us who are lucky enough to have seen the Johannesburg gold miners performing for tourists on Sunday afternoons recognize at once the source of Ipi Tombi's inspiration.... At the end of the gold miners' performances many tourists ask: 'Where are the women?' That question, translated into Zulu, is Ipi Tombi? So the producers of this musical have embellished the miners' programs for the stage by bringing in a body of bronze, bare-breasted beauties."[109] Who knows where the Toronto tabloid writer heard this, but it hardly matters, since the curtain is now drawn from another scene. No matter how many times the spelling of the title is corrected by those who mean well, what is put on stage is a phantasy of white men coupling with black women. But in this phantasy of "bringing in" there remains a destructiveness; in no game of *fort-da* is the murderous *fort* ever more than delayed. The language of the woman—which is the mother tongue, the language of the breast—is mangled as the "tourist" shouts for what he wants to see, jumping up and down, voicing his desire in a kind of infantile quasi-pidgin: "Ipi tombi? Ipi tombi?" Just listen to him, he's learning Zulu! So the translation "Where are the girls?" is not a mistranslation when it is read as a translation into English of what was always already a translation *from* English. "Ipi Tombi" *does* mean "Where are the girls?" when the tourist makes his demand. Well-meaning correction of the spelling tends to draw the curtain across the scene again, eliding the miners' programs as a context of utterance, making infantile into grown-up speech, tourist into native. The force of the demand for the plural joins unevenly, and may be irreconcilable, with the girl of one's own that is longed for in the refrain: "Iphi intombi yami?" *Ipi Tombi* is volatile because it never pretends to reconcile singular and plural, but promises to deliver both at once.

A natural question to pose, when confronted with the testimony of spectators (and a performer) who are male and white, is: Where *are* the girls? It is always possible to pose this question rhetorically, and then not listen for the answer. It is also possible to wait for an answer—in which case one's patience would be rewarded, if one wanted to know how it was, not only for the Jewish women impresarios who were drawn to "Zulu" as a sign,[110] but also for female performers in *Ipi Tombi*. Scholars have for some time asked us to look at how, historically, African women's bodies have been put on display, in a spectacle designed to titillate, or just to satisfy some more diffuse commoditizing "spectatorial lust";[111] there was Sara (or Saartje) Baartman, billed as the "Hottentot Venus," exhibited in Europe in the early 1800s,[112] there was *Ipi Tombi*, one of countless such shows, but the practice of "ipitombification," as Loren Kruger calls it, has proven all too tenacious.[113]

We can look, and we can also listen. In 1999, Thembi Mtshali-Jones appeared onstage in a collaboration with playwright Yael Farber called *A Woman in Waiting*. This is a "testimonial play," with Mtshali-Jones, a well-known actress in film and television, playing herself. She enacts scenes from her life, from gestation and birth, through growing up, motherhood, and work, to being a witness inspired by the women who testified before the Truth and Reconciliation Commission. In the fourth and final scene, "This Museum in Me," Thembi's monologue relates how a role in *Ipi Tombi* took her from domestic service—"the girl in the kitchen"—into a career on the stage.[114] Her memories are mediated in part by lyrics from the songs that she sang, as she recalls moving from Durban to Johannesburg in 1976 with her daughter Phum'zile.[115] Lyrics from the battle finale to *Ipi Tombi* are modified to evoke the schoolchildren's mass protests: "As night fades out . . . / Faded by the sun / Ten thousand kids stood high on the hill."[116] And then, sung softly, to mourn a mother's loss of her child: "Ipi Ntombi yami? Ntombi yami?"[117] Then there is a turning point: "By the late seventies I had performed on the West End and Broadway—but what is smiling and kicking your legs high on Broadway, when your home is on fire? I knew it was time to walk the road that other artists had paved . . . To use the stage to tell the truth."[118] She performs at the Market Theatre, the famous crucible of progressive South African drama.[119] There events come full circle, when, after having sung a song that begins, "My sister breastfed my baby, while I took care of you," in which Thembi recalls once having cared for a little white boy, a young white man from the audience in military uniform visits her backstage.[120]

If the typical male spectator is supposed to be fixated on the breast as sexual object, and this is supposed to have been what Vegas wanted, in this scene we witness quite a different coding of the breast. Metonymically, the little white boy has received the breast of his childhood caregiver—and what he has received with it has been the language of the breast: "I was your only resting place / You seemed to want no other / Your first word was my name / Your first song was in Zulu."[121] Repeating the earlier scene, the scene backstage, which is now on stage, is of atonement and reparation: "But this young man's eyes had tears in them. I had no words. I held him while he cried."[122] Figuratively speaking, this also repeats the infantile one. Some might complain that the symbolism is overdone and suspect the playwright's heavy hand, but can one nevertheless not say that this is an answer, with several layers, from a position that is at least not male, to the question: Where *are* the girls? The "girl" in domestic service has made for herself a professional acting career, and, acting herself, hears the lament of the mother for her daughter: "Ipi Ntombi yami? Ntombi yami?" Now she appears to give her countersignature to the little white boy's secret history of language, producing a scene that repeats the infantile scene, the scene, before he grows up and the breast becomes a sexual object, in which he learns Zulu as his *first* language. Remembering the conscript, Thembi addresses him, declaring: "you showed me something too that night: the damage that had been done to all of us."[123]

One does not want to claim too much on the basis of this single collaborative play, evidently staged for white audiences,[124] but one also risks claiming too little. Can one therefore not say that, if a reparative phantasy is at work in the piece, then it is one that circulates, moving in more than one direction? And can one not also say, in this instance, that *Ipi Tombi*, by bringing Thembi on stage, affords conditions of possibility for this setting to work? *A Woman in Waiting* certainly suggests that one can, not least by the way in which it represents the care given to the little white boy as an abandoning by the mother of her own child: "My sister breastfed my baby, while I took care of you." The point is made graphically in the preceding scene, "Spilt Milk," when Thembi, importuned by an employer's hungry infant, expresses her breast milk into a toilet before "giving her a bottle of formula milk."[125] If there is an attempt at reparation, it is thus also in relation to Thembi's child, who had to go without her mother's breast. At another level, perhaps in a maternalist version of Nyembezi's prescient "On the Throwing of Stones," reparation is in relation to the "ten thousand kids" of Soweto 1976—the original song from *Ipi Tombi* goes "ten thousand men"[126]—and guilt stemming from an abandoning of one's own child, in the face of danger, for white children who lived in comfort.

There are some who pooh-pooh the symbolism of the breast and consider Melanie Klein to be far-fetched. We have, on the contrary, not gone far enough. Referring to the song "My Sister Breastfed My Baby" in a 2001 interview with the *Guardian*, Thembi Mtshali-Jones "tells of how many black women breastfed the babies of white families without those families knowing."[127] The fact that this is not explicitly put on stage should tell us that there is, in the secret history of language, a less-often-voiced counterpart to the reparation attempted on behalf of the little white boy—whether it be by the young man in uniform backstage, or by the one, no longer so young, who remembers his part in *Ipi Tombi*. In different ways, guilt circulates, for African mother and white son.[128] In *A Woman in Waiting*, that son mediates her reparation toward her daughter. And it appears that he makes reparation toward his secret African mother, from whom he received Zulu as his first language.

We cannot know for certain, however, what the soldier's tears meant to him. He has no direct speech in *A Woman in Waiting*. And that is why, in concluding this chapter, I wish to insist on the specificity of what, for the six- or seven-year-old boy, might have stood in the way of his making reparation toward that mother. Although one could justly say that, because of the multiple meanings that it can bear, *Ipi Tombi*—or better, the question "Iphi intombi yami?"—serves as a common idiom or lingua franca for the two figures, it will have had quite a different meaning for the young boy. For him, the sense of an identification with the girl, which, ironically, arises from his being made up for a role as a Zulu boy, actually threatens his distinctness as a boy. At another level, because lipstick connotes the greeting kisses of female relatives, which he tries to elude, being made up for the role also connotes a coupling, and, ultimately, a scene of violation of the mother, which is more deeply repressed. He is not ready for the reconciliation that Johnny Clegg appeared to have achieved as an adolescent. As a symbolic act, wiping the lipstick from his lips is also his way of doing away with the evidence of that act. He could not have known then that, in another secret history, among Zulu gardeners, known as *abaqulusi*, who typically entered work in adolescence, "[o]ne of the myths circulating . . . alludes to the possibility that madams, white women but even more especially Indian women, feed their male servants their expressed breast milk."[129] Consumption thereof is taboo. I therefore retranslate: "Where is the girl?" A rhetorical question, since the boy is the not-girl. The girl is not there, not anywhere in fact, not for him. And not just because he attends an all-boys school, and because this is an all-boys' production, for there are boys among them who are thought of as girls—a way of thinking that, let us say, without letting all the cats out of the bag, may be found at the highest echelons today.

CHAPTER 4

100% Zulu Boy

By the time that news of Jacob Zuma's trial for rape reached New York in early 2006, I had been thinking of taking up my studies of Zulu again. Although I had made no definite plans, I was attuned to anything about Zulu that happened to come my way. And what did come my way was a report in the *New York Times* that said that Jacob Zuma's supporters, demonstrating outside the Johannesburg High Court,[1] wore t-shirts with the slogan "100% Zulu Boy," and that, when examined, Zuma explained his actions in terms of Zulu culture: "His accuser was aroused, he said, and 'in the Zulu culture, you cannot just leave a woman if she is ready.' To deny her sex, he said, would have been tantamount to rape."[2] In short, to be 100% Zulu boy was to be able to say: She asked for it—I am guilty only of giving her what she asked for.

This put me in a quandary. As a learner of the language, was being 100% Zulu boy not what I was seeking? I do not think that I was "begging to be Black"—as Antjie Krog has it[3]—but rather that I wanted to make the grade—get a teacher's stamp of approval: a gold star, a Good News Note to take home, a heartfelt "Well done!" It is one thing to pass a reasonable test with flying colors, and quite another to cheat history. It did not seem even to be a wish to belong; after all I had never thought of wearing one of the ironic "100% Boer" t-shirts that I saw being sold in Johannesburg the year before, alongside the one I did buy—a pre-distressed "Liberté Afrique du Sud '94" by MaGents, with flaming torch in black hand against a yellow ground. Yet there was—in this striving for 100%, for the perfect identity that is a hundred out of a hundred—a powerful identification with the Zulu boy. And that identification was strong because it was mixed up with phantasies of being good, and thus of doing and making good, which is what being good presupposes. Good marks will always have meant a good Mark. I have, in that sense, always been the Jarvis boy reincarnate.

But there was more to it. Had my reluctance to being made up for my little stage part in *Ipi Tombi* not stemmed from a standing up for my boyhood? Lipstick and mascara would have made me into a girl, and at a boys' school one does not want to be a girl. The identification was not going to be dislodged just so. Insofar as I was a boy, I was a Zulu boy, even if my assegai was of cardboard painted brown, with a tinfoil tip—much as if it had come from the props cupboard for a passion play, or, say, *A Funny Thing Happened on the Way to the Forum*, in either of which it might have been a spear held by a Roman soldier. You can see that for me "Zulu boy" was anything but the menial in "A Zulu boy will understand." There was no Fanagalo in Sea Point, and also no Zulus, as far as I knew: Dlamini, whose name I remember A. calling, was just the man on the bicycle who delivered the *Argus*. I had no idea who was on Robben Island just across the water, with my father only confusing me when he tried to explain by singing "The Seagull's Name Was Nelson" as we strolled on the promenade. Maybe it was just another version of "the stork brought you," the *bobbemeise* that he said I never believed, but which "good" children are supposed to accept, even as their own theories of origin are not well founded.[4]

As a Zulu boy, then, I was good, and I was virile—or as virile as a seven-year-old could imagine himself to be. Maybe the right word is puerile—if one can use this term to mean good boy as one can use virile to mean good man. And that is perhaps why what I read in the *New York Times* came as a shock—no, not as much a shock as a confrontation: the mother had been violated, the most deeply repressed phantasy of the boy in his latency thrust before him. To be the boy is to do violence to the girl, who one does not want to be, and to violate the mother, whom one does not want the father to have. There, in the *Times*, were Jacob Zuma's words, and then there was the journalist's construction upon them: "To deny her sex, he said, would have been tantamount to rape." This is not quite what Zuma said, but I did not know that at the time. Their effect was to introduce an alternative that offered no way out of the phantasy: Either he raped her (as accused), or, by not having sex with her, he will have raped her (as he is said to have said). It was disturbing, and it prompted the thought: I want nothing to do with that. The making-good in learning a language—in learning Zulu—was supposed to repair this violence—and you can see this at work in Paton, as the Jarvis boy goes to the Reverend Kumalo's house for his lesson. But even there, back in Ndotsheni, his every word is shadowed by a paranoia and a jealous primal scene that are not his own but rather his birthright, and by a destructiveness of the narrative discourse toward the Zulu language that is a response to the persecutory paranoia. One wants to go on, but one finds oneself drawn into an attack on the Zulu, and on the Zulu boy, which easily amounts to an attack on Zulu. This is only as the *New York Times* instructs: "Mr. Zuma ... effectively argu[ed] that he is being persecuted for his cultural beliefs."[5] Pure projection, pure paranoid projection. This complicity is why the news comes as a shock: it means having to find a way of continuing to make good through a learning of language—this I have not given up—while relinquishing the puerile identification (so painfully overdetermined) with the *name* of the language; a type of fetish, in that it was what stood between me and being a girl—which is, let me come right out and say it, also to be an object for boys, and thus to have boys as one's object. A few months after his acquittal, Zuma himself would unwittingly confirm the extent to which homosexual object-choice was at stake. To continue the endeavor to make good would be to summon the courage to bring the *words* of the language themselves into one's mouth—perhaps as with the ludic speech of Ahmadou Kourouma's Birahima—and so to master the phallic meaning of the *name* of the language, in other words the threat of castration that led to the name being made into a fetish. Something of this was at work late the following year, when I wrote my first composition for Eckson, punning on *ulimi* (tongue, language), *ukuluma* (to bite), and *ukukhuluma* (to speak), circling about the phantasy sentence: to speak a language is to bite one's tongue. No accident, then, that I would a few weeks later, my throat still painful from surgery to remove half my thyroid—my friend Lisa would refer to it as having my throat cut—compose for Eckson an oral presentation on Kourouma's *Allah Is Not Obliged* and child soldiers (*izingane ezingamasosha*).[6] Ahmadou Khuluma? It was only by bringing the words of the language into my mouth, and thereby overcoming intellectual inhibition, that I would have any chance of making sense of the Zuma trial in ways other than the 100%, the for or against, and the phantasmatic alignment—this not only by the metropolitan press—of Zulu with virile masculinity at the cost of the elision of the girl, and the woman. In accepting these positions—and simply *opposing* them amounts to much the same thing—the reporting fell straight into the trap set by Zuma's supporters with their t-shirts, their oversized phallic wooden toy guns, and their "Umshini wami." It was convenient—at the level of phantasy—to mistake extreme partisanship for cultural truth, when, if one looked at the gestures closely, the more hyperbolic among them as equivocal and as ambivalent as the best *izibongo*, one could see the rifts often exposed by symbolic overcompensation.

Judging Jacob Zuma

Until June 2005, Jacob Zuma (b. 1942) was deputy president of South Africa. After being implicated in corruption by the verdict delivered in the trial of his financial adviser, Schabir Shaik, who was sent to prison for soliciting bribes relating to the South African government's purchase in 1999 of $4.8 billion worth of arms, among them a bribe to be paid to Zuma by a French arms company to ensure that investigation into its role would stop, Zuma was dismissed by President Thabo Mbeki. Although it had decided in 2003 not to prosecute him with Schabir Shaik, after the Shaik verdict, the state moved forward with a corruption and racketeering case against Zuma. This deepened Zuma's rift with Mbeki, with whom he had worked closely while in exile, as well as during the negotiations to end white minority rule. Zuma had been the ANC's chief of intelligence, and is widely credited with a decisive role in brokering an end to the civil war between the ANC and the Inkatha Freedom Party that claimed thousands of lives between 1990 and 1994. Accusing Mbeki of leading a relentless conspiracy to prevent him from becoming president of the country, including an abuse of power through selective prosecution, Zuma gained the support of the Congress of South African Trade Unions (COSATU), the South African Communist Party (SACP), and the ANC Youth League against the increasingly unpopular Mbeki, and was able to retain his position as deputy president of the ANC. When, in November 2005, still facing trial for corruption, Zuma was indicted for rape, he and his followers portrayed it as further evidence of a political plot against him supported by a biased mass media. This stance hardly settled doubts, for, as Aubrey Matshiqi astutely observes, "[w]e must bear in mind that the idea of a conspiracy against Zuma and the possibility that such a conspiracy does not exist, and the issue of his guilt or innocence, are not mutually exclusive. . . . Because conspiracies succeed by exploiting the weaknesses of opponents, we must be open to the possibility that the Zuma saga is a story of two seemingly contradictory truths: his guilt and the existence of a plot against him."[7]

According to the indictment, Zuma had on November 2, 2005, raped a family friend who had come to his house in Johannesburg to discuss something with him, and had then decided to stay there for the night. The woman in question, who was thirty-one years old at the time, was the daughter of a senior member of the ANC who had been one of Zuma's fellow prisoners on Robben Island, where Zuma served the full term of a ten-year sentence from 1963–73. Her father had been killed in a road accident in Zimbabwe in 1985, leaving her and her mother dependent on the support of extended family as well as the organization. The overtones of the story were ugly, not only because of the age difference and the fact that Zuma was a married man, and because the complainant was HIV-positive and identified as a lesbian, but also because they seemed to fit with what exiles knew about the predatory behavior of older men, who were labeled, in a bitter play on words, *omalume abalumayo* (uncles that bite). This play on *ukuluma* is insistent. And, indeed, in her testimony, the complainant would refer to Zuma as Malume. In the months before November 2005, she received help from Zuma to raise money from others to pay for her studies in England,[8] and she had sent Zuma numerous text messages, which Zuma said he interpreted as a romantic interest because of their affectionate salutations and valedictions. According to her, Zuma came into the guest bedroom where she was sleeping and offered to give her a massage. She refused, but he insisted, and then he raped her. Confronted by actions such as these on the part of a "father figure," she had frozen, she told the court, and had not physically resisted or protested verbally. Two days after the incident she laid a charge of rape. In a meeting arranged by Zweli Mkhize, an ANC National Executive Committee member and then KwaZulu-Natal Minister of Finance, Zuma met with her mother and apologized, albeit without saying what for. Although not demanding a forfeit (*inhlawulo*), the mother hinted at a contribution to her daughter's school fees.[9] Prior to this meeting, Zuma's intermediaries had even mentioned *ilobolo*.[10] During this time, the complainant denied publicly that she had laid a charge against Zuma. Evidently the negotiations with the family—culminating with a visit from the lawyer Yusuf Dockrat, who suggested she drop the charges—failed, and Zuma was indicted. When he appeared in the witness box in April 2006, Zuma testified that he and the complainant had had consensual sex, and that, having worn a *kanga* (cotton wrap), which he found suggestive, she had come to his bedroom, asked him for a massage, and raised no objection when that massage became more intimate. All of this Zuma described in graphic detail. As in many rape trials in which there are no additional eyewitnesses and in which the physical evidence is inconclusive, the case came down to his word against hers. Zuma's defense counsel, led by Kemp J. Kemp, persuaded Judge Willem van der Merwe to allow the complainant to be cross-examined with regard to her sexual history—the door to which had already been opened by the prosecution—asserting that she had made baseless rape allegations against men in the past, and that this was relevant as to her credibility.[11] Several men then testified in court to having been falsely accused by her of rape. When two others testified to having been her boyfriends, she denied ever having known them, which limited the prosecution in its cross-examination[12] and raised further questions about her credibility. The testimony of the prosecution's main expert witness, a psychologist, was successfully impeached by the skillful direct examination by Kemp of another psychologist, testifying for the defense. Zuma's counsel also convinced the judge to throw out the testimony of a police commissioner who said that Zuma had told him that he and the complainant had had sex in the guest bedroom, not in his own bedroom, but had not noted this in his report or properly read Zuma his rights. The question asked by the Commissioner was, furthermore, phrased in such a way—Was this the room in which the crime took place?—as to trap the accused, and was unconstitutional in that it relied on information in statements made by the complainant and contradicted Zuma's prior sworn "warning statement."[13] Although the prosecution, led by Charin de Beer, doggedly cross-examined Zuma, managing to trip him up on some details of his account, and embarrassing him about showering after sex in order to prevent HIV infection—which lived on in Zapiro's cartoon caricatures—it could not dislodge his representation of the sex as having been consensual. The prosecution also failed to object to hearsay testimony from various witnesses, and to speculation about the complainant's state of mind introduced into evidence through the biased testimony of Duduzile Zuma, the defendant's daughter, who opined that, judging from the way she was dressed on the night in question, the complainant was out to seduce her father in order to get money from him. It may well have helped the prosecution to have more aggressively questioned Zuma's claims about Zulu culture—to have had an African prosecutorial team, as Raymond Suttner suggests[14]—but as

Mmatshilo Motsei, who advocates a greater role for "indigenous justice," correctly observes, "the outcome of the trial . . . was largely influenced by technical evidence provided by Western-trained experts—legal and medical practitioners, scientists, technicians and psychologists."[15] Within that framework, it was not surprising that Judge van der Merwe, having heard a sometimes flat-footed case for the prosecution that was successfully weakened by a more able defense counsel, would decide in favor of the defendant. It was nevertheless noted by Lisa Vetten and others that Van der Merwe's judgment contained conservative circumstantial criteria for deciding on whether a woman has been raped;[16] that, among other things, led campaigners against sexual violence, who had aligned themselves with the complainant to whom they gave the name Khwezi (Morning Star, or Venus), to criticize the verdict. The fact that Zuma joined his supporters to sing "Umshini wami" only aggravated perceptions that the trial and acquittal had set back years of feminist law reform and campaigns to encourage women to report rape, in a country where sexual violence against women and girls is endemic but, as several studies agree, is significantly under-reported.[17]

Obiter Dicta

It appears that I was not the only one learning Zulu. About to deliver judgment in the case, Judge Willem van der Merwe opened his address in Zulu.[18] Accounts differ as to the fluency of his Zulu; whereas the *Star* called it "fluent,"[19] Mmatshilo Motsei writes of his "attempts to address [Zuma] in Zulu."[20] The reporters also differ in their transcription of his words, depriving us of a firm basis for deciding, although in each of the versions it is perfectly clear what Van der Merwe is saying. But all appear to agree that to hear the judge speak in Zulu was a surprise: "Van der Merwe, it turned out," writes Jeremy Gordin, "spoke a credible Zulu, though he hid this until the last day of the trial."[21] Motsei justly commends Van der Merwe for his attempts, as she does the fact that Zuma "testified in his native Zulu"[22]—which he did throughout his evidence. But what is more significant is that Van der Merwe's Zulu was undisclosed until the end. Could it be understood as a secret identification—part of a secret history of making-good through speaking Zulu? When one is not fluent in a language, and one does not *need to* speak it, it is clearer that one's code-switching into that language could be symbolic, a performance of something. One commentator alleges a "meeting of minds" that will have biased him in favor of Zuma,[23] and another a misplaced sympathy for "African culture."[24] It may be that his Zulu was a way of demonstrating that solidarity and sympathy; for his very words, having thanked the court interpreter for his work, which he adds was difficult, were to the effect that the defendant would not need to be addressed in Zulu: "UMnuz Zuma usizwa kahle isiNgisi, kasikho isidingo sokutolika isahlulelo." (Mr. Zuma understands English well, there is no need to interpret the verdict.)[25]

But I do not think that things are quite as simple as solidarity or sympathy. Having once played the Zulu boy myself, the brown poster paint coming off the spear in my sweaty hand, I am tempted to see Van der Merwe's Zulu as masquerade (even if the more obvious masquerade in retrospect is that he appeared to the gallery not to know Zulu, a perfect judicial *eironeia*). Like Zuma's exercising of his right to testify in his mother tongue, when questions were posed in English by the prosecutors as well as his lawyers, it was in excess of utility, greatly burdening the interpreter, Mr. Charles Moloi, who struggled to translate some of the things that Zuma said. I would be the first to admit that there can be a phallic identification with the name of the language—I am 100% Zulu Boy—when one makes a point of switching into it, or of speaking it in a context where one is making a point by speaking it, and that the judge can himself be heard to perform the identification by speaking Zulu. Yet I would also observe that, in relieving Mr. Moloi of his duties, it is as if the judge is saying: The show is over now, all along I have been aware that your performance has been exactly that: a performance. Let us drop our masks, and move on. I may, he seems to be saying, be susceptible to the identification—to wanting to be 100% Zulu boy— but I am well aware that no such thing exists, except insofar as it is a part one plays. So, now that I have shown you, by playing such a part myself, that, in order for *you* to be 100% Zulu boy, *you* also have to perform, although your rendition is, admittedly, more convincing than mine, I shall, as you must too, *aus der Rolle fallen*, and deliver my verdict. I cannot deny that it will bear the trace, somewhere, of that identification that I have now given up and am asking you to give up, since we have, although I have concealed it well, been in a sort of secret complicity all along. It lies with others to locate that trace, and to measure its effects.

If the case was cut-and-dried from a legal perspective and if, for the 100-percenters (on both sides), the verdict represented an exoneration of a certain phallic Zulu culture or "Zulu culture," as Van der Merwe's Zulu performance might have led us to expect by what it seemed to reveal about Jacob Zuma's performance, the trial also revealed, for the one learning Zulu, a number of distinct faultlines within the name *Zulu*. These faultlines are apparent in what was said after the trial by the complainant, and at the trial about attempts to avoid a trial.

In an interview following Jacob Zuma's acquittal, Khwezi was asked by members of the One in Nine Campaign, a coalition of organizations fighting for women's sexual rights formed in February 2006 in solidarity with her and who gave her her evocative pseudonym,[26] what she thought and felt, looking back on the trial, about whether she should or should not have laid a charge. Her answer was unequivocal:

> Yes. Rape is a crime, full stop. On a personal level, I would never have been able to live with myself if I had walked away without doing so. Rapists need to be brought

to justice. Of course this particular rape case was more complicated, malicious and cruel, but still, this was the only thing I could do. . . . It was really hard to keep going once I decided to lay the charge. But, firstly, I know what happened; secondly, I got to tell my story about this rape. I simply had to tell the truth, although this was really not under the right conditions.[27]

Her unequivocal position—it was rape, and rapists should be brought to justice—relates in a complex way, I think, to what she says about being a lesbian. "The fact," she says, "[is] that I am disgusted by semen and a penis."[28] Referring to a counselor with whom she spoke after laying the charge, she adds, "I didn't see her as able to deal with my sexuality as a lesbian. And what the rape meant in that context."[29] Later in the interview, when discussion turns to how her sexual history was introduced at trial—to which she objects because she does not see having been abused as a child as having anything to do with sexual history—she reminds her interviewers that the defense successfully cast doubt on the fact that she was a lesbian:

> Ja, [Judge van der Merwe in his judgment] questions my identity as a lesbian saying how can I call myself a lesbian when I had had sex with men. He reaches the conclusion that I am not a lesbian! He did this without asking me for the details about my identity as a lesbian. Well that is the nature of identity and this judge didn't get that. He doesn't begin to understand the complexity of sexuality. You live in this heterosexual society. You don't see the options because that's how society works. Then you are raped. And you think well if I am a lesbian, people are going to say I am a lesbian because I was raped and yes, I don't want them to think that. So I have to show that this is not so. Anyway what was the relevance of my sexual identity in this judgment? This was not properly explained as far as I am concerned. Was it a matter of my credibility? I am saying something that is not true? [From what we know at the moment, could there be anything that supports the truth [*ubuqiniso*] that I am a lesbian?][30]

She is steering a contorted course. On the one hand, she seems to say that, because she is a lesbian and has an aversion to semen and the penis, she would not have had sex with a man. Yet she concedes that she has on occasion had sex with men; one can be a lesbian and also have sex with men. On the other hand, because of heterosexual norms in the community, people say that if you are raped you were raped because you are a lesbian, implying that if you were not a lesbian you would have consented to sex with a man. When Khwezi's interview is translated into Zulu for publication in *UmAfrika*, this how her words are construed: "If you are raped people take it that you were raped because you are a lesbian."[31] But there is some ambiguity; she could also be saying that people say that if one is a lesbian it is because of a *past* experience of being raped that would be seen as the source of one's sexual aversion to men. These are both constructions that she wishes to avoid. The fact that she is a lesbian, and was raped, does not mean that other women who are raped become lesbians through being raped—or if we take *UmAfrika*'s translation—are lesbians by virtue of not consenting. She is thus insisting on two different things, which are interrelated because of the way in which the community views sexual orientation. The first is that there is such a thing as being lesbian, which means that one is a lover of women, but which does not mean that one never has sex with men. Whether or not to have sex with a man would be up to her; it would come down to consent, which is the second thing on which she insists: the right of *any* woman to withhold consent. The nexus of being lesbian and being raped is broken doubly: not giving consent (being raped) does not *make* one a lesbian or *make* one *into* a lesbian. Breaking the nexus of being lesbian and being raped generalizes consent. Being lesbian may thus be generalized to all women, whether they have sex with women or not, because, when it is rape, it is a matter not of object-choice but of consent. That is what the judge, who decides that "she is bisexual and that she regards her orientation as being lesbian,"[32] confining sexual orientation to object-choice, cannot seem to understand. Those who have read Foucault can see what is going on: being a point at which sex becomes a subject's truth,[33] object-choice can be used as a verifiable fact in order to test whether a subject is telling the truth. This Khwezi seems to realize, at least in retrospect; arguments for and against questioning her about her sexual history were heard by the judge *in camera*, with her absent from the courtroom.[34] But, for her, being bisexual could imply (to others) that one has sex with just anybody: "And then there is his pronouncements about my identity. Who I am? It is so strange to be sitting there like an onlooker, to hear someone telling you who you are. And here is this man telling me I am mad,[35] unable to even know what is consensual and not; promiscuous, bisexual and not lesbian."[36] The bisexual does not discriminate; there is surely a moral element to this, but, viewed within a matrix of possibilities, the bisexual, so runs a certain stereotype, is the one who does not say no, which is to say, constitutionally, cannot say no. And this effectively cancels the very question of consent. That is why, when she takes a stand for consent, she does so not as bisexual but as lesbian. And that stand effectively jams the operations of the heterosexual norm—not by declaring exclusively female object-choice (lesbians never have sex with men), but by asserting "lesbian" as the limit, not to be transgressed, of female sexual prerogative.

To the extent that such a stand could be, and is, made in different social formations—she is no more specific than "society"—it could appear not to apply to Zulus specifically, or to claims made about Zulu culture. But that would not be entirely accurate. Her remarks emphasize that her stand would not have been possible for women of her mother's generation: "We have opportunities today that our mothers didn't have. In our mothers' time, they could not just tell about rape. In a case like this, they would have just been quiet. They wouldn't have told. It was just not an option. Who would they have told and what would have been the response?"[37] In the context of the case, these remarks about the present generation of women having opportunities and "rights"—as *UmAfrika* translates—that their mothers did not have, or were unable to exercise, is also a *break* with the codes of their mothers' generation.

These codes continue to operate. And some of them are, or are said to be, specifically Zulu, or at least specifically African. Khwezi's own mother was asked, under cross-examination, whether, prior to Zuma's indictment, she and Zuma had discussed the matter of a fine or forfeit (*inhlawulo*). Like Jacob Zuma, but in contrast to her daughter, she gives evidence in Zulu through the interpreter. Because it registers what was said in Zulu, I quote first from Fraser Mtshali's report—based, he informs me, on what he took down in his notebook—instead of from the record of the court, which preserves only the English rendering of the interpreter. Although she maintains that "I did not say that I wanted *inhlawulo*. What I did say was that my child needed to go back to school because it is her right to study," Kemp's assistant, Advocate Brauns, goes on to ask her: "What is *inhlawulo*?"

Here is her reply:

> Well, that is a difficult question. I think it may be said that for a woman to be taken without her consent [*ukubanjwa ngenkani*] is a misfortune [*ibhadi*]. According to the ways of black African people misfortune must be expiated [*Ngesintu ishwa liyagezwa*]. Just as with a person if he has recently been in jail, on his return he is usually purified with protective medicines [*uye agezwe ngezintelezi*]. According to black African ways [*ngokwesintu*] the matter of *inhlawulo* is discussed if a man enters the head of household's cattle enclosure or sleeps with a woman [*engene esibayeni somnumzane noma elale nowesifazane*].[38]

According to the mother's testimony, *inhlawulo* can be discussed in cases where a woman has not consented to sex, as well as in cases where consent is not at issue, or not the main issue. Such cases might once have been tried as "seduction" under the 1891 Natal Code and other systems of "customary law." Referring in his classic study of women and customary law to a 1936 case tried in the Native Appeal Court of the Cape of Good Hope and the Free State Provinces, H. J. Simons draws parallels between the legal regime in force in the Cape and Free State and the provisions of the Natal Code:

> Scott, P. remarked in the case of *Mkupeni v. Nomungunya & others* that, though the custom of *thwala* was largely practiced, the court would not "countenance its use as a cloak for forcing unwelcome attentions on a patently unwilling girl." The defendant in this case, aided by two other men, had abducted and raped a girl who rejected his advances. The court awarded her damages of £25 for forcible abduction and seduction. Abduction is an offence under the Natal Code and constitutes a common law crime if the girl is under 21 years and is taken away without her guardian's consent for the purpose of marriage and carnal intercourse. *Thwala* followed by sexual intercourse without the girl's consent can give rise to

a charge of assault and rape. Parents, however, seldom invoke the criminal law. They often acquiesce, sometimes before the abduction, and usually prefer to settle the matter by claiming damages or arranging a marriage.[39]

As Elizabeth Thornberry tells us, magistrates in colonial Transkei would sometimes try cases of non-consensual sex as civil matters of seduction and adultery in order to weigh the forfeitures expected by Xhosa plaintiffs, whereas they would have to try rape as a criminal matter not subject to the award of damages. A compromise took place, in other words, between two systems of punishment, in which the expected punishment determined the name of the crime.[40] This judicial practice evolved into a system wherein black South African women would through the twentieth century have little recourse to the criminal courts in the case of rape by black men.[41] This juridico-legal history is an important context for understanding the implications of Khwezi's mother's testimony.

I am not the first to observe that the mother's sexual lexicon, in its impeccable propriety, reflects a patriarchal figuring of the sexual act. As Mark Hunter tells us, to speak of the vagina as the "head of household's cattle enclosure"—or "her father's cattle enclosure," which is the name Hunter discusses—is to tie sex with an unmarried woman to the prosperity of her father, whose property will be increased when bridewealth (*ilobolo*) is paid, in the form of cattle or money equivalent, when his daughter marries. To the extent that sex by a man with another man's unmarried daughter jeopardizes that payment by jeopardizing her chances of marriage, the man has entered the enclosure to rob the father of his cattle.[42] The complainant's mother, interrupting the court interpreter, specifies: "I also know that if you have impregnated some girl or . . . (witness interrupts: deflowered her) . . . had intercourse with somebody's wife you have to pay some sort of compensation."[43] In the case of an unmarried woman, the father—or surviving parent—is entitled to compensation in the form of *inhlawulo*. These sexual metaphorics work in southern African social formations in which wealth, materially and symbolically, has taken the form of cattle.[44]

As Fraser Mtshali, without whose extensive reporting on the trial for *UmAfrika* we would be almost entirely in the dark about certain facets of the testimony, avidly notes, the mother's lexicon is highly idiomatic Zulu; the court interpreter, Mr. Moloi, has trouble translating the ideophone *damu*, appears not to know what *izintelezi* are, and, as Mtshali relates, "[a]t the time that there was talk about the head of household's cattle enclosure, Mr. Moloi was completely silent and was no longer doing his job that he was hired to do, namely to interpret. [The witness having just assisted Mr. Moloi], I too ended up wishing to help him."[45] Mtshali's repeated references to the interpreter being unequal to the task of Zulu idiom, which bespeak an investment by him in the being-idiomatic of what is testified to, show us that, in the negotiations by Zuma and his intermediaries with the complainant's mother, what was at stake was not simply whether a settlement could be reached, but whether it could be reached *ngo-kwesintu*. The mother having testified that she did not raise the matter of *inhlawulo* with Zuma, although she dropped the hint about school fees, Brauns asks her: "Did you speak in that direction with Dr. Mkhize?" She replies: "Indeed [although] another person might see it differently." (*Phela omunye umuntu angabona ngokwehlukile.*) It is not entirely clear here whether she is saying that there might be different views as to what is *inhlawulo*, or whether she is saying that Mkhize might not agree that their discussions went in this direction.[46] Be that as it may, an unnamed "reliable source" quoted by Fraser Mtshali says that the judge held a meeting in chambers with counsel in order to explore the question of whether the negotiations about payment involving Mkhize and the complainant's mother were part of an effort to get the rape charge dropped. "[A]t that meeting there was an expert explanation concerning the black African practice that is the custom with the Zulu people [*inqubo yesintu ewusiko esizweni samaZulu*], the custom that is forfeiting [*ukuhlawula*] and perhaps ritual purification [*ukugezwa*] at a man's household if it is found that there is a sexual act."[47] "It is said," Mtshali adds, "that the prosecutor having now accepted this expert explanation, there was a failure for 'firecracker' witnesses [*izi"klwibhisi" zofakazi*] to be called." Having been expected to call further witnesses, who might have brought some fireworks to the proceedings, De Beer rests her case; or, as Mtshali puts it, "says 'Maluju,'" as is done when you concede in a stick fight. The prosecutor appears to have followed the red herring of whether payment *is* or *is not* a custom, when the real issues are *which* custom was in play, and whether or not there is a contestation of that custom, or a decision *not* to follow it. Perhaps the central issue is whether there had been an admission of wrongdoing, as *inhlawulo* would normally imply. In analyzing the moves of the prosecution, we might again appeal to Foucault: if the truth of culture is produced by the expert, say the ethnographer, just as it will have been produced by "customary law," then propositions about culture, like those about sex, become subject to procedures of verification. But, as with Khwezi's sexual orientation, those propositions are not what are most relevant when the entire set of cultural propositions in question has been set aside by the complainant, who insists on pursuing the criminal charge. Mtshali, who mocks the mother by reporting that when, apparently overwhelmed by Brauns's cross-examination, she requested a bathroom break, he overheard one of her companions say "hhayi, usayokhipha i-stress semibuzo" (hhayi, she is busy going to relieve herself of the stress of the questions),[48] is as blind to this as the prosecution appears to have been; for him, it is enough that, yes, what the mother spoke about was *echt*.

The opportunity for a different line of questioning that would insist on *inhlawulo* as a sign of a wrong having been committed is also missed. In her cross-examination of Zuma, De Beer broaches the question of compensation without pursuing it, and rapidly moves on to ask Zuma about how his intermediaries attempted to resolve the situation through payment of *ilobolo*.[49] Here is the summary by Mtshali: "Mr. Zuma wrapped up his testimony with the efforts that he made to negotiate [*ukuxhumana*] with the accuser; he asked her why she laid a charge of rape against him, being that they had consensual sex. Umsholozi said that he wanted to negotiate with the accuser's mother with the intention of explaining to her too that it was not an instance [*isimo*] of rape there, and that the situation [*isimo*] that happened could be made right by means of Zulu custom [*ngosiko lwesiZulu*]. In the efforts to resolve this matter, they [the intermediaries] at first even suggested that Umsholozi pay *ilobolo* for the accuser, which was a scenario [*isimo*] with which he had no problem."[50] In contrast to *inhlawulo*, the full significance of which is only explored by *UmAfrika*,[51] and the specificity of which De Beer appears not to have grasped when she cross-examined Zuma, the matter of *ilobolo* is more widely reported.[52] In Kemp's closing arguments, it goes to Zuma's *mens rea*: "The court will ... remember the time that he was speaking about the matter of *ilobolo*. That means that the matter of matrimony was then on his mind."[53] Kemp is not specific about which words of Zuma's he is referring to, but presumably it is to what Khwezi testified to in her direct examination—namely that he had asked her whether she had had *ilobolo* paid for her, which she testified having understood as something that, in days of exile, an *umalume* such as Jacob Zuma might have inquired about in loco parentis, and might have negotiated *ilobolo* on her behalf when she married.[54] By all reports, the prosecution—and for obvious reasons, the defense—appears to have stuck to *ilobolo*, seeming to bypass the possibility that for the complainant's mother and Zuma's representative to have discussed *inhlawulo* may have entailed, or at least implied, that Zuma had raped her; as the mother says, *inhlawulo* is contemplated when "a woman is taken without her consent."[55]

If, during the negotiations after the charge was laid, but before Zuma was indicted, talk turned to *inhlawulo* or *ilobolo* to be paid by Zuma, then it is clear that this was not accepted as a resolution by the complainant. As she testifies, "when [Zweli Mkhize] was talking to me I said I do not have anything to do with the compensation, that is something that he should talk to with my mother [sic] because the discussion they were talking about it was for her and not for me and that I was just carrying on with the route that I had taken of laying the charge."[56] The path of Zulu culture was not taken because, I state the obvious, a Zulu decided not to take it, and not because a court rejected it. There was a time when the case might, in certain jurisdictions, have been heard and settled under "customary law"—but, for most people, those days are gone. The closed circle of the cattle economy, in which cattle can be exchanged for cattle, is broken—as its metaphorics will always have been in the sex talk of the accused, who is reported to have used the term *isibaya sendoda* (the man's enclosure) as a synonym for *isibaya somnumzane* (the head of household's cattle enclosure; or, to translate with less sentimentality, the Mister's enclosure). The son will, for a long time, have usurped the place of the father. Once he has broken the circle, it cannot be remade. Cattle can no longer be exchanged for cattle, since what was entered was the enclosure not of the cattle but of the penis. That the father, or his survivors, can make claims on his daughter's sexual partners is a patriarchal fiction. When this ennobling fiction, like the old Shakespearean resolution in which the father comes in at the end to preside over his daughter's nuptuals, falls away because of what men do, or is cast aside by women who have had enough, what remains looks decidedly shabby—or simply out of date, since, in general, as Mark Hunter has shown, in a time when so many men are simply too poor to pay *ilobolo* or *inhlawulo*, men and women have been able to find other ways, and women have found ways without men.[57] Yet for people of means, among whom are men able to afford to maintain a household with more than one wife, a crisis occurs when the pretense at a governing patriarchy is dropped, and "Zulu" becomes one name among others, no better and no worse.

Even if the crisis of "Zulu" can be generalized, the faultline emerging in this trial has a definite contour. The codes of *ilobolo* and *inhlawulo* reduce everything to a set of heterosexual assumptions, functioning within a patriarchy, but more importantly—like the idea that if one is raped one must be a lesbian—they tend in practice to leave aside, or negotiate away, the matter of consent. I say "tend to" because clearly, for Zulus, and especially for people whose political education was in the ANC—remember that Khwezi was in 1987 able to have her allegations against two men heard by a panel of ANC women in Zimbabwe[58]—rape is considered a serious crime, even if in this case an attempt appears to have been made to plead down to a less serious offense. One could speculate that, in the discussions about *inhlawulo*, the sticking point might have been that Zuma was not prepared to admit that the sex was non-consensual. And it is in order to bring the question of consent back in that Khwezi and others break as activists with the heterosexual paradigm by declaring themselves to be lesbians—and thereby generalizing non-consent to all women. The systematic tendency to set aside, or negotiate away, the matter of consent is surely also what prompts an unequivocal stand to be taken: "Rapists need to be brought to justice."[59] Even here, however, the stand is not quite unequivocal, since "to bring to justice" can mean both to bring somebody before a court of law, and for that court to mete out punishment should that person be found guilty. The attendant ambiguity is retained and displaced when *UmAfrika* translates it as *ukubopha*, which, literally meaning to tie or bind, can in Zulu mean both "to arrest" and "to imprison." Historically, plaintiffs would sometimes have men accused of rape arrested in order to pressure them to pay compensation, without the intention of going through with a criminal trial.[60] It may be that a history of somewhat effective use of the police to effect arrest and / or arbitrary imprisonment in order to intimidate men accused of rape (and surely also of other offences) is being transposed into expectations for what will be achieved through the criminal courts, which, under apartheid, were not typically where rape cases involving black complainants and accused were heard. In other words, two narratives of *ukubopha* collide—the first being that of pressure, with the aid of the police, for a settlement of *inhlawulo* (between Khwezi's mother and Zuma), the second being Khwezi's insistence, following unsuccessful negotiations, on a criminal trial so that Zuma would be imprisoned—or perhaps just found guilty of rape, as the draft of a memoir she was writing says she was content with in the case of one of the men brought before the ANC commission in Zimbabwe.[61] The long shadow of the first narrative could go to explain why the complainant might have been confident that not only the police, but also the criminal court, would work in her favor. This explanation could apply even if Khwezi was not looking for money—as Kemp tried to imply—but simply wanted Zuma to admit to having raped her (which his lawyers would probably have advised him against doing, given that a formal criminal charge had been laid). And Zuma himself is heard to explain to De Beer under cross-examination that "[i]f a certain agreement is reached [between the families], that would mean the end of the matter and decisions will then be taken as to do what next [*sic*]. But if the matter is already in the hands of the police discussions are held to see how the police can be approached in this connection."[62]

We know that not all of those guilty of a given crime are, or even should be, charged with that crime and punished in accordance with the law. The unequivocal stand by Khwezi that "[r]apists need to be brought to justice" is, however, a response to a crisis of impunity: if not all are punished, then nobody ought to be. The same logic was applied to criticize the state's corruption case against Zuma as selective prosecution. This brings about the response: one day a stand has to be taken in order to remind everybody what the law is. In the absence of effective reminders by the courts, all that remains is the kind of advocacy in which Khwezi and her supporters are engaged.

But if the name "lesbian" and an unequivocal stance on the prosecution and / or punishment of rapists sought to insist on consent within the context of cultural codes that operate in ways that, in practice, have sometimes tended to set consent aside—making for a juridico-legal subtext that was not readily apparent except to the well informed—the trial also produced a highly visible faultline within "Zulu" as it relates to its others, or presents itself as relating to its others. This was apparent in the testimony of Jacob Zuma himself—in the part of that testimony that, one cloudy spring morning in New York City, shocked—or confronted—me because of my old, and unexamined, identification with the name "Zulu."

I re-open the *New York Times*: "His accuser was aroused, he said, and 'in the Zulu culture, you cannot just leave a woman if she is ready.' To deny her sex, he said, would have been tantamount to rape."[63] I look at the *Star*: "Zuma said he was also aware that 'in Zulu culture, you don't just leave a woman ... she will have you arrested and say you are a rapist.'"[64] This is already different from the *Times*: to say that an action or inaction is tantamount to rape—repeated uncritically by Vetten[65]—is very different from saying that one might be accused of rape as a result of one's actions or inactions. Zuma's narrative is of somebody who fears retaliation; the accuser in this imaginary scenario, who would be a *false* accuser, is far from declaring that leaving her in an aroused state *is* rape and that "Zulu culture" would support such an accusation. And so is Zuma, I believe. It is far from being a "cultural defense"; Van der Merwe only cites her words as recalled by Zuma, not Zuma's construal of them.[66]

If he was not making claims about Zulu culture, with a view to making them part of his defense, why then should Zuma have embarked on cultural explanation at all at this crucial moment in his testimony? What status does it have in his narrative? One comes up with two, interrelated, answers. One, he is explaining for a non-Zulu court—he is being examined by Kemp and will be cross-examined by De Beer—how things are with Zulus. This would make what he said another episode in the more or less constant extraversion that, for more than 150 years, is the history of the name "Zulu." It could, as Steven Robins writes, thus be a part of a politically motivated performance.[67] Van der Merwe, with a performance of his own, appears to have realized this. Two, Jacob Zuma is revealing that as a Zulu, *he* will have had to *learn* Zulu (*isiZulu*) just as would any non-Zulu. How can I say this? Because this is what Zuma says. You glance back up at what I have quoted from the *Times* and from the *Star*—Where from? Let us open a different newspaper:

> Ngingabazile ngoba ngicabange ukuthi ngabe ingakanani ingozi kulokhu okwase kuzokwenzeka, kodwa kulowo mzuzu ummangali ukhulume wathi umuntu wesifazane akayekwa uma esekuleso simo. Nami ngisheshe ngakhumbula ukuthi ekukhuleni kwethu bengazi kamhlophe ukuthi ngokwesiZulu akayekwa umuntu wesifazane uma esesesimweni esithile, angakubopha ngisho ukukubopha athi umdlwengulile.
>
> (I hesitated because I thought that there might be some danger with what was going to happen [because the complainant was HIV-positive and a condom was not available], but at that moment the complainant spoke and said that a woman cannot be left when she is in that state. I also quickly remembered that in our growing up I knew very well that according to *isiZulu* a woman is not to be left if she is in a certain state, she could have you arrested I mean having you arrested and say that you raped her.)[68]

This is from *UmAfrika*, as reported by Fraser Mtshali. I do not know, however, whether this is a verbatim transcript of Zuma's testimony; the version in *Isolezwe* is slightly different, but it shares the traits that I want you to see: "Ngazitshela ukuthi ngiyazi uma sisakhula ngokwesiko lakwaZulu awumshiyi owesifazane ekulesi simo ngoba uma wenze njalo angakubopha akubize ngomdlwenguli." (I told myself that I know if we are growing up according to the custom of KwaZulu you do not leave a woman who is in this state because if you do so she can have you arrested and call you a rapist.)[69] This reads like a paraphrase, even a Zulu re-translation of the English of the interpreter; the record of the court has the following: "She then said you see you cannot just leave a woman if she is already at that stage, in that situation, in that position and I said to myself I know as we grew up and in Zulu culture you do not just leave a woman in that situation because if you do she may even have you arrested and say that you are a rapist."[70] But what it contains, which neither the *Times* nor the *Star* does, is the fact that Zuma refers to his "growing up." He uses the verb *ukukhula*, to grow or grow up; or, in a more specific sense, to reach puberty. It is his upbringing that told him what to do. If "Zulu culture" is on trial, it is Zuma himself who is unwittingly putting it on trial. He is implicitly questioning his *Bildung*—or at least opening it to question. He can be heard as accusing it of having produced in him a certain paranoia: I will be arrested, charged with rape, even put in jail. (For somebody who spent ten years of their life on Robben Island, this is not an abstract idea.) I breathed a sigh of relief when I finally read Waetjen and Maré,[71] who state what should be obvious when they read Zuma's excuse as a demonizing narrative of the vindictive woman, and not as a Zulu cultural commonplace that says that to leave a woman in a state of arousal is "tantamount to rape." A day after the South African newspapers print their reports—but five days before the *New York Times* prints its own—Zuma actually spells this out under cross-examination: "it is said she becomes so infuriated that she can even lay a false charge against you and allege that you have raped her."[72] But there is more to it when one thinks psychoanalytically. The word *ukubopha* brings about the boy's worst nightmare; the woman who insists that men who rape must be "brought to justice"—which *UmAfrika* translates as *baboshwe*—becomes a figure in a paranoid phantasy; if we translate more directly, as has been pointed out to me, both reported versions say that *she can arrest you* (*angakubopha*) and not simply that she can have you arrested. The force of law is invested in the woman herself. It sounds like a feeble if not outrageous excuse, but the paranoia has invested itself deeply for him in the name "Zulu" or *isiZulu*. Again, this is a version of phantasmatic Oedipal wish fulfillment and punishment: leave the mother alone / make your mother happy, or she'll call your father. Among the more aggressive phallic symbols of Zuma's supporters—the avid "Boy Scout" with his obelisk-like "Mshini Wami" appears in several photographs—were sorry images of persecution: Zuma crucified, his photograph pockmarked by what look like bullet holes; Golden Miles Bhudu of the South African Prisoners' Organisation for Human Rights in his heavy chains with a placard reading "Why was Zuma Raped?"—which led one wry commentator to find that "[t]his slogan was confusing because it was known perfectly well that it was Zuma who was accused of rape but it asked why he was raped."[73] Zuma himself is reported to have compared himself to Jesus facing Calvary.[74] Heard as paranoia, it is a confession of sorts, but it is not heard in this way. All that is said is: no, that is *not* Zulu tradition, it is Zuma's tradition (De Beer), or that it *might not* be, but that is up to expert witnesses to judge (Suttner, Robins). Somebody told me that, yes, this is what some men say among themselves, you cannot leave a woman and so forth, as a kind of joke—but what exactly is the joke if it is not an allaying of castration anxiety? Simple negation / affirmation within the horizon of verifiability without any investigation of the motivation—which lies in an identification with the name, a doing in its name, and a paranoid fear of punishment if I do not do what it calls upon me to do (which is what I wish to do but which, according to the Oedipal phantasy, at the same time it bars me from doing). Hang on, you say, we're talking about a 63-going-on-64-year-old man here, how does all this apply? Well, here the older man is remembering—and we need not ignore the effects of *Nachträglichkeit*—himself as a subject in the process of growing up: as a boy, in other words. And remember how he was called out for saying, in a Shaka's Day speech at Stanger a few months after the rape-trial verdict, that "when he was growing up, 'an *ungqingili* [homosexual] would not have stood in front of me. I would have knocked him out.' "[75] What he told Jeremy Gordin some time afterwards was that "[a]ll I was doing—it was Shaka's Day, after all—was explaining the kind of values, for better or worse, I had been brought with up [*sic*] as a Zulu boy. I didn't say that I went around knocking out gays. I meant that, when we were young, gays were not acceptable to most people and anyone suspected of being one, or was somewhat effeminate during our stick-fighting training, would get knocked down."[76] In other words, to have been a boy—a Zulu boy—is to have been not-a-girl. He knew that as well as I did when I tried to wipe the makeup off my face applied for my bit part in *Ipi Tombi*. Like Zuma's remarks about the *ungqingili*, what he refers to in explaining his behavior in his Forest Town house needs to be placed in the correct chronological order. The words are uttered by a man in his sixties, but they are, arguably, those of a boy or youth speaking. And this anachrony, which makes it possible to suspect an implicit though almost silent critique—"for better or for worse"—would also apply to his position vis-à-vis the complainant; much was said about his position as father-figure,[77] and his betrayal of trust, as Khwezi claimed in her testimony, but what about her actual father, whose name the court effectively rules out in order to safeguard her identity, as is customary in South African rape trials? Although he was about the same age as Jacob Zuma, he was better educated,[78] and on Robben Island helped Zuma, who had received little formal schooling, become a better reader and writer.[79] Pupil-teacher is not son-father, but when the father of the woman in question was once one's teacher—the one who had what one did not have, and hence "deprived" one of—can one help but enter into a quasi-Oedipal rivalry? One cannot *know*, but I, myself never able to resist transference in relation to certain teachers, would hardly wish to exclude this possibility.

Rape or not rape, these remarks are (as all the newspapers in the world seem to sense, even if not all of them report his words fully) the most revealing moment in Jacob Zuma's testimony. It is the point at which Zulu is comprehended as something that is *learned* and which therefore has been taught, and could therefore also have been *taught differently* (since what is the point of perpetuating paranoid fear, let alone feeble excuses?). This is the crux for Mmatshilo Motsei, who wonders about the kind of sex education uMalume uZuma is providing to males on the brink of maturity.[80] *Learning*, one could say, has been *generalized*, so that the one who has received his Zulu from his mother's breast stands on the same footing as the one learning it as a second language. It is the repression of this generalization of learning—which also occurs when in 2008 xenophobia identifies Zulu with South African as being native—that produces all of the purisms of 100% and the polemicism of for-or-against. This is not to say that this opening toward the generalization of learning is actively perceived and pursued—but it is worth noting that, following the verdict, Zuma emphasized that his supporters came from all over the country,[81] even if many of them hailed from KwaZulu-Natal, and that, in 2008 in response to the xenophobic violence, he, like Thabo Mbeki, referred to the difficult dynamics of hospitality in exile whereas Mangosuthu Buthelezi appealed to shared ethnicity. He thereby abides by the ANC's founding principles of non-racialism. The latter are, however, not contradicted by what he says about his early formation. The point is that at the very moment that "Zulu" is produced as *pure*, and "JZ" as "100% Zulu Boy," it is demonstrated—if one perceives the demonstration—that it is *anything but* pure, since even—and perhaps especially—for the one proclaiming his Zuluness as the ultimate excuse for going ahead, Zulu will have had to be learned: do like so, a kind of "Fana ka lo" in fact. There are parallels here with what Benedict Carton writes about Zuma's *isizwe*, the Nxamalala, who, like the Ndwandwe and other peoples, were incorporated into Shaka's kingdom, but remained peripheral and also subaltern. For them, as for Thonga from northern Zululand seeking mine contracts, there may have been "deeper reasons to be self-conscious" about their Zuluness.[82] We shall see a comparable forgetting of marginality and migrancy in some intellectuals' responses to xenophobia in 2008. An extreme dispropriation of *isiZulu*, then. If realizing this generalization of learning is not ready to be admitted to consciousness, it nevertheless remains for the learner of Zulu, as historically determined—the Jarvis boy, the white reader of Fanagalo handbooks and Nyembezi's *Learn More Zulu*, the non-Zulu African migrant, me—to join the critical Zulu scholar or intellectual in order to effect this generalization by loosening the identification with the name—which in the story that I am telling myself about myself—is also the masculinist and heteronormative phantasy-identification with the agent of sexual violence. Whatever the size of the phalli outside of the court, and of the carnivalesque wooden *imishini*, the Presidential penis is just a penis.[83] And Zulu is, after all is said and done, just another language.

CHAPTER 5

2008

> AbakwaGileyadi bavimba amazibuko aseJordani phambi kwabakwa-Efrayimi; kwathi lapho ababalekileyo bakwa-Efrayimi bethi: "Mangiwele," abantu bakwaGileyadi bathi kuye: "Ungowakwa-Efrayimi na?" Uma ethi: "Cha," bathi kuye: "Shono uthi: 'Shiboleti,'" abesethi: "Siboleti," ngokuba engaqaphelanga ukuliphimisa kahle; base bembamba, bambulala ngasemazibukweni aseJordani; kwawa ngaleso sikhathi abakwa-Efrayimi abayizinkulungwane ezingamashumi amane nambili.
>
> —Judges 12: 5–6

It is early June 2008. I have just returned to Johannesburg from Cape Town, to where the xenophobic attacks that began in Gauteng in the weeks following my return from Jozini have spread, when a friend shows me a disturbing clipping from the *Mail & Guardian*. Under the headline "The 21st-Century Pencil Test,"[1] it describes how, at the height of the violence against migrants, armed mobs demanded that people demonstrate knowledge of obscure and archaic Zulu words in order to prove that they rightfully belonged in South Africa:

> As attacks on foreigners intensified and spread across Johannesburg, mobs began pulling people out of shopping queues and forcing them to take "tests" to establish their nationality.... A language test is first, where one is asked to label certain body parts in isiZulu. Certain words in the Zulu language are no longer used on a daily basis. For example, people generally speak of their fingers as *iminwe* rather than *ucikicane*, the more formal word for the pinky finger. South Africans are still familiar with these more archaic words[;] however, foreigners would probably not know them. While speaking to displaced victims of the violence in Alexandra, one of our reporters was warned by a woman to find out what an elbow is called in isiZulu, or he might find himself under attack if stopped by the mob and unable to give the correct answer. Angeline Motowanyika, a Zimbabwean woman who used to live in Jeppestown, was not so fortunate. "They took my money and my passport and asked me what is the name of this [elbow] in Zulu and I did not

know and they started attacking me." The formal Zulu word for elbow, *indololwane*, has also become extinct; most people now refer only to arms and hands. Another test is to ask people to give the Zulu name for toes—*inzonzwane* [sic].

This report by Nosimilo Ndlovu compares these Zulu language "tests" to the "pencil test," once used by apartheid government officials to help them refine racial classifications: you were African if the pencil stayed in your hair, you were coloured if it slipped out. At a time when the perception is widespread that South African national identity documents are meaningless because so many are forged, and immigration policies are said to be in disarray, the tests are an improvised form of popular border control. They are perhaps also a hyperbolic parody of policing that reveals some of the less openly acknowledged impulses guiding policies, regulations, and their enforcement. What these incidents show is that possession of a language is being aligned with the right to own a house or have a job, and even to reside in a particular place. Ownership of a language is being asserted—for what stronger claim to ownership can be made than to profess knowledge of the ancient and arcane?—in order to assert an exclusive right to ownership of property and opportunity. Jealousy of material things is being expressed through a jealous possessiveness over a language.

The word "shibboleth" comes to us from the Old Testament, where the Gileadites used it to identify and kill enemy Ephraimites moving among them, who pronounced it "sibboleth." When used to test pronunciation, the Zulu word *indololwane* is a shibboleth in the precise Biblical sense. *Ilanga* quotes a young Alexandra woman from Malawi: "Now the majority of us are not able to pronounce this word properly just as some were saying 'ingololwane' and then they are attacked with sticks accordingly."[2] In the *Mail & Guardian* report, however, *indololwane* is being used in a somewhat different way. In the incidents it describes, the ostensible targets of the shibboleth are Zimbabwean migrants. Many speak Ndebele, which, being the language of the descendents of the Khumalo people under Mzilikazi who broke away from Shaka's rule in 1823 and migrated north, differs little from contemporary Zulu. The mob logic appears to be that, even if Ndebeles have learned to make the adjustments in speech necessary to make themselves pass for speakers of Zulu, they would be unlikely to know certain obscure words. In a non sequitur—for, although Ndlovu is not consistent about what is common knowledge or not, and her claims are open to debate, let us accept for argument's sake that *not all Zulus* would know the word *indololwane* nowadays—it would prove that he or she was a "foreign national."

The phenomenon of mobs discriminating in the name of Zulu is widespread in 2008. A resident of the George Goch informal settlement, south of the Johannesburg city center, testifies: "On Saturday night the gangs came. They said that if you do not *khuluma* [speak] Zulu, then you are Makwerekwere and then you must go! My mother and father were murdered in the DRC [Democratic Republic of Congo]. With whom must I find refuge now?"³ But, as I have already learned, the people attacked also include South Africans. If the shibboleth is Zulu, there is no guarantee that non-Zulu South Africans would, as the King James Version has it, "frame to pronounce it right."⁴ In informal settlements on the East Rand, speakers of Shangaan from Mpumalanga, and of Venda from Limpopo, are being told by mobs that they must leave the places they live because they do not speak Zulu: "'The problem is my language. . . . They say that the president [of the ANC, Mr. Jacob Zuma] is Zulu, and therefore the country belongs to the Zulus.' 'It doesn't help even to show them our identity books.'"⁵ And, according to Bishop Paul Verryn, who has opened the doors of Johannesburg's Central Methodist Church to refugees ever since attacks flared up in January, "[t]he people who are resorting to police stations [as places of refuge] are not just foreigners. Among them are Sotho-, Venda-, and Shangaan-speaking South Africans."⁶

This news falls on me like a hammer blow: Zulu is the language of xenophobia.⁷ Zulu is being used to discriminate against, and to deprive. Although it is not clear how being South African comes to mean being Zulu,⁸ in the name of being Zulu, foreigners—as well as people from within the borders of South Africa—are being persecuted and attacked, their houses and shops set alight. In some cases, shot, beaten, and burned, they lose their lives. What is more, among them are people who are trying to learn Zulu in order to better equip themselves for life in South Africa's economic heartland, but whose endeavors are being used as a reproach and an accusation against them. As a learner of Zulu myself, I cannot help but identify with those migrants, and thereby occupy a position that, when I began learning Zulu in earnest the year before, I had never anticipated taking up. It is not a position free of fear: Who will be next? Yet the identification also produces the sense that people like me are no longer at the center of the secret history of language that I am tracing. If the phantasy of 100% Zulu boy has gone haywire, the small white boy and his faltering endeavors have become somewhat irrelevant, a quaint throwback to a simpler time when, if whites might have used Fanagalo in interactions with black people, it would have been better had they learned more Zulu instead. That irrelevance threatens to swallow me like an abyss. As with the lines drawn at Jacob Zuma's trial, can I nevertheless not use this irrelevance to map the terrain—aware of the structure of my own investment, without any longer assuming that it is an investment that "counts?"

But when my friend shows me the *Mail & Guardian* clipping, I feel that I am also being asked another version of the usual question: Why are you learning Zulu? It is like those unbearable family dinners when, as a student at UCT marginally involved in leftwing politics, I was asked to defend the policies of the UDF and COSATU. Now I get the sense that, because I have ever so slightly loosened the bonds of white solidarity by trying to learn an African language, I have to answer for all of the worst things that are done in its name.

I have always hated being put in such a position. Accusation—which can always be self-accusation—leads to a paranoid fear of punishment. And that fear, sooner or later, leads to an inhibition of learning—which is the last thing I need. But are the question and the accusation it implies entirely without merit if they lead one to consider what complicities one might be entertaining? One can pose the question in an even more pointed way: Is the song "Umshini wami," as reports in *Beeld* and the *Star* insinuate,[9] a red thread connecting the crass ethnic posturing of Jacob Zuma's supporters during his trial for rape two years before, and these new events, where the song is being sung by some of those engaged in xenophobic violence? In other words, now that Zulu is a signifier of immense polarization, and one is compelled to be on this side or that, on which side do you stand? Push it a little further and you have: Are you for Zulu, or against it?

Do these questions and demands make sense outside of a white South African world? Phrased in this starkly polarizing way, they could not easily be assimilated with what I was experiencing myself, as I conversed with people in Johannesburg and Jozini, and read the Zulu papers.

Thanks to Eve, who at our very first meeting led me to a newsstand on Jorrisen Street in Braamfontein to buy the Zulu newspapers *Isolezwe* and *Ilanga*, my reading had a definite direction. At our twice-weekly sessions we would read an opinion column from each of the papers: in *Ilanga*, the serious "Ngisika elijikayo" (I add my bit) by Professor O.E.H.M. Nxumalo, and in *Isolezwe*, "Ngeso likaVolovolo" (Through the sight of the Revolver), a satirical column signed by Volovolo Memela. Once my lessons with Eve drew to an end, I continued to make a point of reading the two columns regularly. This was easy to do with "Ngeso likaVolovolo," since *Isolezwe*, the country's only Zulu-language daily newspaper, was also available on the internet. Founded by John Dube in 1903, and since 1987 owned by Inkatha,[10] the venerable *Ilanga*, which appears twice a week, was not yet online. Although it is ubiquitous in KwaZulu-Natal, in the northern suburbs of Johannesburg copies of the Monday sports edition in which Nxumalo's column appears would sell out quickly in the couple of shops in Melville and Parkview where I was able to find it. Did these two very different newspaper columns provide a counterpoint to the white opinion that I was finding so persecutory? Did they address the fear associated with an identification with the migrant?

Events and Responses

Beginning in Alexandra on a Sunday night on May 11, the violence soon also erupted in Diepsloot and other townships and informal settlements around Johannesburg, before spreading to KwaZulu-Natal and the Western Cape. Whereas in Alexandra people originally from Zimbabwe, Mozambique, and

Malawi, as well as South Africans, were driven from their shacks in a kind of ethnic cleansing, in Diepsloot those targeted also included traders from Pakistan, India, China, and Somalia, whose shops were looted and burned.[11] Although the events of May 2008 were not unprecedented, they were more widespread and of greater duration than episodes in Alexandra dating back to 1995,[12] the well-publicized violent attacks that occurred against foreigners in different parts of the country between 2005 and 2007, and a series of incidents in the first few months of 2008 in which foreigners were targeted.[13] Among labor migrants, tensions along the Zulu-Shangaan divide are much older.[14] These events were taking place in a country beset by uncertainty. Some friends described it as an apocalyptic time. When Louise and I arrived in Johannesburg in January 2008, the power would suddenly go out in the evening. Electrical "load shedding" was a fact of life all over the country, and the explanations given by Escom never properly clarified why there was not enough electricity to go around, or why there had to be a 27% cost increase. New words came out across the airwaves as the languages of the country adapted; in Afrikaans, load shedding was euphemistically called *beurtkrag*, a taking-it-in-turns to have power; in Zulu it was simply *ukwehla kwamandla kagesi*, a sinking of electrical power. Although the global recession was not yet affecting South Africa as seriously as other countries, the economy was slowing down, and perennial problems of joblessness and lack of housing were aggravated by the price increases in electricity, as well as of food and fuel. The government was being blamed for slow or inadequate "service delivery"—the all-encompassing term for the promises, incompletely met, of the Reconstruction and Development Programme (RDP) to provide basic amenities, such as housing, to poor people. On top of this, the national government was divided at its highest level. At the ANC's conference in Polokwane in December 2007, Jacob Zuma had been elected president of the ruling party by an overwhelming majority, in a humiliation for President Thabo Mbeki, orchestrated in significant part by an alliance of Mbeki's detractors, COSATU, the South African Communist Party, and the ANC Youth League. Yet Mbeki remained president of the country until he resigned in September 2008, having been under pressure to resign ever since Zuma's election, and having been cited for prosecutorial interference by the judge who dismissed corruption charges faced by Zuma, opening the way for Zuma to be elected State President in April 2009.

In response to the May violence in Gauteng, large numbers of police are deployed, and hundreds of people suspected of taking part in it are arrested. Mbeki decides to send in the army to help the police restore order. The Minister of Home Affairs, Nosiviwe Mapisa-Nqakula, promises that, for the moment, no undocumented foreigners will be deported. Displaced people are placed in temporary refugee camps, some of which rapidly become overcrowded. In early June at the bleak and rain-swept Soetwater camp south of Cape Town, the situation appears desperate as several Somalis stage a suicide attempt by walking into the sea.¹⁵ People in the affected communities interviewed by the press blame foreigners for taking their jobs, and for being illegally granted or sold RDP houses. Corruption comes into it, some allege. It is also said that foreign traders unfairly compete with local traders and that the foreign business owners give nothing back to the communities that provide them with a livelihood. The Inkatha Freedom Party, which issues instant and emphatic denials, is blamed.¹⁶ Thabo Mbeki and other leaders allege a criminal element,¹⁷ and yet others, remembering the violence of the early 1990s, speculate about a "third force," but the stamp of a generalized xenophobia is unmistakable.

Academic experts soon register and relay the popular explanations for violence, adding analyses of their own. One frame of analysis in particular interests me: relative deprivation. It is not merely that people are poor, Adam Habib writes, but that, in relative terms, they are deprived of the basic means of existence while others are not. The point is that inequality in the distribution of benefits and opportunity is palpable.¹⁸ This leads people to look for scapegoats. Critics of this idea, such as Michael Neocosmos, point to the fact that xenophobia is rife among the well-to-do as well as the poorest of the poor. Neocosmos maintains that a deeper cause is a "political subjectivity" that, instead of actively claiming rights by various democratic means, passively appeals to the government, which has reinforced this passivity by whittling away at civil society, to provide a livelihood and basic conditions of existence.¹⁹ Neocosmos is persuasive. But I would nevertheless maintain that, although it can be a decisive factor, there does not need to be actual deprivation in order for there to exist a sense of deprivation. If there is indeed an undermining of political subjectivity, a perceived failure to be provided for by the government can reinforce a sense of deprivation when others are perceived to be favored by the government—or by the economic system. For Daniel Bell, who analyzed the discourse of the American right of the 1950s and '60s in "The Dispossessed," this resulted in a "politics of frustration," which, rather than being a conflict over doctrine, was a "psychological politics."²⁰ In order to be envied one does not actually need to possess anything. All envy needs is for somebody to believe that one does,²¹ and, moreover, in a paranoid turn, to believe that one has stolen it from him or her. In other words, forces of envy, and the unacknowledged dynamics seated in phantasy, as analyzed by Melanie Klein, can come strongly into play to set in train the secret history that I am telling.²²

Of what do South Africans feel deprived? Not simply houses and jobs, I begin to think, but their very identity as South Africans. After 1994, all South Africans should have been able to think of South Africa as *their* country. But somehow not all have been able to, and those who are perceived to have taken away portions of their patrimony are the ones to be persecuted and punished. Rights understood to be exclusively those of the citizen—such as an RDP house or a decent job—seem to them to have been usurped by outsiders. South Africa is still widely and unreflectively viewed as different from Africa proper.

Surely thanks in part to decades of imposed Bantustan citizenship, the allegiance of many black South Africans is still regional, even local, rather than national, thus creating a further instability: alienation from within and without. South African immigration policy is full of ambiguities and uncertainties, and reputed to be inconsistently, even corruptly, applied. In this light, possession of the country and of a national identity by its people is shaky and tenuous. My analysis is, admittedly, highly speculative, hurried, and based on comparatively little information. It does, however, attempt to synthesize what I have gleaned from the press—and from the learned commentators to whom it affords space, among whom Mamphela Ramphele stands out in her seriousness[23]—with my own sense of how the country has struggled to change in the years since 1994. Does what I am reading in Zulu take me any deeper into these painful matters?

A Professor's View

The Zulu of O.E.H.M. Nxumalo's *Ilanga* columns is difficult, and he tends to make his points by allusion. In the beginning I need a great deal of help from Eve. I know little about Nxumalo (b. 1938) save for his co-authorship with Sibusiso Nyembezi of the invaluable compendium of Zulu vocabulary, figures of speech, and proverbs, *Inqolobane yesizwe* (1966), until Liz Gunner tells me that, in addition to being an eminent academic and prominent public intellectual, he is well known as a poet and novelist in Zulu. Subsequently I learn that he is also one of King Goodwill Zwelithini's authorized biographers, and participated, along with Sibusiso Nyembezi and others, in the refounding of Inkatha in 1975.[24]

By the time I am in Jozini in April, I am tentatively reading "Ngisika elijikayo" on my own. I find fascinating Nxumalo's series of three articles on "Izinselelo zesiZulu esiyingcwenga" (Challenges of refined Zulu),[25] even if the purism apparent in his first installment raises questions for me, as somebody who has been practicing his Zulu in suburban Johannesburg by conversing with security guards whose mother tongue is Xhosa, Ndebele, or another language, and some of whom say *-cedile* instead of *-qedile*. Is there a place in Nxumalo's thinking for those who speak Zulu, not as a mother tongue, but as a language they have learned, for one reason or another, in later life?

Writing against the background of a colonial history in which the conquerors impose their language, debasing in the process the language of indigenous people, Nxumalo emphasizes from the opening paragraph of his first article that "[o]ur language is our patrimony [*ifa*] and that of our children."[26] His observations about language are strongly informed by a notion of ownership, implied here by his metaphoric use of *ifa*—legacy, inheritance, patrimony—to the extent that he chides Zulu speakers for switching to English or translating when white people are present, and doing so even in Parliament where interpreters are employed for that purpose.²⁷

But Nxumalo is not primarily defending Zulu against the depredations of colonialism, and of an incompletely achieved mental decolonization. The conversation conducted in his columns is an internal one in which the possibility of a non-Zulu readership is scarcely imagined. For the most part, the enemies of Zulu are not whites but Zulus who speak the language in a careless way. His first set of examples of misuse is not surprising, as they show how Zulu usage has undergone a narrowing under the influence of English—its most powerful linguistic neighbor for well over a century—and is still present in the "Natal" on the other side of the hyphen that Nxumalo prefers to elide when using "Kwa-Zulu" as the name of the province.

His examples can be difficult to translate, precisely for the reason that Nxumalo gives; whereas when it comes to dress, English tends mainly to use the words "wear" or "put on," an eloquently idiomatic Zulu would call for specific synonyms depending on the garment or item of adornment being worn or put on: "Sithi sibhinca ibheshu noma isidwaba—hhayi ukuligqoka noma ukusifaka.... Sithi sithwala isigqoko—hhayi ukusifaka." (We say that we gird on a skin buttock-covering or skin skirt—not that we wear it or put it on.... We say that we sport a hat—not that we wear it). Displaying a dry didact's sense of humor, Nxumalo writes: "This *faka* [put on, wear] comes from the English word that 'puts on' all things: hat, shirt, trousers, tie."²⁸ In his second installment, printed two weeks later, he writes, perhaps using the verb *ukufaka* ironically, that "[t]he main thing is that we must not mix the language, and that we really fight the temptation to put on [*ukufaka*] English words when we speak Zulu."²⁹

Nxumalo's second type of example of linguistic misuse is more confusing, equivocal even. "We ought to feel bad [*siphatheke kabi*] if we speak Zulu badly in a way similar to when we are learning the language of other nations."³⁰ Figuratively, the foreign language learner is being used as a bad example. "It should not be easy," he continues, "just to say that *uyashiselwa* [you are being heated] and you mean that *uzwela ukushisa* [you feel the heat]; and to say that *uyaqwashisa* and you mean that *uyexwayisa* [you are put on the lookout], or you say *ubogawula ubheka* [look before you leap]; and to say that *liyanetha* [it gets wet with rain] and you mean that *liyana* [it is raining]; and to say that *ufana njengoyise* [he or she resembles like his or her father] instead of saying that *ufana noyise* or *unjengoyise* [he or she is like his or her father]."³¹ Yet, as he more explicitly acknowledges in the second column in the series—where *ukushiselwa* and *ukuqwashisa* are included in a list of regionalisms—among those speakers whom Nxumalo confronts are those of regional variants of Zulu in KwaZulu-Natal.³² They are not people who are learning Zulu as a second language. Although in the second and third installments of his series on language he is more welcoming of regional differences in speech, perhaps in response to readers of

Ilanga who have contacted him in the intervening weeks, in his first article he introduces a standard for linguistic correctness that stems directly from the Zulu monarchy: "there are places that are known that if the majority there speak thus, it can now be said that that Zulu resembles that which is spoken in the Royal Household [*eNdlunkulu*]. In fact the language that is refined [*ulimi oluyingcwenga*] ought to have originated from the royal house [*lwalufanele luphume endlunkulu*]."³³

Nxumalo is nonetheless at pains not to impose his purism on those who speak regional variants of Zulu—as had Colenso in *First Steps in Zulu*, he notes that "kwakukhona abathefuyayo (abathefulayo!) kwakuthiwa ngabakwaQwabe nabakwaMthethwa" (there were those who *thefuya*-ed [those who *thefula*-ed!] and it was said that they are the Qwabe and the Mthethwa)—even if, according to Nxumalo, the way they speak ought not to be emulated by people from other regions: "Some of this is regional speech [*yinkulumo yezigodi*] . . . it can appear that it is a carelessness [*ubudedengu*] that is now set loose in all regions."³⁴ From the early nineteenth century, as one might expect from Colenso's appeal to the fact of political dominance of the amaZulu as his criterion for linguistic standardization—whereby *tefula* and *tekeza* become non-standard—differences of dialect were strongly aligned with relations of domination and subordination within the Zulu Kingdom; as Carolyn Hamilton and John Wright note, referring to testimony from the James Stuart archive, "[t]he [social status] category [of *amaLala*] seems to have been defined primarily in linguistic terms, being reserved for speakers of the *tekela* or *tekeza* dialect, which appears to have been common south of the Thukela and which differed from the dialect used at the Zulu court."³⁵

Casting his glance beyond his home province, Nxumalo, who must, in certain respects, be seen as the inheritor of these linguistically defined criteria of social distinction and political hierarchy, displays a tolerance toward those who speak Zulu as their mother tongue, but who do not speak the Zulu of KwaZulu-Natal—in part, he says, because they have been in contact with people who speak different languages. He even acknowledges speakers of Zulu for whom the language is not their mother tongue:

> There are many people, especially in provinces outside of KwaZulu[-Natal], who speak the Zulu language. From the way in which they speak it, it sounds like there is another language that they suck from the breast. . . . With others there is no language that they suck from the breast apart from this variety of Zulu that they speak. This language of theirs mixes with other, neighboring languages, and takes from Xhosa, Swati, and also translates . . . words from Sotho and Afrikaans. That is why you hear words like "canda" instead of "iqanda" [egg], "ivinkeli" instead of "isitolo" [shop], "irok" instead of "ilokwe" [woman's dress]. . . .
>
> There is a differing . . . in thinking between people who say every language that is spoken should be the finest [*ingcwenga*], and those who say about the

people who speak the language that is said to be of Johannesburg or of places like the far edges of the Bhaca country, this—it is a variety of Zulu.

It appears that there is intolerance when people are speaking a language that is not the old Zulu that is firmly based in KwaZulu, and it is said that they are murdering the language.

... [E]ven if this language is not written down, and also it is known that it is a fresh shoot of Zulu, we must not discriminate against those who speak it.

... [E]ven in England, ... some different regions simply do not understand what some English people say. The main thing ... is that the main language is known and understood [*luyaziwa ulimi olusemqoka*].[36]

I pause to examine these paragraphs more closely. Proud of the fact that, even in my limited experience, I have also noticed the transposition by some speakers of the dental and palatal clicks (*c*, *q*), I observe, parsing Nxumalo's other examples, that a high degree of standardization will have been reached by the language when distinctions are made among loan words for the same thing, and between alternate lexicalizations of the same loan word. In this instance, *ivinkeli*, which comes from the Afrikaans *winkel*, is the usual Xhosa word for "shop," whereas *isitolo*, from "store," is the Zulu equivalent. For a Zulu to say "irok" would be to defy the rule that, since Zulu does not have an "r," although Xhosa does, the "r" in loan words containing the letter is lexicalized as "l." Hence, in Zulu, the Afrikaans *rok* (dress) becomes *ilokwe*, just as *broek* (trousers) becomes *ibhulukwe*. Even a loan word can be used as a shibboleth. As Derrida observes, when a word is used as a password, what it means goes beyond its semantic sense (*sens*). I would add that its meaning may also transcend its origin—for who is to say that "shibboleth," supposedly Hebrew, was not itself a loan word?[37] Just as English speakers can learn to pronouce the *hl*, however, Zulus can pronounce the "r"; whereas one hears *idolobha* (town, from the Afrikaans *dorp*), one usually hears *edrobheni* (to / in / from town) when the locative is used, although the word would be written *edolobheni*. Artificial—or at least historically contingent—boundaries are being maintained, and the separations that they impose are not purely linguistic. Perhaps Nxumalo realizes this. The parallel that he draws between British English and Zulu is interesting, as it registers a shift in advocacy from a language that is the finest (*ingcwenga*) to a main, or standard, language (*ulimi olusemqoka*). On the analogy with English, one could say that, in these remarks, Nxumalo advocates a Standard Zulu rather than the King's Zulu.

Nxumalo is subtle. Although he does not elaborate upon his views on non-native Zulu speakers—and thus on the migrant who is learning Zulu, and who is the victim of shibboleths—he is careful to avoid simply imposing a single standard of correctness. This restraint is at the heart of his discourse. Although he begins his series of articles by admonishing Zulu speakers against the use of regionalisms, he goes on in his second article to approve of regionalisms within their regions as long as they do not spread. In his final article on the subject, Nxumalo suggests that any variant of Zulu is acceptable as long as a Standard Zulu, which is also that of the orthography, is known and understood. This I would term a qualified purism.

But I remain curious about his attitude toward non-native speakers of Zulu. What of the migrant? And what about me, who, in traumatic fashion, has, at least in his mind, found himself in the position of the migrant? The penultimate paragraph of Nxumalo's final installment on language constitutes something of an answer, and it is a rather discomfiting one. This paragraph expresses his disapproval of a 2008 radio infomercial recorded in Zulu to motivate Grade 12 students by KwaZulu-Natal MEC for Education Ina Cronjé. Let me confess, before I continue, that I myself found the ad irritating to listen to because, like the language laboratory sessions at UCT, it reminded me of how "white" my own intonation of Zulu was. Ostensibly Nxumalo is restricting his critique to Zulus who, just as they speak their language in a careless way, he imagines disingenuously telling Cronjé: "Sikuzwile, cha uyashaya." ("We have heard you—indeed, you speak well.")[38] If the discourse on white people learning Zulu remains fixated on the spectacle of the Reverend Kumalo praising the Zulu of young Jarvis—who, in Nyembezi's translation, is said to draw it from his nostrils[39]—one could say that at least Nxumalo advocates putting an end to the charade in which "our people continue with not complaining when Whites make mistakes with their things [*ngezinto zabo*]." The trouble is that, in advocating candor in matters of linguistic competence, and, to my way of thinking, thereby offering to dissipate the paranoia that can arise when one is praised even though one knows that one's command of the language does not merit it, Nxumalo also imposes silence: "They do not say that this advertisement demeans [*siyathunaza*], it is better it was done by a black person." With Ina Cronjé, and with the imperfect white speaker of Zulu more generally, Nxumalo reaches the limit of his tolerance of non-native and non-standard speech. Cronjé occupies the place that the white Fanagalo speaker used to occupy.

Nxumalo's overarching logic remains: our language is our patrimony—vigilance is necessary "in order that it be a patrimony that is a treasure for our children in the time to come, we having already put ourselves to rest" (*ukuze lube yifa elingaba yigugu ezinganeni zethu ngesikhathi esizayo, thina sesazithulela*)—and, like our country, perhaps the only one we have. Misuse and mixing of the language erode our patrimony. Responsibility falls in the first place to speakers of the finest form—or at least the standard form—of the language, and not to the speaker of a regional or otherwise variant form. Although it would be preferable to speak the purest Zulu, it is understandable that not everybody does (analogous with English). Whereas regionalisms and mixed forms spoken by people as their mother tongue are arguably acceptable, it is not clear that the coinages of radio personalities or the halting Zulu of white politicians ought to be encouraged.[40] Wherever the line is drawn, the structure of thought remains: if our patrimony is under threat, there are identifiable agents of ruin both among native speakers, and, although the discourse resists this implication almost until the end, among outsiders who are learning the language as adults.

Like many a nationalist—or at least the early Afrikaner nationalists who founded *Die Afrikaanse Patriot* in 1876[41]—Nxumalo retails a fable of the infant receiving language at the maternal breast. In Zulu, one's mother tongue is *ulimi lwebele* (language of the breast), and, as we see from Nxumalo, native speakers suck the language from the breast (*baluncela ulimi ebeleni*). The infant receives from its mother words, songs, and stories. I am going to risk speculating that an outcome of subscribing to this idealized dyad as the privileged transmission point of the patrimony (*ifa*) is that a sense of deprivation and paranoia can set in, should others be imagined to gain access to the breast. The phantasy that one is being attacked by those others would then lead to a violent defensive reaction. On the other hand, following what Klein writes about *envy*—which she distinguishes from jealousy, which involves a third party—one can witness the breast itself as being attacked for its very capacity to nourish.[42] In other words, the purist who stands for love of the language-giving breast may punish it through his lording and disdainful strictures on usage precisely because it has the capacity to nourish far and wide, a capacity that no individual speaker or writer could ever have. The word *ingcwenga* comes from the verb *cwenga*, to clarify, filter, or strain. *Ukucwenga umlaza* means to strain off the whey, from cow's milk, leaving the delicious and nutricious *amasi*, and *ukucwenga amazwi* means to choose words with care.[43] The speaker of the Zulu that is *ingcwenga* is the one most harshly constrained. And, as is commonly the case, when the mother is idealized as the child's first teacher of language, symbolically the figure of the woman becomes the nodal point for a racial nationalism. In O.E.H.M. Nxumalo's nationalism, which is also a monarchism, this symbolism is reinforced by the fact that *Indlunkulu*, the name for the Royal House, from which "the language that is refined [*ulimi oluyingcwenga*] ought to have originated [*lwalufanele luphume*],"[44] is a synecdoche of *indlunkulu*, the house of the principal royal wife. And, indeed, Nxumalo tends to suggest this by writing the word *indlunkulu* in this sentence in the lower case.

The question then becomes: Is the discourse that writes Nxumalo sufficiently aware of these pitfalls that, when his purist meditations on language are overtaken less than a week later by the wave of xenophobic violence that began on May 11, 2008, and he has no option but to confront the presence of migrants and the inevitable mixing of indigenes with them, it will restrain itself, as it does from censuring the majority of non-native speakers of Zulu, from simply making (counter-)attacks on the mother-tongue speaker's phantasied attackers—or, for that matter, on the language-giving breast itself? Or will its relatively mild censure of misusers and mixers of language other than Ina Cronjé (who appears to symbolize the envied breast held out to KwaZulu-Natal schoolchildren) be intensified when it comes to addressing the alleged usurpers of material elements of patrimony such as jobs, houses, hard-earned income, and rights?

Of Migrants and Migration

O.E.H.M. Nxumalo does not mention the shibboleths directed at migrants. He nevertheless begins with language, opening the first of his two columns on "Ukuqhubukusha abantu bokufika" (Elbowing out immigrants),[45] with the careful reflection on the meaning of words that stands out as the hallmark of his writings in *Ilanga*. He is against the word *izifiki* (arrivals) for example, which is the word on everybody's tongue in public discourse to refer to migrants.[46]

Having proposed other, less dehumanizing, words (*abafiki*, people who arrive; *abafuduki*, people who move away), Nxumalo proceeds to summarize some of the reproaches leveled at migrants by those who attack them: "they take jobs, they do not have papers to enter the country, there is being released a 'flood' of people and they enter at will; there is crime, including the selling of drugs." He then adds: "Over and above all of this, all of those who emit opinions on the airwaves and in the newspapers say that there is no need for violence. But some say that it is not going to help that what has now been started be stopped when at the same time there are people who are not promised a certain thing that goes forward, or a trying to find a remedy for the outbreak that is here now."[47] Here, as elsewhere, it is a matter of a promise: of something not given, or of something taken away by the migrant. That something has not been given, or withheld, is a condition necessary but not sufficient for a violent response. The latter requires the sense that it has been taken away—by a "thief." Even in the absence of actual deprivation—say, among the well-to-do—the accusation of the "thief" in itself has the power to generate a sense of loss or lack, because of the phantasy that he or she has what I do not have. These are dynamics of envy, dynamics well understood in Zulu auto-critique; as the writer of a letter to the newspaper *UmAfrika* declares: "Sekuvela ngokusobala-ke ukuthi abamnyama banomgolo oxaka uSathane ngoba abanye bezithuthukisa." (It really appears now that black people have envy that overwhelms Satan because other people are improving themselves.)[48] Having noted the demand for a promise, does Nxumalo say anything to meet the underlying psychopolitics of deprivation and relative deprivation?

His first appeal is to custom: "We have a fine custom in the culture of black people. That custom is the one that says that ubuntu is the treating of migrants well [*ubuntu yikuphatha kahle izihambi*]." A stranger should be fed and given a place to sleep, even supplied with livestock to provide him with milk. Inquiries should be made as to the guest's customs so that his mores (*usikompilo*) can be met, and he is to be given the opportunity to inquire about those of the host. But above all, according to custom, the stranger should be presented before the chief or induna, who has the power to grant a place to reside. The stranger and his background are carefully examined in the process. Nxumalo concedes that nowadays some people live in places that do not have a chief of the people or induna, although there are councilors, ward heads, and other leaders. He has a confidence in local authorities that *Ilanga*'s own editorial the previous week had shown to be misplaced: "Bebekuphi abaholi ngaphambi kwalolu dlame?" (Where were the leaders before this violence?).[49] *Ilanga*'s answer is: absent from their communities, living it up in the "suburbs," and visiting their constituencies only to win votes come election time. In this light, the vision that Nxumalo offers is decidedly nostalgic. Although he admits that practices have changed, his solution is an unequivocally conservative one in which newcomers must conform to the practices of the places to which they come: "It is not recalled that these migrants were presented to communities in whatever way. Perhaps the problem lies there also. . . . Maybe when the problem that exists is spoken about, it should be observed in what manner these new communities are prepared in order that they become accustomed to the new place—in order that the calf is now accustomed to the hobble."[50]

This conservatism—consistent with his linguistic purism—will continue to dominate Nxumalo's discussion, as he proceeds to enumerate the grounds on which people are attempting to quell the violence, and, adding to what he has already said, which its perpetrators give for their actions. In vindication of migrants, Nxumalo reports, people have pointed to neighboring countries' hospitality to exiles during the struggle against apartheid and declared that xenophobia is not the custom of South Africans. It has also been observed, as Nxumalo relays, that some migrants do have papers, and many create work for themselves without waiting to be hired by South Africans; that South Africans are in fact among those being attacked; and that it is not migrants that have caused prices to rise. Also held, Nxumalo reports, is the opinion that South Africans are lazy, and when they get a job they play games, always taking off for a death in the family whereas migrants never do.

Against what is said in vindication of migrants, Nxumalo relays accusations commonly leveled against them, noting that "[a]batolika isimo bengena ezicathulweni zabathukuthele" (those who interpret the situation enter the shoes of those who are angry).[51] It is said that employers, especially white employers, deliberately employ migrants; that instead of employing all, migrants without papers are hired because they will work for low wages and not go on strike; and that it does not matter whether a migrant has papers or not, any migrant is welcomed. It is also said that during the days of exile, South Africans lived in camps and not in local communities, and that they were not allowed to start their own businesses. It is further reported that migrants in Durban Point draw a red line that South Africans cannot cross; that corrupt officials give migrants RDP houses; and that young South Africans unwittingly marry migrants because so many forged identification documents are in circulation. "The list is long," Nxumalo declares, "we brought it to an end in vain."[52]

Many of the complaints on Nxumalo's list are the familiar ones relating to deprivation—of a decent job, or just any job, of an RDP house, and so forth. Migrants are, furthermore, stealing our women; *izingane zabantu* (children of the people, or young people) may,[53] technically, refer to young men too, but in this context probably just means young women. As Pumla Gqola observes, "The story of threat and competition [in the oft-heard retort: 'These guys come here and steal our women and jobs'] ... shows that if women and jobs are a resource and also an entitlement for heterosexual South African men, then obstacles can be eliminated and indeed must be. This is a bizarre inversion. But then again, inversions always accompany violent epistemic projects."[54] By "inversion" I take Gqola to mean that when the migrant is branded a thief the question of ownership and entitlement is begged, since the "right" to a woman—as of to a job—is routinely arrogated by South African men without question. This is paranoia in its most basic Oedipal form: the father / brother (foreign men) is doing bad things to the mother (South African women). If one's assumption is that women must accept local men, in the end it is one's own patriarchal violence that is doing the harm, and, fearing the punishment that will ensue, one loads the blame onto the phantasied rival. One can take this further and ask: Would a "rival"—or a "thief," or indeed, in this particular context, a "foreigner"—even exist in the absence of this paranoid fear of punishment?

Added, and possibly not unrelated, to this violent masculinism is a new and ugly accusation—namely that the hospitality offered to South African political exiles in Zimbabwe, Mozambique, and elsewhere was a hard hospitality; when Thabo Mbeki and Jacob Zuma, and other leaders who were exiles,[55] point to the fact that "[d]uring the time of apartheid many took refuge in the countries of those people who are being assaulted now," they forget that "[t]hose who took refuge in other countries in the time of apartheid were settled in camps, they did not roam about among the people, to the extent of even buying houses that they should not be being sold. Those who were taking refuge never owned a store or spots for selling beer, or owned cars."[56] Whether the latter is factually true of exile or not is less important than that these two points directly contradict the reconciliatory statements made by the leaders of the ANC, whose government, Nxumalo says, in conclusion, in fact has no policy on immigration. The points also insinuate without question the canard that houses are being bought and sold illegitimately by migrants in South Africa today. But what is worse is that impoverished neighboring countries like Zimbabwe and Mozambique are being reproached for a hospitality that was, in the apartheid years, an act of enormous political courage. In other words, not only are the people of neighboring states depriving us of our patrimony and livelihood now, but, through their restricted hospitality to the exiles, which might have included not making available their women to our men, they also deprived us in the past.

Getting toward the end of this litany of accusations, I sense that, despite his vehement condemnation and his careful semantics, Nxumalo's sympathies may not be wholly with the ones being attacked. Those who interpret (*abatolika*), of whom he is in turn an advocate, allow the reproaches so much force. Whereas some of the accusations that he relays directly contradict points made in vindication of migrants that they follow, the accusations themselves are never subject to critique. When he returns to the subject of "Elbowing Out Immigrants" two weeks later, *Ilanga*'s editorial on the opposite page, under the rubric "Bayekeleni bagoduke abafuna ukubuyela emakhaya" (Let them go those who want to return home), aggressively confronts the refugees with the reproach, reported two weeks before by Nxumalo, of a hard exile: "According to our understanding the young men who crawled on their stomachs under the electric fence did not in the least have time to run businesses and perhaps to find themselves jobs or to settle in the communities of those countries, whereas we see that happening in our country where immigrants are running businesses for themselves at will."[57] I am thus curious to learn what Nxumalo has to say in his sequel. After picturing the high financial cost to the country of aiding the displaced, he praises communities for calming one another down, and emphasizes, as do Thabo Mbeki and others, that "[w]e must confront problems in a way that has ubuntu."[58]

But then he produces a further series of reproaches against immigrants: "Many people are complaining by saying that immigrants, not only those from Africa, among them those from Pakistan and those from China, have a certain uncaringness [*ubudedengu*] when they are here, especially as they are running their businesses." What follows is a litany of underhanded business practices and other unacceptable conduct—inter alia, the selling of defective or inferior goods, refusing to allow customers to return such merchandise, not paying staff, and "[t]o be going to sell at social grant disbursement events the very items that were previously sold to people who were going to sell them at grant disbursement events themselves."[59] The final point is a reproach of a different order: "Not to show respect in the township or in the town, especially when old people cross, they are chased like they want to run them over because they walk slowly or they are confused by the traffic lights."[60]

I can hardly believe what I am reading, and have to read his list of ten bullet points several times to make sure that I am not misunderstanding the crass slurs for which Nxumalo, with scarcely a word of censure, is acting as go-between. The point about selling merchandise at social grant disbursement events is particularly puzzling. Once I discuss it with Mbongiseni Buthelezi, who has generously gone over my translation, I realize that the complaint is that wholesalers are competing in the same market with, and probably underselling, the very retailers to whom they sell. This is widely considered an unfair trading practice. But, like the other business practices enumerated, is it one engaged in only by migrant traders? All Nxumalo says in response is: "This does not require the police. It requires that the community caution at the appropriate time."⁶¹ Who is to be cautioned, though? The accusers, or the ones accused? Such accusations about trading practices have been leveled by Zulus at Natal Indians and Chinese traders for more than a hundred years (recall the crooked Chinese shopkeeper in Nyembezi's *Mntanami! Mntanami!* and the cheating Indian employer in his *Ubudoda abukhulelwa*).⁶² And, in the midst of the present wave of xenophobia, the accusations are not isolated; the writer of the letter to the editor of *UmAfrika* whom I quoted above on the subject of envy among black people, asks a rhetorical question: "These people who arrived here, they sell merchandise that they came out with from their countries and other merchandise they are buying from wholesalers in South Africa. If it is the case here that immigrants are being driven out, why then are left alone the Chinese because they too are now spread all over this country?"⁶³

What comes next? I am relieved to see that it is a turn toward history, a field in which Nxumalo displays considerable erudition, criticizing former Minister of Education Kader Asmal (1934–2011) for stating that, since no jobs exist in music, African languages, history, and religion, university departments devoted to those subjects must be closed.⁶⁴ Here is what Nxumalo says about the relevance of history:

> Thanks to the demeaning of the dignity of history, there was an attacking of people who are from here, it having been said that they were migrants [*abokuhamba*]. It appears that there are people who think that Shangaans and other peoples who are here in South [*Ningizimu*] Africa are immigrants [*abantu bokufika*]. The Shangaans are a people that was formed after it was that Soshangane quarreled with King Shaka. Soshangane was begat by Zwide, son of Langa.⁶⁵ He went to Mozambique and also to Gazankulu. The peoples that they found there are of different names, and so were those they arrived with, they called them by saying that they were the peoples of Soshangane.
>
> Observe the names of hospitals and schools at Thulamahhashi and even in Limpopo. Shangaan people came into being. There are the Sitholes, Mthembus, Nxumalos, Mdakas, Langas, and many other names. It is not even that they are our people [*abantu bakithi*], but they are people of our homeland [*abantu basekhaya*]. There they are, all the peoples that we have here that have customs that coincide with ours: they make lobola; they give in marriage; they brew people's beer; they observe customs of respect [*ziyahlonipha*]; they esteem the old person; they have a forum for discussing matters; the woman has her place, the man has his place; they believe that a person does not die and really stop existing forever [*aphele nomphela*], they believe in the power of the creator; they are our people [*ngabantu bakithi*].⁶⁶

Coming after the back-and-forth of bullet points relaying a dueling vindication and accusation of migrants, with little intervening comment on the substance of what xenophobes say, this is Nxumalo's first statement of reasoned opposition to xenophobia. His response is rather complex. Like Mangosuthu Buthelezi—who made xenophobic statements while serving as Minister of Home Affairs in the mid-1990s,[67] but who in 2008, when addressing the displaced people from Zimbabwe and Mozambique sheltering at a police station in Cato Manor in KwaZulu-Natal, stated that "bayizihlobo zegazi zabantu bakulesi sifundazwe" (they are blood relatives of the people of this province),[68] and that "Zulus and Ndebeles [from Zimbabwe] share the same ancestry,"[69]— Nxumalo appeals to historical kinship, and a history of migration and conquest with which most readers of *Ilanga* would probably only be roughly familiar. He directly engages with one of the points made by those wishing to end the violence that he enumerates in the first installment: "There is now also the beating of people from South Africa who speak different languages, and who are from here, because bush behavior does not analyze anything." (*Sekukhona nokushaya abantu baseNingizimu Afrika abakhuluma izilimi ezahlukene, abangaba khona lapha ngoba inqubo yasehlathini kayicwaningi lutho.*)[70] Not only are there Shangaans who are resident in South Africa, as Nxumalo rightly notes, but, historically, Shangaans in Mozambique are descended from the people that took up residence there under the leadership of Soshangane, and from those people who were subjugated by him to form the Gaza Kingdom. The latter remained an independent monarchy until Gungunyama was defeated and exiled by the Portuguese in 1895, leading some of his followers under Mpisane Nxumalo to flee to the Transvaal, where they settled at Bushbuckridge in present-day Mpumalanga.[71] In a sense, then, just like the Ndebele people whom Mangosuthu Buthelezi invokes, for O.E.H.M Nxumalo their early history makes Shangaans a remnant of peoples who preferred to migrate instead of submitting to Shaka's rule—although it is also observed that the name "Shangaan" has "proud[ly]" been used by people in southern Mozambique whose forebears were once subjects of the Gaza Empire. "To this day," J. D. Omer-Cooper wrote in 1966, "mine-workers from this area who go to work in South Africa call themselves Shangaans."[72] And, of course, because this is also what South Africans call them, the Shangaans of Mpumalanga championed by Nxumalo are sometimes subject to mistaken identity.

But things grow more complicated, and what Nxumalo writes depends on a more detailed knowledge of nineteenth-century history than he explicitly provides, as well as an acquaintance with relatively obscure contemporary ethnic-identity politics. Historically, the followers of Soshangane were a part of the Ndwandwe people, who, having been ruled by Zwide, had been defeated by Shaka in 1818 at the battle of Mhlatuze.[73] According to the report of the Nhlapo Commission, which in 2010 ruled on the king- and queenship claims of various South African "traditional leaders," "[a]fter the defeat of Zwide by Shaka in

1819 [sic], Soshangana refused to be incorporated into the Zulu Kingdom. He fled with his followers along the eastern foothills of the Lubombo mountains to the upper Tembe River. Soshangana and his followers later crossed the Tembe River to Delagoa Bay. He fought, defeated and subjugated the vaThonga communities he found in the area."[74] Historians now think that, even after the defeat at Mhlatuze, the Ndwandwe remained a significant rival power and were only finally defeated by the Zulu at Izindololwane in 1826, after Zwide had died and a struggle for succession between his sons Sikhunyana and Somaphunga had split the Ndwandwe. Those under Somaphunga gave their allegiance to Shaka, and the survivors of those under Sikhunyana were allowed to "resettle in the former Ndwandwe territories south of the Phongolo, but now under the rule of the Zulu royal house."[75] Those Ndwandwe who had migrated under Soshangane eventually became Shangaans, whose language, although sharing many features with Zulu, is Tsonga, the principal language spoken in southern Mozambique. The declaration of kinship being made by Nxumalo thus does not depend on the Shangaans being, or having been, Zulus, but rather on their having been Ndwandwes. There is, today, as Mbongiseni Buthelezi explains, a movement afoot to organize the Ndwandwe that, although centered among Zulu-speaking Ndwandwes in northern KwaZulu-Natal, crosses linguistic lines—Zulu, Shangaan—and the national borders of South Africa and Mozambique.[76] Compared to Zulu nationalism, the Ndwandwe movement is a minority one. It is different to claim kinship on its basis than to do so on the basis of shared Zuluness, as does Mangosuthu Buthelezi, who is an uncle of King Zwelithini. What Nxumalo does not say out loud but hints at when he includes the name Nxumalo among the Shangaan names of hospitals and schools in Limpopo and Mpumalanga, but which anybody conversant with the relevant genealogy could tell you, is that the Nxumalo were and are the ruling clan of the Ndwandwe, and also of the Mpumalanga Shangaans; the Nhlapo Commission, for instance, ruled against the kingship claim of Mpisane Eric Nxumalo, "senior traditional leader" in the Bushbuckridge area.[77] Despite the fact that the Ndwandwe were a twice-conquered people, it nevertheless remains true that the Ndwandwe-Shangaan identity for which Nxumalo stands is, from the perspective of Thonga history, one formed through conquest of its own. As Henri Junod writes: "Let us only say that the history of the Thonga tribe during the XIXth century was dominated by the invasion and migrations of the Zulu conquerors, who left Chaka and for their own sake enslaved the poor Ama-Thonga of the coast, just as Mosilekatsi did among the Mashonas."[78] Although O.E.H.M. Nxumalo's ties to the Zulu monarchy are strong—he is an authorized biographer of King Zwelithini and is handsomely paid to write speeches for him[79]—his investment in this minoritarian politics is more than one guided by a knowledge of his clan's history. Nxumalo is a participant in the Ndwandwe movement, and has on occasion addressed its gatherings.[80] Could Nxumalo's history lesson therefore be read as an allegory of his own clan and people's position within the Zulu nation:

its subjugated status, and the risks involved in asserting an identity that is not a Zulu one?[81] Viewed in this light, as John Wright first suggested to me, the irony of Nxumalo's activity as a writer and public intellectual is stark. To judge from his columns in *Ilanga*, nobody is more fastidious than he is when it comes to the Zulu language, the finest form of which emanates from the Royal Household, and his commitment to elucidating and commenting on matters of concern to Zulus is nothing short of exemplary. Yet here we have a reasoned appeal against xenophobia that risks marginalizing the one making it: to declare as an Ndwandwe that the Shangaan *ngabantu bakithi* (are our people) and even *ngabantu basekhaya* (are people of our homeland) is different than declaring it as a Zulu, even if the declaration is made in the Zulu language and in a venerable Zulu newspaper.

To appeal to historical memory in order to take up the position of the marginalized—and even of the alien—may be an act of the responsible intellectual. But no matter how strategically exigent it may be to do so, the problem is that the response of declaring ethnic and linguistic kinship is of limited reach; even if Thonga people of Mozambique and South Africa *not* historically under the domination of migrant Ndwandwes are accepted by Nxumalo as his own—which is doubtful, just as is his advocacy of Shangaans from *outside* of South Africa—how can Pakistanis and Chinese, who are the targets of the worst prejudices, be included? Although so different in its context, Nxumalo's *ngabantu bakithi* reminds me of N. P. van Wyk Louw's 1960 declaration that "die Bruinmense is óns mense, hóórt by ons" (the brown-people are *our* people, *belong* with us), which he made on the basis of language, culture, religion, and history shared between white Afrikaners and coloureds.[82] Louw's gesture had no way of including Africans. To avoid falling squarely into the trap of racism, but perhaps also to avoid digging up the history of nineteenth-century conquest in what are today Zimbabwe and Mozambique, is perhaps why Mbeki and Zuma appeal to a shared history of hospitality, albeit a complicated one, dating back to the years of struggle in exile. Mbeki and Zuma declare that xenophobia is against "our tradition," and invoke a more general Pan-Africanism, instead of asserting a kinship-based diasporic Africanism that, if it is applied consistently, can ultimately only accord a selective welcome to migrants. As an alternative not based in racial kinship, the migrant labor system could also be cited, but it isn't here. Although the Ndwandwe were once migrants from what is now KwaZulu-Natal, and were later migrants from Mozambique, the conceptual path of a generalized migrancy, and the consequent advocacy of the migrant, is never explored by Nxumalo. The last straw for me, however, is when I read that, like us—Zulus, Ndwandwes?—Shangaans esteem older people (*zazisa umuntu omdala*). The Pakistanis and Chinese are thus explicitly "not like us" because, the unanswered slur goes, they show no such respect: "Ukungahloniphi elokishini noma edolobheni, ikakhulukazi uma kuwela abantu abadala." (Not to show respect in the township or in the town, especially when old people are crossing.)[83]

Whether the reproach is factually true makes no difference when it is juxtaposed without question with the stipulation that others, by virtue of adhering to customs like our own, can, by definition, not be subject to this reproach.

Although thoughtful and erudite, Nxumalo's response to the violence was equivocal, and, to me, disturbing even. Whereas he might have given moral and political direction to an implied reader who shared his assumptions about who is answerable for what, he provided me with no clear answers. I would even say that his division between those who are like us and those who are not like us mirrors the white question: Are you for Zulu or against it? His answer is that *they* are against it—the abusers of language, the closers-down of the teachers' colleges,[84] the disrespecters of the elderly. This is, in effect, a paranoid answer, bound up with the envy of the one who succeeds, perhaps learning just enough Zulu to get by (remember Jabulani in Nyembezi's *Mntanami! Mntanami!*, who is assured that a "'fana ka lo' of Afrikaans or Sotho" is good enough for the work he is getting into), and a projection of envious violence onto the latter. Faced with its mirror image, the white question also gains in clarity: By learning Zulu, are you not succeeding where we—your fathers and forefathers—have failed, competing unfairly, as it were, engaging in a kind of parricide (Arthur Jarvis's murder is the punishment here)? This *envy*, for the other's success, can turn into a kind of *jealousy*, in which, if the learner him- or herself is not persecuted for being a *kafferboetie*—in a certain American idiom, a nigger lover—the supposed loved object is attacked. In the phantasy, that object is nothing other than Zulu itself.

The import and power for me of this paranoia, and its violent acting out—of which I am by no means innocent, as my Zulu fossilizes and my criticisms become less and less relenting, as if I am trying to please my own fathers and forefathers by taking sides against a language with which I identify the Professor—is far more consequential than anything I can find in Nxumalo himself. Nevertheless, from the time that I read his columns on xenophobia, I find that I take only an occasional glance at what he writes in *Ilanga*. I continue, however, to make the time to read Volovolo's columns every Wednesday. Considered a light diversion by most of the people I know who read "Ngeso likaVolovolo," they are for me a lesson in what other forms public dissent might take in Zulu. They are also a lesson in how the reading culture, whose beginnings in the nineteenth century are so well analyzed by Hlonipha Mokoena in her book on Magema Fuze and by Vukile Khumalo on the "Class of 1856,"[85] has evolved in ways that exceed the tradition of didactic opinion of which Nxumalo is obviously an inheritor. Even if at first "Ngeso likaVolovolo" appears to have no direct bearing on the xenophobic violence, it does show me that, in the hands of a skilled writer, there is a certain dialogism that runs contrary to linguistic purism, in the presence of which a unitary and unreflective Zuluness could not easily be alleged; the question was: could "Ngeso likaVolovolo" address xenophobia without resorting, as Nxumalo does even as he appears to take up the minoritarian Ndwandwe position, to an assertion of ethnic and racial sameness? Volovolo's columns, which, after I returned to New York in the autumn of 2008 were eagerly taken up by Eckson and distributed by him to his Zulu-language students at Columbia, also became a respite from the aggression of family and of white friends, and from the platitudes and pieties of some of those who, animated with the best intentions in the world, teach foreign students about Zulu culture. Volovolo's quips were in fact closer in feel to the lighthearted exchanges that I was having with people I met, and conversed with in Zulu, in Johannesburg, Jozini, Imbali, and Amaqongqo. (I am not saying, of course, that there is no place for serious didacticism, or that I never had conversations that dealt with serious matters in a serious way.) If Nxumalo's swipes at Ina Cronjé for her bad Zulu, and Kader Asmal for not knowing any,[86] could easily aggravate a paranoia in a learner who happened to read them—How much do I really know? What is he saying that I do not even understand?—and thereby actually inhibit the learning of the language, Volovolo's columns somehow provided relief by not triggering in me a paranoid reaction. But how would Volovolo respond to xenophobia? And what bearing might any response of his have on the desire to learn Zulu? When it eventually came, some time after my return to the United States, his response would be oblique and equivocal, like all of his best writing.

The Chief of The Point

A few weeks before soccer's World Cup was held in South Africa in 2010, readers of *Isolezwe* will have come across an announcement by somebody calling himself the Chief of The Point (*inkosi yasePhoyinti*) that "[a]fter fasting for three days the vision has come to me that it might be a mistake to prevent prostitutes from other countries from trading their bodies in this country [*abaqwayizi bakwamanye amazwe ukuthi bazohweba ngemizimba kuleli*]."[87] The Chief has changed his mind: "It will be worth remembering that at a time not so long ago I released a proclamation as Chief of The Point in which I said that I did not want for the foreign Babies to clash with the ones here at the time of the World Cup."[88] The "proclamation" in question, published two months earlier, was headed "Abaqwayizi bangaphandle abahambe bayoqwayiza ngakubo" (Let the foreign prostitutes go and prostitute themselves in their own countries), eerily echoing the title of the xenophobic editorial published in *Ilanga* in June 2008.[89]

What has led the Chief to change his mind? Although a clear reversal of an arbitrary xenophobia, being against xenophobia is not the ostensible reason that the Chief has come to a different view. For the two years leading up to the World Cup, sex work became a veritable obsession among local, provincial, and national politicians in South Africa: Would there be a vast influx of foreign sex workers?⁹⁰ Should sex work be legalized for the duration of the tournament, how might it be regulated, taxed, and so forth?⁹¹ Applying the same logic as the politicians who envisaged a tax on sex work, the Chief of The Point proceeds: "At that time I did not perceive the need for bringing traders from other countries, given that we had ones from our country. In my mind I told myself that my people will continue to look after me with money in commission available from the purchasing of men who are customers."⁹² But whereas "the Babies of this country continue to leave off looking after me as chief," "foreign prostitutes have now promised me that they are going to bear me my portion as chief [*bazongiphathela isipheko sami njengenkosi*]. It now also happens that that portion of mine is going to be a load of money in American dollars."⁹³

What is going on here? And who is the Chief of The Point? Tempting as it might be for some to read it as an allegory of the World Cup, with the South African state supine before FIFA—the view of critics of neoliberalism, and vividly drawn in Zapiro's cartoon of Jacob Zuma as a streetwalker accepting a tip from FIFA president Sepp Blatter out of the tournament's profits⁹⁴—it should be apparent from the fact that this leader openly declares his willingness to sell out to profiteers from abroad, in exchange for a suitable "portion" in American dollars, and to leave his "people" unprotected from foreign competition, that we are firmly in the realm of make-believe.

The Chief of The Point is a satirical persona adopted by Volovolo Memela in his newspaper column, "Ngeso likaVolovolo." Appearing each week on a Wednesday in *Isolezwe*, Volovolo's column pokes fun at the news. If *Isolezwe* (Eye of the nation), which bears on its nameplate the proverb "iso liwela umfula ugcwele" (the heart's desires reach where a human being does not have the power to reach; literally: the eye crosses a flooded river),⁹⁵ is thus both witness and advocate of aspirations, the *iso likaVolovolo*—Volovolo's eye or view, also the sight of a revolver or gun (*ivolovolo*)—can provide pointed commentary. Referring to himself as "gun of truths, boy who resembles the case docket that goes missing while in the hands of the police" (*isibhamu samaqiniso, umfana ofana nedokodo lecala lona eliduka lisezandleni zamaphoyisa*),⁹⁶ Volovolo explains, "I was given the nickname because they saw my striking contributions [*amagalelo*]. It does not denote a gun for shooting people."⁹⁷ Appearing below the editorial and Qap's Mngadi's daily cartoon, the column displays in its upper right-hand corner a line drawing of a rotund man with a bald head in a singlet seated in his armchair, guffawing at what he has read in *Isolezwe*, a copy of which he holds aloft in his left hand. Lest we take his laughter to be entirely harmless, in his right hand he holds what looks like a knobkierie with rather a large head.

We know nothing about Volovolo Memela apart from his columns, even if in some of them biographical details appear that might be taken to refer to their author, such as that "he was born and grew up in the country and pursued his education in schools in the towns,"⁹⁸ or, in a column I return to below, that he is "a boy from Bulwer." Volovolo—or Volos, as he frequently refers to himself, and as many of his readers call him—can thus itself also be understood as a persona. Indeed in the very first installment of "Ngeso likaVolovolo" the name Volovolo Memela is placed in quotation marks.[99] For regular readers of Volos, what stands out in the piece published just before the World Cup is how the identity of the "Chief of The Point" or "Chief of the People of The Point," which from 2007 features in many of Volos's columns, is elaborated.

According to *Isolezwe*'s then-editor, Thulani Mbatha, the newspaper, which began publication in Durban in 2002, "cater[s] for the modernising Zulu. Someone who may go back home to the rural areas to slaughter a cow to the amadlozi [ancestors], but is equally comfortable taking his family out for dinner and a movie in a shopping mall."[100] In a society that elects its government, even as a king is recognized, and among whom the authority of chiefs and their headmen is respected, especially in rural areas, it is an audacious gesture to assume the persona of a chief—even if that chief is the chief of a place that, being in a city center, has no official chief, and the people of which he is chief are the city's sex workers.

A residential and commercial area beside the Durban harbor mouth, known in the past for its traders, ships' chandlers, seamen's institutes, and the usual dockland mix of rough bars and seedy hotels, The Point has seen decline in recent years, its older residential buildings falling into disrepair and neglect, even as luxury apartments and a small-boat marina have been built in an effort to stimulate urban renewal. Point Road, controversially renamed Mahatma Gandhi Road, remains notorious as a hub of prostitution and drug dealing, despite the luxury housing and tourist development projects, including uShaka Marine World, that have sprung up in the vicinity.[101]

The Chief of The Point's people are the *abaqwayizi* or *omahosha* (prostitutes)—or, given a proper name, the *amaNu* (which, assuming that the word, an abbreviation of *Amanunuzana*,[102] derives from *inunuza*, or baby, I translate as Babies). In return for material support, he is their champion. Despite constantly complaining about it, the Chief of The Point is accorded no recognition by the powers that be,[103] is never consulted about the proposed legalization of prostitution ahead of the World Cup,[104] and even his "people" are remiss in bearing him his chiefly "portion."

Because money and power and sex are involved, the Chief of The Point is a figure that allows satire of the machinations and excesses of leaders, especially those of the province of KwaZulu-Natal (Volos has conducted regular insider "interviews" with leaders of an Inkatha Freedom Party on the wane and a clueless Congress of the People).[105] What is at stake in Volovolo's persona of Chief of The Point is perhaps clearest when, in a few sentences at the beginning of a 2008 column ostensibly about a rumored merger of Ukhozi and Gagasi radio stations (probably an April Fool's joke), the Chief comments on King Goodwill Zwelithini kaBhekuzulu's rejection of a new house built for him in Hillcrest:

"Until when will people not want to listen to *iSilo samabandla*[106] when he says that there is something that he does not love with all his heart? *UBhejane phuma esiqiwini kade babekuvalele*,[107] he already spoke at length saying that he is not committed to living in this house that has been bought for him in Hillcrest, west of Durban. Volos fails to understand why *uHlanga Lwezwe*[108] is pummeled about the house though he has already said that this house does not go down well in his throat."[109] Including several of King Zwelithini's praises, Volovolo— or the Chief of The Point—does not directly criticize the king for his extravagance and profligacy, but instead reproaches those people who ignore the king's complaints. In so doing, he employs the tact of an *imbongi*, whose *izibongo* can be masterpieces of ambiguity.

This is, incidentally, one of the problems of translating the word *izibongo* as "praises," of translating *imbongi* as "praise poet," and of regarding any given *isibongo* as either simply laudatory or, for that matter, simply critical; when a man or woman has made a name for him- or herself, it is understood that, in his or her deeds, there will be things to extol and things to censure.[110] Archie Mafeje, in his classic essay, "The Role of the Bard in a Contemporary African Community" (1967), was timely in showing how the Xhosa *imbongi* engages in political criticism—but his translations, I believe, sometimes remove a telling ambiguity. In the midst of a struggle over the implementation of the Bantu Authorities Act in 1959, the Minister of Bantu Administration and Development, De Wet Nel, is addressed "Ndithi kuye Aa! Zanelanga!!! / Nguzanelanga kumhlaba wemvula." Mafeje renders these lines as "To him I wish to say, 'Hail! Bringer of barrenness!' / He is a bringer of drought in a land of rain." According to Mafeje, the poem "has an obvious political implication that Mr. de Wet Nel, as a representative of the Nationalist Government, is not seen as a protector of the people of the Transkei, but rather as one who takes bread out of their mouths."[111] *Zanelanga* means "Comes with the Sun." Despite the context delineated by Mafeje, which undoubtedly overdetermines the meaning of the *isibongo* in the way that he shows, the convention used by the *imbongi* is, I submit, for the words themselves to remain equivocal nevertheless, allowing that the sun may, in conjunction with rain, give life just as it may take it away.

But Volos, although he is practiced in the art of the *imbongi*, is not the King's *imbongi*, and his Chief of The Point is, well, a *chief*, and not a chief's praise poet. Although in previous years he played for a while with the persona of *indunencane* (minor induna, or sub-induna), as the Chief he comes right out and says: give me the house: "The Chief of The Point does not have a private royal enclosure in which to reside in order that he might bask in the reverence of his people of The Point [*isigodlo sokuhlala ukuze ikwazi ukothiwa yisizwe sayo sasePhoyinti*].[112] The provincial government must stop changing the subject [*ukubika imbiba nebuzi*], it must be announced officially at the end of this week that He-Who-Baths-with-a-Cellphone [*umaBhavaneselula*] will now occupy this house that *iMbube*[113] has refused."[114]

Mafeje famously compared the *imbongi* to the medieval European court jester;[115] but with the Chief of The Point, I think, we have something a little different. When the teller of home truths symbolically usurps the place of the chief or king, we are closer to what Mikhail Bakhtin describes in *Rabelais and His World* (1965) as taking place at popular carnivals during the same era: "Civil and social ceremonies and rituals took on a comic aspect as clowns and fools, constant participants in these festivals, mimicked serious rituals.... Minor occasions were also marked by comic protocol, as for instance the election of a king and queen to preside at a banquet 'for laughter's sake' (*roi pour rire* [king for a laugh])."[116] Laughter, which is the goal of "Ngeso likaVolovolo" from its inception, is, as it was in Rabelais, declared to be therapeutic: "Those who know say that to laugh cures many ailments, especially those of fatigue of the body and the mind, and it even makes people whose faces do not look good think that they are a little bit better."[117] Reference may also be found to a Volos Church of Smiling Philosophy.[118] The Chief of The Point, who could be said to be "chief for a laugh," parodies the *imbongi*, just as he parodies *izibongo* and the protocol of *ukubonga*, in order to expose folly and excess among the powerful. Typically referring to himself as *okaVolos* or *thina zinto zoVolos* (roughly: His Volos or We, His Volos), his most striking self-praises of the period in which I have been reading his column are *umaBhavaneselula* and *umaBhavangekliveji*: respectively, He-Who-Baths-with-a-Cellphone and He-Who-Baths-with-Cleavage. These praise names, along with his demands for a luxury house and car,[119] connote the decadence that he satirizes—even if he has written that having his cellphone with him in the bathtub is just to avoid having to get out of the bath to answer it.[120]

From its inception, with Volos's tell-all "interview" with soccer bad-boy Jabu Pule, "Ngeso likaVolovolo" has made sex one of its main subjects. The column has often included polite comments on people's sex life, and has regularly dispensed advice to the lovelorn, especially when Volos replied periodically, as he did from 2003–2004, to letters from readers in a kind of agony column. It should be obvious that there is much that is emphatically male (and even masculinist) about Volos's satire. Whereas the Chief of The Point is the unsung champion of Durban's sex workers, He-Who-Baths-with-Cleavage identifies women with their breasts—or, rather with their breasts as creators of a now-it's-there-now-it-isn't fetish effect for the male eye.[121] Analyzing this somewhat ironically, through thick-lensed psychoanalyst's spectacles, we sense a man who is attached, in phantasy, to the maternal breast and its substitutes—which he at once venerates, sometimes in the form of a fetish, and reproaches, for not yielding the Chief his "portion" (the word *isipheko* is culinary).

The Chief's turnabout with regard to foreign sex workers comes with an admonition to local ones faced with competition: "As I speak, the prostitutes of this country have never troubled themselves to learn the languages of other countries in order to facilitate communication with customers who speak foreign languages. When I tell the Babies that they should go into a stokvel for saving up money to find teachers who will teach them the languages of other countries, then they ignore me." (*Ngikhuluma nje omahosha bakuleli abakaze bazihluphe ngokufunda izilimi zakwamanye amazwe ukuze kube lula ukuxhumana namakhasimende akwitizayo. Ngathi uma ngithi amaNu awadlale isitokofela sokubeka imali yokuthola othisha abazowafundisa izilimi zakwamanye amazwe angishaya indiva.*)[122] As somebody learning Zulu himself, I found in this admonition a certain resonance. I could not help recalling a column from two years before, in which the Chief mocked the Fanagalo or broken Zulu spoken by some of the Babies, who, because they do not speak English, have trouble communicating with their white clients: "'Hello do you want me? Mina zokusondeza loduze kwalosifuba sami.' . . . 'Lomzimba wami shibhile sesipeshelini today, first come first served Baba.'" ("Hello do you want me? Me going to bring you up close to this my bosom." . . . "This body of mine cheap on special today, First come first served Baba.")[123] In 2008 Volos's ostensible target is the Babies' lack of ability in "the language of King George" (*ujoji*), and the *national origin* of the *amaNu* has not yet come into the foreground; yet his parody also suggests that, on the streets of The Point, in a city and region where African people are overwhelmingly native speakers of Zulu, foreign sex workers, who may speak neither a good Zulu nor a good English, may already have been plying their trade, and were, furthermore, also being recognized as members of the Chief's "people." Indeed, a survey of South African sex workers just before the 2010 World Cup found 30% to be of foreign origin.[124]

But what came closest to home was that the non-native speaker's discourse and inflection were being recognized at all. Typically, Volovolo's Zulu—although it spans multiple registers, from royal praises to township slang you won't find in a dictionary—is self-enclosed. It was the occasional deviation, in the form of a fractured Zulu—in a column I missed at the time, he parodies the Fanagalo of South African Indians[125]—that suddenly "interpellated" me, or allowed me to intercept a parodic interpellation and make it my own. Was I, a learner of Zulu, suddenly being hailed, not as an outsider to the Chiefdom, but as a potentially welcome newcomer? If so, did this not tally with my personal experience, which had included being graphically instructed by an exasperated trainee teacher at Sinethezekile on the difference in tongue placement between *dl* and *hl*, and hearing some time after the fact that my tone-deaf pronunciation of *ngiyabonga* (thank you) was a source of amusement in the staff room?

Two years later, in the Chiefdom of The Point, the boot is on the other foot. The xenophobia of May 2008, which has not stopped threatening to reignite, remains a painful memory. For some, no matter how much one distances oneself from the violent and bigoted mobs, the implication of self-identifying Zulus in the events must surely be a source of shame.[126] Even if it could be a gesture of acceptance, to make fun of the foreigner may not be good enough—as the portrayal of attitudes to "prawn" language in *District 9* brings home (despite being science fiction, Neill Blomkamp's 2009 film may be one of the most realistic South African films ever made). Now it is the local sex workers who ought to learn foreign languages; the satire, of course, is that this will increase the Chief's revenues just as it increases their business. But the use by Volovolo of the persona, and the distance it allows from implied author—in contrast, say, to a newspaper editorial—allows anti-xenophobia to emerge as the main issue precisely because the Chief's ostensible reasons for welcoming foreign sex workers are ridiculous. Even if his proclamation is entirely meretricious, he is, at least for the duration of the World Cup, Chief of the Babies of the entire world: "At the time of the matches of the World Cup, I am going to be chief of the Babies of the whole world, this Baby and that Baby will be judged by the portion that she brings to the chief."[127]

Read in the context of South African xenophobia circa 2008–2010, I would venture to say that this column represents a *play* at being usurped. The mimicry of the early column in which the Chief encourages the Babies to learn English harbors this play, in which locals are supposedly being usurped, as its secret, just as the abyss of mimicry and counter-mimicry in the two known versions of the "Fanagalo" song represents this play in its extreme form: who can possibly know who is usurping whom? If there is usurpation, then—of language, of rights and privileges, of a position of authority, anything really—it is usurpation *in play*. Although it can elucidate the phantasy-scene of usurpation that is part of the psychopolitics of language that I am investigating, there is a way in which, because of its possibility of instant reversal *pour rire*, it is not in itself reducible to that psychopolitics—or not entirely.

The Chief's Induna

In September 2010 I send a draft of "The Chief of The Point" to Volovolo Memela via the editor of *Isolezwe*. I receive no reply until, on Wednesday, February 2, 2011, a column appears in the newspaper entitled "Inkosi yasePhoyinti isinenduna ezinze eNew York, kwelaseMelika." (The Chief of The Point now has an induna who is settled in New York, in America.)[128] As a response, it goes beyond what I could ever have imagined. Before moving on to express his concern for a ninety-two-year-old Nelson Mandela, who is in hospital and has him and the rest of the country anxiously on edge, Volovolo expresses his pride at the fact that his column has been the subject of scholarly analysis, and thanks all of those at *Isolezwe* who have supported and encouraged his writing over the years: "It can be I am making a mistake if I do not thank the one who was then editor of *Isolezwe*, Mr. Philani Mgwaba, who was the one who gave me the opportunity to show myself during the past six years. The sun can set if I can count all of the people who have supported me since I began to write this column, people like the one who became editor, Thulani Mbatha, let me never forget them. How can I forget Zanele Msibi, Skhumbuzo Miya, Eric Ndiyane, Lindani Buthelezi, Mazwi Xaba, and Qaps Mngadi, who encouraged me in different ways?" By implication, I can thank all of these people too.

But what blows me off my feet is what comes next. Giving me a special praise name, the Chief of The Point anoints me his induna in New York: "Just as Volos has now entered New York, it says for itself that a seat of the chiefship of The Point is now in America, and the person who is standing against that chiefship, it will be necessary for him to write there and explain why he is fighting against it. I wish to announce officially that Professor Mark Sanders (He Who Sleeps Wearing Sunglasses), I now anoint him officially as induna of The Point who is settled in New York. His Sanders has not been voted in, it is the Chief of The Point who has given him the nod, therefore people must not ask what methods were followed at the time he was being selected." (*Njengoba uVolos esengene e-New York kuyazisho ukuthi ikomkhulu lobukhosi basePhoyinti seliseMelika, umuntu omelene nalobukhosi kuzofanele abhalele khona achaze ukuthi kungani elwisana nabo. Ngifisa ukumemezela ngokusemthethweni ukuthi uSolwazi uMark Sanders [Umalala efake izibuko zelanga] sengiyamgcoba ngokusemthethweni njengenduna yasePhoyinti ezinze e-New York. OkaSanders akavotelwangwa, yiNkosi yasePhoyinti emkhombe ngentshebe ngakho akufanele abantu babuze ukuthi kulandelwe ziphi izindlela ngesikhathi eqokwa.*) Having presented myself as one who is *learning* Zulu—as evidenced by the less-than-perfect Zulu of my e-mail to the editor—I am being embraced, and not derided as Ina Cronjé was by O.E.H.M. Nxumalo. The gratitude I experience is immeasurable. When I write thus, I sense the truth of what Melanie Klein writes: when envy is alleviated, gratitude is possible. But for envy to be alleviated, paranoid fear of punishment must first be lessened. Klein's emphasis is on inner processes. Yet who would doubt that what a teacher says and does can resonate with what goes on inside? There is that transference. When one learns a language, every speaker of that language is a teacher, and so is every writer. It matters a great deal what their attitude is to the one learning their language. Does he want you to learn it? Might she be ambivalent about your gaining anything approaching advanced knowledge in it? Call this the counter-transference if you will. In other contexts it shares its conditions of possibility with xenophobia and its shibboleths.

Volovolo's response is particularly apt in that it addresses the style of my analysis while also taking up my observation that praise names are in themselves irreducibly equivocal. Although it may also allude to my having noted De Wet Nel's having been addressed as Zanelanga, I believe that the *isibongo* I have been given by Volos—Umalala efake izibuko zelanga (The One Who Sleeps Wearing Sunglasses)—refers to my having donned my "thick-lensed psychoanalyst's spectacles," which, although powerfully magnifying things latent, may also ward off the enlightenment represented by the sun, or simply lead one to mistake what is plainly visible to others in the clear light of day. It seems to be saying: What you write is all very well, but why complicate things so? Such a question would be a healthy check on academic habits of analysis. It would also be a reminder of how infrequently scholarly modes of discourse allow for a change of tone, or for a rhetoric that salutes the achievements that have earned somebody a name without, however, sparing that person's shortcomings.

I reply, again via the editor, thanking Volovolo for anointing me his induna, and for the *isibongo* that he has given me. Then I begin to reflect. Since being an *induna* means being subordinate to the superior authority of a king or chief, and I have lent the Chief my word, I am knowingly entering into a complicity. Volos and I will not, however, always see eye to eye; in a column published shortly after Jacob Zuma's acquittal in his trial for rape, he implies that Zuma, like other prominent men, was falsely accused by a woman after money,[129] whereas I am less than confident that I know the facts of the matter, and thus wary of remaining silent while a chorus of men and women condemn the complainant.

Is it possible, in the end, to know for certain in what it is that I am complicit when I lend the Chief my word? Of course, there is the play of mother-substitutes, in which I would readily declare myself as being as deeply implicated, having undertaken to learn Zulu as somebody whom history gives that project only under the sign of *envy*—mine, to be sure, but not only. This is what makes for reparation, and the plea—to the father and to the mother—*ngicela uxolo*.

But what is more important, and what renders everything unknowable as well as unverifiable, is that my exchange with Volos is in the realm of fiction and of the figural. It is to a series of personae—the Chief of the People of The Point in particular—that I respond, in a persona of my own: the one who wears spectacles. And, never having made contact with me in private correspondence, it is in persona that he has responded to me. If I am the Chief's induna in New York, it is only because there is a Chief of The Point. If I have lent him my word, then he has lent me his as well. It is nothing, this exchange, and it is also everything.

Acknowledgments

First and foremost, my gratitude goes to Eckson Khambule, whose gifts as a teacher are second to none. Combining a love of language with an ability to make his students laugh, he opened the door for me to learn Zulu in a way that had eluded me for a long time. Although I was not thinking of writing a book when we began our lessons, *Learning Zulu* would never have come about without Eckson's skill, dedication, care, and confidence in me as his student.

Eve Mothibe at the University of the Witwatersrand helped me to deepen my knowledge of the language, and of the stakes for me of learning it. My three weeks at Sinethezekile Combined School in Jozini, KwaZulu-Natal, were nothing short of transformative. I can never thank enough Mr. N. H. Mkhwanazi, principal of the school, for requesting that teachers at the school speak to me only in Zulu, or Mr. Nzuza, for inviting me to attend his Grade 12 Zulu class. I am grateful also to Mr. Mkhwanazi and MaGumede for generously opening their home to me during my stay at Jozini. Their neighbor, Mr. Thembeka Ndlovu, principal of the nearby Mavela High School, was a constant friendly presence; toward the end of my stay, he gave me the honor of addressing the school's Grade-12 Usuku Lokukhuthaza (Motivational Day), an experience as moving as it was enlightening, and which I will always remember. The teachers at Sinethezekile graciously followed Mr. Mkhwanazi's request, helping me with my Zulu, some of them offering me companionship along with conversation. I hope that I have not forgotten anybody when I thank S'fiso Dlamini, Mnelisi Ntombela, Sakhile Mpontshane, Fani Ntombela, Musa Mthembu, and Sibusiso Nkosi, as well as Mr. Mthethwa, who let me guest-teach his Grade 11 English class.

I subsequently had the privilege of being awarded a fellowship to take part in a Fulbright-Hays Group Projects Abroad (GPA) for study of Zulu in and around Pietermaritzburg, KwaZulu-Natal. This excellent program helped me to build on the work I had already done, through two months of classroom study and language immersion. I thank Audrey Mbeje and her fellow teachers, Nelson Ntshangase and Thabile Mbatha, as well as the Khanyile family of Imbali and the Mngadi family of Amaqongqo for hosting me during this time.

Many people have been interlocutors, in different ways, in the course of writing *Learning Zulu*, and in the time leading up to it. In this regard, I thank David Attwell, David Brown, Mbongiseni Buthelezi, Carli Coetzee, Lucy Graham, Liz Gunner, Antjie Krog, Peter McDonald, Joe Napolitano, Vanessa Place, Michael

Rothberg, Meg Samuelson, Jonny Steinberg, Liz Thornberry, and Corina van der Spoel. Patricia Ngxiya patiently conversed with me in Zulu and shared with me her memories of learning Zulu as a newcomer to Johannesburg.

Lily Saint, Andrew van der Vlies, Stephen Clingman, and Loren Kruger read early versions of the entire manuscript. Their candid comments have contributed a great deal to making *Learning Zulu* a better book, as have those of the anonymous reviewer for Wits University Press. Mbongiseni Buthelezi and Eckson Khambule took the time to answer my translation queries, although, because I have not always followed their suggestions, final responsibility for any mistranslations rests with me. Rajend Mesthrie kindly checked my translations from Fanagalo and Chilapalapa.

For assisting me with my archival research, special thanks go to Najwa Hendrickse at the South African Library in Cape Town, and to Sandra Naidoo at the Bessie Head Library in Pietermaritzburg, as well as to Peter Michel at the University of Nevada, Las Vegas Libraries, Special Collections.

A sabbatical leave from New York University in 2007/2008 made it possible for me to take the time required to embark on intensive language study. In 2008, I was hosted by the Wits Institute for Social and Economic Research (WISER), which provided a stimulating academic environment, for which I thank Deborah Posel, then-director of WISER. An American Council of Learned Societies ACLS / SSRC / NEH International and Area Studies Fellowship gave me time in 2010/2011 to write the first draft of my book.

For so much that cannot be put into words, my most profound thanks go, as always, to Louise Kuhn.

Notes

Introduction

1. Nkosinathi I. Ngwane, *Ngicela uxolo*, 2nd ed. (Pietermaritzburg, South Africa: New Dawn Publishers, 2006).
2. Melanie Klein, "Love, Guilt and Reparation," 1937, in *Love, Guilt and Reparation, and Other Works, 1921–1945* (London: Hogarth Press, 1975), 306–43.
3. Klein, "Early Analysis," 1923, in *Love, Guilt and Reparation*, 100–1. Klein, who draws details from her case histories, also cites Sabina Spielrein, "Die Entstehung der kindlichen Worte Papa und Mama: Einige Betrachtungen über verschiedene Stadien in der Sprachentwicklung" [The origin of the childlike words Papa and Mama: Some observations about different stages in speech development], *Imago* 8 (1922): 345–67.
4. Klein, "Mourning and Its Relation to Manic-Depressive States," 1940, in *Love, Guilt and Reparation*, 350–52; Hanna Segal, *Introduction to the Work of Melanie Klein* (New York: Basic Books, 1964), 95–96.
5. D.B.Z. Ntuli, *Ngicela uxolo*, in *Woza nendlebe* [Lend me your ears] (Pietermaritzburg, South Africa: Shuter & Shooter, 1988), 41–52.
6. Ngwane, "Isethulo" [Author's note], *Ngicela uxolo*, n.p.
7. Ngwane, *Ngicela uxolo*, 1.
8. Ngwane, *Ngicela uxolo*, 119.
9. KwaZulu-Natal Department of Education, Republic of South Africa, IsiZulu Ulimi lwasekhaya [Zulu—Home language] (HL), Iphepha lokuqala [First paper] (P2), Novemba [November] 2008, www.ecdoe.gov.za/files/exams/110209151302Q.pdf.
10. Ngwane, *Ngicela uxolo*, 70–72.
11. Ngwane, *Ngicela uxolo*, 70.
12. Ngwane, *Ngicela uxolo*, 119. See John 8:7.
13. Ngwane, *Ngicela uxolo*, 117.
14. Jacques Derrida, "Force of Law: The 'Mystical Foundation of Authority,'" trans. Mary Quaintance. *Cardozo Law Review* 11.5/6 (1990): 997.
15. *Census 2011: Census in Brief* (Pretoria: Statistics South Africa, 2012), 23, http://www.statssa.gov.za/census2011/Products/Census_2011_Census_in_brief.pdf.
16. This point is emphasized by Pumla Dineo Gqola, "Brutal Inheritances: Echoes, Negrophobia and Masculinist Violence," in *Go Home or Die Here: Violence, Xenophobia and the Reinvention of Difference in South Africa*, ed. Shireen Hassim, Tawana Kupe, and Eric Worby (Johannesburg: Wits University Press, 2008), 214–15.
17. For a synopsis of African American imaginings of Zulus, see Robert Vinson and Robert Edgar, "Zulus, African Americans and the African Diaspora," in *Zulu Identi-*

ties: Being Zulu, Past and Present, ed. Benedict Carton, John Laband, and Jabulani Sithole (Pietermaritzburg, South Africa: University of KwaZulu-Natal Press, 2008), 240–42. An invaluable collection of critical scholarship on various aspects of Zulu identity and its historical genealogies, *Zulu Identities* is a work that I shall cite frequently in what follows.

18. See Patrick Harries, "Imagery, Symbolism and Tradition in a South African Bantustan: Mangosuthu Buthelezi, Inkatha, and Zulu History," *History and Theory* 32.4 (1993): 110; John Wright, "Reflections on the Politics of Being 'Zulu,'" in *Zulu Identities*, ed. Carton et al., 39; Michael R. Mahoney, *The Other Zulus: The Spread of Zulu Ethnicity in Colonial South Africa* (Durham, NC: Duke University Press, 2012), 117–49.

19. See Gerhard Maré and Georgina Hamilton, *An Appetite for Power: Buthelezi's Inkatha and South Africa* (Johannesburg: Ravan Press / Bloomington: Indiana University Press, 1987), 218–20; Thembisa Waetjen and Gerhard Maré, "Shaka's Aeroplane: The Take-Off and Landing of Inkatha, Modern Zulu Nationalism and Royal Politics," in *Zulu Identities*, ed. Carton et al., 355.

20. There are similarities between *isiZulu*, in this sense, and *Setswana* (Tswana ways), which, in relation to *Sekgoa* (European ways), "came to be constructed, in opposition to one another, as distinct, objectified cultures"; Jean Comaroff and John Comaroff, *Of Revelation and Revolution: Christianity, Colonialism, and Consciousness in South Africa*, vol. 1 (Chicago: University of Chicago Press, 1991), 194.

21. A sense is given by Jacob Dlamini, *Native Nostalgia* (Auckland Park, South Africa: Jacana, 2009), 135–50. Further complexities and contradictions are explored by Rustum Kozain in "Moedertang," *LitNet Seminar Room*, October 19, 2005, http://www.oulitnet.co.za/seminarroom/kozain_moedertang.asp.

22. Chinua Achebe, "The African Writer and the English Language," in *Morning Yet on Creation Day* (Garden City, NY: Anchor, 1976), 74–84; Ngũgĩ wa Thiong'o, "The Language of African Literature," in *Decolonising the Mind: The Politics of Language in African Literature* (London: James Currey, 1986), 4–33. The locus classicus of language acquisition and racial alienation remains Frantz Fanon, *Black Skin, White Masks*, trans. Charles Lam Markmann (London: Pluto, 1986), 17–40. Arguments are developed in a South African context along related lines by Njabulo Ndebele, "The English Language and Social Change in South Africa," *South African Literature and Culture: Rediscovery of the Ordinary* (Manchester: Manchester University Press, 1994), 98–116. For a useful recent commentary on Ndebele, see Carli Coetzee, *Accented Futures: Language Activism and the Ending of Apartheid* (Johannesburg: Wits University Press, 2013), 45–60.

23. An important exception is Johannes Fabian, *Language and Colonial Power: The Appropriation of Swahili in the Former Belgian Congo, 1880–1938* (Cambridge, UK: Cambridge University Press, 1986). See also Diana Jeater, "Speaking like a Native: Vernacular Languages and the State in Southern Rhodesia, 1890–1935," *Journal of African History* 42.3 (2001): 449–68.

24. The census cited above tells us that about 16,700 Indians, and about 16,500 whites, spoke Zulu as their first language. Also counted, out of a total population of nearly 52 million people, were nearly 24,000 coloured first-language speakers of Zulu. *Census 2011: Census in Brief*, 26.

25. *Miners' Companion in Zulu: For the Use of Miners on the Witwatersrand Gold Mines*:

Issued by the Prevention of Accidents Committee of the Rand Mutual Assurance Co., Ltd. (Johannesburg: Argus, 1920), 2.

26. See Carolyn Hamilton and John Wright, "The Making of the AmaLala: Ethnicity, Ideology and Relations of Subordination in a Precolonial Context," *South African Historical Journal* 22.1 (1990): 19; John Wright, "A. T. Bryant and the 'Lala,'" *Journal of Southern African Studies* 38.2 (2012): 362.
27. Procopius, *Secret History*, trans. Richard Atwater, 1927 (Ann Arbor: University of Michigan Press, 1961), 3.
28. On the *Daily Sun*, see Anton Harber, "Two Newspapers, Two Nations? The Media and the Xenophobic Violence," in *Go Home or Die Here*, ed. Hassim et al., 161–69.
29. O.E.H.M. Nxumalo, "Izinselelo zesiZulu esiyingcwengwa [sic]" [Challenges of refined Zulu], *Ilanga*, April 14–16, 2008: 5; "Izinselelo zesiZulu esiyingcwenga (Isigaba sesibili)" [Challenges of refined Zulu (Part two)], *Ilanga*, April 28–30, 2008: 5; "Izinselelo zesiZulu esiyingcwenga (Isiqephu sesithathu)" [Challenges of refined Zulu (Part three)], *Ilanga*, May 5–7, 2008: 5.
30. See, for example, Philip Bonner and Noor Nieftagodien, *Alexandra: A History* (Johannesburg: Wits University Press, 2008), 418–19.
31. Judges 12:6.
32. Jacques Derrida, *Monolingualism of the Other; or, The Prosthesis of Origin*, trans. Patrick Mensah (Stanford, CA: Stanford University Press, 1998), 24.

CHAPTER 1: LEARN MORE ZULU

1. Harriette Emily Colenso, preface to J. W. Colenso, *Zulu-English Dictionary*, 4th ed. (n.p., Natal: Vause & Slatter, 1905), vi–vii. Rajend Mesthrie speculates that the word "cadan" might derive from "cha" ("no" in Zulu) and "don't" (personal communication).
2. Jeff Guy, *The Heretic: A Study of the Life of John William Colenso, 1814–1883* (Johannesburg: Ravan Press / Pietermaritzburg, South Africa: University of Natal Press, 1983), 64, 80.
3. Along with the name, "*Sokululeka*, 'Father of raising-up,'" it was, Colenso writes, a name "entirely of their own invention, and constructed out of the notions which they have formed of the Bishop's duties from what they have been told of them." J. W. Colenso, *Church Missions: To the Members of the Church of England, The Earnest Appeal of the Bishop of Natal on Behalf of the Heathen Tribes within and on the Borders of the Diocese* [1854], in Colenso, *Bringing Forth Light: Five Tracts on Bishop Colenso's Zulu Mission*, ed. Ruth Edgecombe (Pietermaritzburg, South Africa: University of Natal Press / Durban: Killie Campbell Africana Library, 1982), 6.
4. Jeff Guy, *The Heretic*, 95–190. For a more detailed discussion of the role of Ngidi, see Guy, "Class, Imperialism and Literary Criticism: William Ngidi, John Colenso and Matthew Arnold," *Journal of Southern African Studies* 23. 2 (1997): 219–41.
5. Guy, *The Heretic*, 105. In 1856 Cetshwayo's brother, Mkhungo, a rival for the succession of their father Mpande, had been given refuge by Colenso. Guy, *The Heretic*, 64.
6. See David Welsh, *The Roots of Segregation: Native Policy in Natal, 1845–1910* (Cape Town: Oxford University Press, 1971). The received view is complicated by Jeff Guy, in *Theophilus Shepstone and the Forging of Natal: African Autonomy and Settler Co-*

lonialism in the Making of Traditional Authority (Pietermaritzburg, South Africa: University of KwaZulu-Natal Press, 2013).
7. John William Colenso, *Ten Weeks in Natal: A Journal of a First Tour of Visitation among the Colonists and Zulu Kafirs of Natal* (Cambridge, UK: Macmillan, 1855), 145–51.
8. Guy, "Class, Imperialism and Literary Criticism," 225.
9. Colenso, *Ten Weeks in Natal*, 146. For further details on Shepstone's early life, see Guy, *Theophilus Shepstone*, 57–60.
10. *Report of the Expedition Sent by the Government of Natal to Instal Cetywayo as King of the Zulus, in Succession to His Deceased Father, Panda* (London: William Clowes & Sons, 1875), reprinted in *Accounts and Papers of the House of Commons: 1875* (London: British House of Commons, 1875), vol. 12 [1137], 21–22. For a fascinating exploration of Shepstone's role in Cetshwayo's installation, see Carolyn Hamilton, *Terrific Majesty: The Powers of Shaka Zulu and the Limits of Historical Invention* (Cambridge, MA: Harvard University Press, 1998), 72–85.
11. In using the word "tribe," I reproduce the official discourse of the period. A large body of critical scholarship has challenged the use of this term to describe South African polities of different kinds.
12. Guy, *The Heretic*, 212; Hlonipha Mokoena, *Magema Fuze: The Making of a Kholwa Intellectual* (Pietermaritzburg, South Africa: University of KwaZulu-Natal Press, 2011), 109–15; Guy, *Theophilus Shepstone*, 405–13. The principal source document for these commentators is J. W. Colenso, *Langalibalele and the amaHlubi Tribe: Being Remarks upon the Official Record of the Trials of the Chief, His Sons and Induna, and Other Members of the amaHlubi Tribe* (London: William Clowes & Sons, 1875), reprinted in *Accounts and Papers of the House of Commons: 1875* (London: British House of Commons, 1875), vol. 12 [1141].
13. Guy, *The Heretic*; *The View across the River: Harriette Colenso and the Zulu Struggle against Imperialism* (Cape Town: David Philip, 2001); "The Colenso Daughters: Three Women Confront Imperialism," in *The Eye of the Storm: Bishop John William Colenso and the Crisis of Biblical Inspiration*, ed. Jonathan Draper (New York: T & T Clark International, 2003), 345–63; Shula Marks, "Harriette Colenso and the Zulus, 1874–1913," *Journal of African History* 4.3 (1963): 403–11; Vukile Khumalo, "The Class of 1856 and the Politics of Cultural Production(s) in the Emergence of Ekukhanyeni, 1855–1910," in *The Eye of the Storm*, ed. Draper, 207–41; Mokoena, *Magema Fuze*.
14. Colenso, *Ten Weeks in Natal*, 236. Commenting on this passage, Rachael Gilmour compares and contrasts the role of language study in the respective missionary endeavors of Grout and Colenso; Rachael Gilmour, *Grammars of Colonialism: Representing Languages in Colonial South Africa* (Basingstoke, UK: Palgrave Macmillan, 2006), 142–43.
15. J. W. Colenso, *First Steps of the Zulu Mission (Oct. 1859)*, 1860, in Colenso, *Bringing Forth Light*, 50.
16. Colenso, *First Steps of the Zulu Mission*, 54–55.
17. Guy, "Class, Imperialism, and Literary Criticism," 224, quoting J. W. Colenso, "William, the Kafir Teacher," *The Mission Field* 2 (1857): 151.
18. Guy, "Class, Imperialism, and Literary Criticism," 224, note 6; Khumalo, "Class of 1856," 239.

19. J. W. Colenso, preface to *Zulu-English Dictionary*, 2nd ed., viii. See also J. W. Colenso, *First Steps in Zulu: Being an Elementary Grammar of the Zulu Language*, 5th ed. (Pietermaritzburg and Durban, South Africa: P. Davis & Sons, 1904), 1–4.
20. Hlonipha Mokoena points to the influence of Colenso's standardization by quoting an 1893 letter by Magema Fuze to the editor of the newspaper *Inkanyiso*: "For one who doesn't want to be troubled, one who would like to read the book that is our proper [correct] language, must take Sobantu's [Colenso's] book and that will lead him/her on the correct path which s/he desires, if s/he wishes to abandon the Lala dialect, Mpondo language, Bhaca dialect and the Xhosa language, and Zunglish [*isiZulu-mLungu*]." Mokoena, *Magema Fuze*, 225, first two interpolations by Mokoena. Mokoena thinks it likely that the book to which Fuze refers is Colenso's *Zulu-English Dictionary* (1861). Having been J. W. Colenso's convert and printer, and Harriette Colenso's aide and intermediary with the Usuthu, Fuze—who is best known for his book *Abantu abamnyama lapa bavela ngakona* (The Black People and Whence They Came) (1922)—was a key figure in early Zulu letters. Noting J. W. Colenso's distinctions between dialects, John Wright observes that "certain colonial lexicographers and dictionary compilers of the late nineteenth and early twentieth century . . . were driven, in a way that their predecessors were not, by something of an obsession with delineating and preserving what they saw as a 'pure' form of the isiZulu language." John Wright, "A. T. Bryant and the 'Lala,'" *Journal of Southern African Studies* 38. 2 (2012): 359.
21. Khumalo, "Class of 1856," 238–41. Like the converts whom Khumalo calls the "Class of 1856," alluding to the year in which the first pupils entered the school at Ekukhanyeni, Harriette Colenso advocated her father's system. She spoke in its favor at the second of two Zulu orthography conferences, held by the Natal Missionary Conference in 1905 and 1906, in Durban and Pietermaritzburg. J. Stuart, ed., *Zulu Orthography: Being Some Account of the Proceedings of the Zulu Orthography Conference Held in Pietermaritzburg in 1906, Especially in Regard to Speeches Delivered, Rules Submitted, Etc., to Which Is Added the Set of Rules Recently Passed (March, 1907) by the Zulu Orthography Committee* (Durban, South Africa, 1907), 24, 38. The question debated at the 1906 conference was "whether Zulu should be written in a 'conjunctive' or 'disjunctive' manner." Following that of Wilhelm Bleek, Colenso's system was "conjunctive." Although the latter is the basis of the Zulu orthography in use today, the rules decided upon in 1906 were a compromise with "disjunctive" orthography, as was set out in Rule 1 of the Zulu Orthography Committee: "The different Parts of Speech shall be written separately, except as modified by these Rules. E.g.:—Ilanga li ya kanya; isinkwa ngi ya si tanda; umuti u baba kakulu; abantu ba mpofu; ba kona abantu; izwi li ka Mpande." Stuart, ed. *Zulu Orthography*, 33. In the conjunctive orthography, these phrases would have been written *ilanga liyakanya* (the sun is shining), *isinkwa ngiyasitanda* (I am liking the bread), and so forth. At one level, the debate was between rival missionary societies, represented by followers of Colenso versus followers of Grout. Stuart, ed. *Zulu Orthography*, 16, 23. Much of the substantive debate revolved around which orthography best represented how the language was spoken. Advocates of the disjunctive system also argued that it would make it easier to learn Zulu by making reading easier. The moral and political stakes were clear when the arguments of the "disjunctivists" were countered by those, such as the Reverend Sebastian Msimang, who foresaw damage being done to the language:

"They (the Natives) were jealous on account of their language, and hoped it would not be mutilated in any way merely for the sake of learners." Archdeacon Roach seconded the Reverend Msimang, and other Zulu delegates, when he declared: "We are accused of spoiling this country, and destroying some of [the Natives'] good old customs; let us not also be charged with mutilating their language." The Reverend Abner Mtimkulu takes a stand that is more definitely purist: "The Zulu language is the language of a particular people, with its history, connections, and ties; its peculiar characteristics should be preserved untainted and uncontaminated." Stuart, ed. *Zulu Orthography*, 10, 13, 27. J. L. Dube, editor of *Ilanga lase Natal*, also addressed the conference, which was attended by King Dinuzulu, who had for some time been interested in questions of orthography. Guy, *View across the River*, 435; Harriette Colenso, preface, v. At a third conference, held in Durban in 1907, debate was reopened on Rule 1, and, after two days of discussion, a "conjunctivist" amendment proposed by Archdeacon Roach that "[p]ronomial particles used in the formation of all tenses, moods, and voices, positive and negative, shall be written together with the verb root or adjective as one word," was narrowly outvoted. *Report of Proceedings of Zulu Orthography Conference Held at Durban, Natal, South Africa, May 29, 30, 31, 1907* (Pietermaritzburg, South Africa: P. Davis & Sons, [1911]), 20–74. The frequent initiatives undertaken subsequently by the South African government and its advisory bodies to reform Zulu orthography lie beyond the scope of this book.
22. Rachael Gilmour, "'A Nice Derangement of Epitaphs': Missionary Language-Learning in Mid-Nineteenth Century Natal," *Journal of Southern African Studies* 33.3 (2007): 531.
23. A comparable pattern is observed by Patrick Harries, who traces the historical roots of Tsonga / Shangaan ethnicity to the linguistic classifications of French and Swiss missionaries, and their standardization of a Tsonga language and orthography. Patrick Harries, "The Roots of Ethnicity: Discourse and the Politics of Language Construction in South-East Africa," *African Affairs* 87/347 (1988): 25–52. Harries briefly introduces a similar analysis in his account of the formation of elite Zulu ethnic identity. Harries, "Imagery, Symbolism and Tradition in a South African Bantustan," 109–12.
24. Khumalo, "Class of 1856," 241.
25. Commenting on a plan by Theophilus Shepstone to return King Cetshwayo to Zululand from exile in 1881, Harriette Colenso expressed her mistrust: "'any scheme involving the Shepstones . . . *means virtual annexation* . . .'; 'they are dreadfully cunning, and will play false somehow, and it makes my heart sick to see them at work.'" Guy, *Theophilus Shepstone*, 511. At the time, John Shepstone, brother of Theophilus, as well as two of the latter's sons were also involved in native administration. Guy, *Theophilus Shepstone*, 508.
26. Marks, "Harriette Colenso and the Zulus," 404, quoting a letter from Sarah Frances Colenso to Mrs. Lyell, June 1883, in *Colenso Letters from Natal*, ed. Wyn Rees (Pietermaritzburg, South Africa: Shuter & Shooter, 1958), 374.
27. Guy, "The Colenso Daughters," 347.
28. Referring to the dictionary, Harriette Colenso writes, addressing a subsection of its readership—namely, colonial magistrates whose job it was to adjudicate cases under African customary law: "Above all it is aimed against the exaction of bricks without straw for which we are responsible as a community, so long as we require that justice

shall be administered in our name and on our behalf, without providing those—often new-comers—to whom we commit the task, with at least the means of understanding one another and those over whom they are placed." Preface, vi. The allusion is to Exodus 5: 6–19. On language learning by administrators in a comparable context, see Jeater, "Speaking like a Native."

29. J. W. Colenso, *Zulu-English Dictionary*, 723. Most of the *isiPiki* words are of Dutch and English provenance.
30. Knowledge of Zulu had provided missionaries with the "means to assert superiority over other whites." Gilmour, "'A Nice Derangement of Epitaphs,'" 537.
31. Procopius, *Secret History*, 3.
32. Colenso, *Church Missions*, 1–2. Also see Colenso, *Ten Weeks in Natal*, 16.
33. See Harries, "Imagery, Symbolism and Tradition in a South African Bantustan," 110; Wright, "Reflections on the Politics of Being 'Zulu,'" 39; Mahoney, *The Other Zulus*, 117–49.
34. John Wright, "Turbulent Times: Political Transformations in the North and East, 1760s–1830s," in *The Cambridge History of South Africa*, ed. Carolyn Hamilton, Bernard K. Mbenga, and Robert Ross, vol. 1, *From Early Times to 1885* (Cambridge, UK: Cambridge University Press, 2010), 211–52; "Rediscovering the Ndwandwe Kingdom," in *500 Years Rediscovered: Southern African Precedents and Prospects*, ed. Natalie Swanepoel, Amanda Esterhuysen, and Philip Bonner (Johannesburg: Wits University Press, 2008), 217–38; "Revisiting the Stereotype of Shaka's 'Devastations,'" in *Zulu Identities*, ed. Carton et al., 69–81; "Political Transformations in the Thukela-Mzimkhulu Region in the Late Eighteenth and Early Nineteenth Centuries," in *The Mfecane Aftermath: Reconstructive Debates in Southern African History*, ed. Carolyn Hamilton (Johannesburg: Witwatersrand University Press / Pietermaritzburg, South Africa: University of Natal Press, 1995), 163–81; "A. T. Bryant and 'The Wars of Shaka,'" *History in Africa* 18 (1991): 409–25; "Political Mythology and the Making of Natal's Mfecane," *Canadian Journal of African Studies* 23.2 (1989): 272–91; John Wright and Carolyn Hamilton, "Traditions and Transformations: The Phongolo-Mzimkhulu Region in the Late Eighteenth and Early Nineteenth Centuries," in *Natal and Zululand: From Earliest Times to 1910*, ed. Andrew Duminy and Bill Guest (Pietermaritzburg, South Africa: University of Natal Press / Shuter & Shooter, 1989), 49–82. One of the key archival sources for the historical revision undertaken by Wright and Hamilton is the James Stuart archive, a unique collection of oral histories by African as well as European informants taken down over twenty years by a Natal magistrate and amateur scholar; on Stuart and his informants, see Hamilton, *Terrific Majesty*, 130–67. Selections have been published as *The James Stuart Archive of Recorded Oral Evidence Relating to the History of the Zulu and Neighbouring Peoples*, ed. John B. Wright and Colin de B. Webb (Pietermaritzburg, South Africa: University of Natal Press, 1976–), now into a sixth volume. For critical reflections on the legacy of Shaka, also see Mbongiseni Buthelezi, "The Empire Talks Back: Re-Examining the Legacies of Shaka and Zulu Power in Post-Apartheid South Africa," in *Zulu Identities*, ed. Carton et al., 23–34.
35. Wright, "A. T. Bryant and the 'Lala,'" 355–68; Hamilton and Wright, "The Making of the AmaLala," 3–23.
36. For a useful synopsis, see John Laband, "The Rise and Fall of the Zulu Kingdom," in *Zulu Identities*, ed. Carton et al., 87–96.

37. Laband, "Rise and Fall of the Zulu Kingdom," 90–91.
38. For William Ngidi, however, *ngapetsheya* was England. Guy, "Imperialism and Literary Criticism," 226, quoting J. W. Colenso, *Three Native Accounts of the Visit of the Bishop of Natal in September and October, 1859, to Umpande, King of the Zulus: With Explanatory Notes and a Literal Translation and a Glossary of All the Zulu Words Employed in the Same: Designed for the Use of Students of the Zulu Language*, 3rd ed. (Pietermaritzburg, South Africa: Vause & Slatter, 1901), 147. The Zulu is in the same volume, 34–35. Here, as throughout, with the exception of Nyembezi's *Mntanami! Mntanami!*, I reproduce the orthography used in the text I am quoting.
39. Colenso, *First Steps of the Zulu Mission*, 124. In mid-nineteenth-century colonial parlance, a distinction was made between "Frontier Kafirs" or "Cape Kafirs," and "Natal Kafirs," respectively the African inhabitants of the Cape Frontier and Natal. For a penetrating discussion of how the word *ikhafula* was used, see Mokoena, *Magema Fuze*, 218–22.
40. *Report of the Natal Native Commission, 1881–82* (Pietermaritzburg, South Africa: Vause, Slatter & Co., 1882), 32–48.
41. See, for instance, Colenso, *Langalibalele and the amaHlubi Tribe*, 50.
42. See Jeff Guy, *The Destruction of the Zulu Kingdom: The Civil War in Zululand, 1879–1884* (London: Longman, 1979).
43. For a detailed account of these events, see Guy, *The View across the River*, 185–238.
44. Guy, *The View across the River*, 309.
45. Shula Marks, *The Ambiguities of Dependence in South Africa: Class, Nationalism, and the State in Twentieth-Century Natal* (Baltimore: Johns Hopkins University Press, 1986), 15.
46. "Ties of culture, language, and kinship (through both marriage and birth) had always linked Natal Africans with Zulus. What was lacking was Natal Africans' self-identification as Zulus; instead there was active rejection. This changed after 1898." Mahoney, *The Other Zulus*, 158.
47. Mahoney, *The Other Zulus*, 182–216.
48. The definitive account remains Shula Marks, *Reluctant Rebellion: The 1906–1908 Disturbances in Natal* (Oxford: Clarendon Press, 1970).
49. Guy, *The View across the River*, 436.
50. Marks, *Ambiguities of Dependence*, 28–30; Guy, *The View across the River*, 446.
51. On Solomon kaDinuzulu, see Marks, *Ambiguities of Dependence*, 15–41.
52. Marks, *Ambiguities of Dependence*, 69–71; Hamilton, *Terrific Majesty*, 169–70.
53. See Mahoney, *The Other Zulus*, 218–21.
54. On the Industrial and Commercial Workers' Union (ICU), see Marks, *Ambiguities of Dependence*, 72–109.
55. Mzala, *Gatsha Buthelezi: Chief with a Double Agenda* (London: Zed Books, 1988), 61–62. See also Jabulani Sithole, "Chief Albert Luthuli and Bantustan Politics," in *Zulu Identities*, ed. Carton et al., 331–40.
56. Mzala, *Gatsha Buthelezi*, 78.
57. Ibid., 85.
58. Ibid., 116–38. For further details on the revival of Inkatha, see Maré and Hamilton, *An Appetite for Power*, 45–60.
59. See *Truth and Reconciliation Commission of South Africa Report* (Cape Town: Truth and Reconciliation Commission, 1998), vol. 2, 584–85; vol. 3, 249, 672.

60. This has included the intimidation of non-Zulu traditional leadership claimants within KwaZulu-Natal. Jabulani Sithole, "Preface: Zuluness in South Africa: From 'Struggle' Debate to Democratic Transformation," in *Zulu Identities*, ed. Carton et al., xv–xvi.
61. Rajend Mesthrie, "The Origins of Fanagalo," *Journal of Pidgin and Creole Languages* 4.2 (1989): 211–40.
62. Basil Davidson, *Africa in History: Themes and Outlines*, rev. ed. (New York: Touchstone, 1995), 20–21. For a critical account of this historiography and its nineteenth-century precursors, see Saul Dubow, *Scientific Racism in Modern South Africa* (Cambridge, UK: Cambridge University Press, 1995), 78–82, 110–11. For a genealogical interrogation of the term "Nguni," see John Wright, "Politics, Ideology, and the Invention of the 'Nguni,'" in *Resistance and Ideology in Settler Societies*, ed. Tom Lodge (Johannesburg: Ravan Press, 1986), 96–118.
63. C. M. Doke, "Early Bantu Literature—The Age of Brusciotto," in C. M. Doke and D. T. Cole, *Contributions to the History of Bantu Linguistics* (Johannesburg: Witwatersrand University Press, 1961), 15–18, 25–26. Evidently the existence of Brusciotto's grammar was not known to the early-nineteenth-century philologists who, after "an almost complete blank in Bantu publications" of about a century, revolutionized the study of African languages. Doke, "Early Bantu Literature," 20. Sweeping claims were sometimes made on the basis of the noun-class system: "The Kafir tongue is spoken, substantially the same, though with dialectic variations, by all the tribes which stretch from the southern extremity, along the eastern side, to the very centre of Africa, even as far north as the equator, and probably beyond it." J. W. Colenso, *Church Missions*, 17. Colenso may have been influenced by the work of the philologist Wilhelm Bleek, who accompanied him to Natal in 1855, before leaving for Cape Town the following year to work for the Governor of the Cape, Sir George Grey. Wilhelm Bleek, *The Natal Diaries of Dr. W.H.I. Bleek, 1855–1856*, trans. O. H. Spohr (Cape Town: A. A. Balkema, 1965). In a paper read before the Philological Society shortly before his departure to Natal, Bleek, whose name lives on for his work on the San languages, had posited a "great African family of languages" characterized by "the distribution of nouns into classes." Wilhelm Bleek, "On the Languages of Western and Southern Africa," *Transactions of the Philological Society* 4 (1855): 42. Bleek did not claim, however, that *all* of the languages spoken in those parts of Africa belonged to this family. Magema Fuze, who, in paragraphs unfortunately omitted by the English translator of his book, *Abantu abamnyama lapa bavela ngakona*, explicitly acknowledges Bleek as cited by Colenso in *First Steps in Zulu* (1859), and uses the fact of near mutual intelligibility and cognate words among different languages to speculate that black people in different parts of Africa "sprang from a common source" (*bavela 'mtonjeni 'munye*). M. M. Fuze, *Abantu abamnyama lapa bavela ngakona* (Pietermaritzburg, South Africa: City Printing Works, 1922), xi–xii; Magema M. Fuze, *The Black People and Whence They Came: A Zulu View*, trans. H. C. Lugg, ed. A. T. Cope (Pietermaritzburg, South Africa: University of Natal Press / Durban: Killie Campbell Africana Library, 1979), vi. For more on Bleek, see Andrew Bank, *Bushmen in a Victorian World: The Remarkable Story of the Bleek-Lloyd Collection of Bushman Folklore* (Cape Town: Double Story, 2006).
64. *Miners' Companion in Zulu*, 2.
65. J. D. Bold, *Dictionary, Grammar and Phrase-Book of Fanagalo (Kitchen Kafir): The*

Lingua Franca of Southern Africa as Spoken in the Union of South Africa, the Rhodesias, Portuguese East Africa, Nyasaland, Belgian Congo, Etc., 5th ed. (n.p., South Africa: Central News Agency, 1958), 6. One of the reasons for the promotion of Swahili in the Belgian Congo in the early decades of the twentieth century was to counter the use of Kitchen Kafir and English, and thus British influence, in Katanga, which borders on Northern Rhodesia (known as Zambia today); Fabian, *Language and Colonial Power*, 64.

66. *Miners' Companion*, 24. For an accessible linguist's account of the structure of Fanagalo, see Rajend Mesthrie, "How Non-Indo-European Is Fanakalo Pidgin? Selected Understudied Structures in a Bantu-Lexified Pidgin with Germanic Substrates," in *Pidgins and Creoles beyond Africa-Europe Encounters*, ed. Isabelle Buchstaller et al. (Amsterdam: John Benjamins, 2014), 85–100.
67. Bold, *Dictionary*, 6.
68. Daniel Defoe, *Robinson Crusoe*, 1719, ed. Michael Shinagel (New York: Norton, 1975), 164.
69. David Brown, "The Basements of Babylon: Language and Literacy on the South African Gold Mines," *Social Dynamics* 14.1 (1988): 49.
70. See Njabulo Ndebele, "The English Language and Social Change in South Africa," esp. 112–14.
71. David Brown, "The Rise and Fall of Fanakalo: Language and Literacy Policies of the South African Gold Mines," in *Language in South Africa: An Input into Language Planning for a Post-Apartheid South Africa*, ed. Victor N. Webb (Pretoria: LiCCA Research and Development Programme, 1995), 324. For more recent news about Fanagalo on the mines, see Ed Stoddard, "Lingua Franca of South Africa's Mines Set to Fade Slowly," *Chicago Tribune*, April 4, 2012, http://articles.chicagotribune.com/2012-04-04/lifestyle/sns-rt-us-safrica-mines-languagebre8330ft-20120404_1_harmony-gold-english-and-afrikaans-mines; see also "Beyond Marikana: The Crisis—Miners Draw Battle Lines to Shut Down Shafts," *City Press*, September 15, 2012, http://www.citypress.co.za/features/beyond-marikana-the-crisis-miners-draw-battle-lines-to-shut-down-shafts-20120915/.
72. *Miners' Dictionary English—Fanakalo / Woordeboek vir Mynwerkers Afrikaans—Fanakalo* (n.p., South Africa: Mine Safety Division of the Chamber of Mines of South Africa, 1985), iv. The title of this book reflects the growing use of "Fanakalo" as the standard spelling for the name of the language. This is consistent with the spelling of the word in Zulu: *isiFanakalo, uFanakalo, iFanakalo*. My preference for "Fanagalo," however, means to reflect how, historically, the Zulu "soft-k" in "ka" has typically been heard and reproduced by English-speakers as a hard "g." See C. M. Doke et al., *English-Zulu, Zulu-English Dictionary*, 1953, 1958, combined ed. (Johannesburg: Witwatersrand University Press, 1990), entry for "k." I have, incidentally, not found an entry for *-Fanakalo* in this dictionary.
73. Ralph Adendorff, "Fanakalo: A Pidgin in South Africa," in *Language in South Africa*, ed. Rajend Mesthrie (Cambridge, UK: Cambridge University Press, 2002), 179–98.
74. D. T. Cole, "Fanagalo and the Bantu Languages in South Africa," *African Studies* 12.1 (1953): 1–9.
75. Mesthrie, "Origins of Fanagalo," 224–29.
76. Adendorff, "Fanakalo," 192.

77. "Those whites who are proficient in Zulu are the few lucky ones who grew up on the farms amongst Zulu-speaking communities. Other non-Zulu speakers often lack the political will, accompanied by feelings of indifference and hostility, when it comes to the question of having to learn an African language"; Phyllis Jane Zungu, "The Status of Zulu in KwaZulu-Natal," in *Multilingualism in a Multicultural Context: Case Studies on South Africa and Western Europe*, ed. Guus Extra and Jeanne Maartens (Tilburg, Netherlands: Tilburg University Press, 1998), 40. This good fortune, however, does not always lead to academic success, as is noted by the principal of Durban High School: "We have had farm boys who speak isiZulu fluently, but cannot manage the subject as a second language." Noleen Turner, "The Status of isiZulu Second-Language Learning in UKZN [*sic*], with Particular Reference to the Case against Durban High School (2008)," *Language Matters* 41.1 (2010): 101. Historically, whites speaking fluent Zulu have also included the sons and daughters of missionaries. Harriette Colenso has already been mentioned. Another interesting example is the versatile R.C.A. Samuelson, who says he learned Zulu before his "mother tongue," and whose Zuluness made him stand out among his white schoolmates; R.C.A. Samuelson, *Long, Long Ago* (Durban, South Africa: Knox, 1929), 57, 71.
78. I am indebted to David Brown on this last point, which orients the next two paragraphs. I also owe to him the observation below regarding a quotidian acceptance of pidginization among whites in the 1950s (personal communication).
79. Quoted by Cole, "Fanagalo and the Bantu Languages," 8.
80. Jacob Nhlapo, *Bantu Babel: Will the Bantu Languages Live?* (Cape Town: African Bookman, 1944).
81. Colenso, preface to *Zulu-English Dictionary*, 2nd ed., viii.
82. Colenso, *First Steps in Zulu*, 1–2.
83. Gilmour, *Grammars of Colonialism*, 120–26. With regard to the dialect spoken by members of the royal house, the picture may be more complicated. In a footnote to his translation of Magema Fuze's *The Black People and Whence They Came* (1922), H. C. Lugg writes: "It is reported that Mpande (and other members of the Zulu royal family) used to affect the *thefuya* accent, which would render [the name of Mpande's son] Mbulazi as Mbuyazwe. It would also render *balethe* (bring them forth) as *bayethe*, an explanation of the royal salute." Fuze, *The Black People and Whence They Came*, 168–69. Lugg, unfortunately, does not supply a source for his report.
84. Harriette Colenso, preface, vi.
85. For a notorious example, see Antjie Krog, Nosisi Mpolweni, and Kopano Ratele, *There Was This Goat: Investigating the Truth Commission Testimony of Notrose Nobomvu Konile* (Pietermaritzburg, South Africa: University of KwaZulu-Natal Press, 2009), 2–3.
86. Aletta J. Norval, *Deconstructing Apartheid Discourse* (New York: Verso, 1996). On the SABRA intellectuals, and their ideas for "separate development," see John Lazar, "Verwoerd Versus the 'Visionaries': The South African Bureau of Racial Affairs (SABRA) and Apartheid, 1948–1961," in *Apartheid's Genesis, 1935–1962*, ed. Philip Bonner, Peter Delius, and Deborah Posel (Johannesburg: Ravan Press and Witwatersrand University Press, 1993), 362–92. The Afrikaans is from J. A. Engelbrecht and D. Ziervogel, "Die keuse van 'n Bantoetaal op skool" [The choice of a Bantu

language at school], *Journal of Racial Affairs* 2.2 (1951): 29–30, quoted by Cole, "Fanagalo and the Bantu Languages," 8, n.1.
87. In addition to Bold's handbook, in print at the time were B. G. Lloyd's *Kitchen-Kafir Grammar and Vocabulary* (n.p., South Africa: Central News Agency, Ltd., 7th ed., 1950; 10th ed., 1960), and K. Hopkin-Jenkins' *Basic Bantu* (Pietermaritzburg, South Africa: Shuter & Shooter, [1948]), as well as R. R. Mayne's *Conversational Zulu for the Home* (Pietermaritzburg, South Africa: Shuter & Shooter, 1947), which, notwithstanding its title, is a manual in Fanagalo. The handbooks for Zulu published or reprinted in the 1950s are more numerous, and include Isaac Fox, *Juta's First Zulu Manual: With Vocabulary* (Cape Town: Juta, 1950); G. L. Nel, *Simple Zulu with Household Phrases* (Durban, South Africa: Knox, 1955); *An Easy Zulu Vocabulary and Phrase Book: With Simple Sentences for Use in the Home and Garden and on Other Everyday Occasions* (Pietermaritzburg, South Africa: Shuter & Shooter, 1955); J. A. Engelbrecht, *Zoeloe-leerboek met oefeninge, leesstukke, woordelys en 'n aantal raaisels en spreekwoorde* (Johannesburg: Voortrekkerpers, 1956); D. McK. Malcolm, *A Zulu Manual for Beginners* (London: Longmans, Green, 1956); C. L. Sibusiso Nyembezi, *Learn Zulu* (Pietermaritzburg, South Africa: Shuter & Shooter, 1957); and G. D. Campbell and Harry C. Lugg, *A Handbook to Aid in the Treatment of Zulu Patients for Doctors, Nurses, Medical Students, Pharmacists and Administrative Staff* ([Pietermaritzburg, South Africa: Natal University Press], 1958). Prior to that, the largest concentration of Zulu language manuals was in the first decade of the twentieth century, which saw the publication of the following: Charles Roberts, *A Zulu Manual; or, Vade-Mecum* (London: Kegan Paul, Trench, Trubner, 1900); Samuel Gibbs, *An Easy Zulu Vocabulary and Phrase Book: With Grammatical Notes* (Johannesburg: Central News Agency, 1902); A. T. Bryant, *Incwadi yesingisi nesizulu: Zulu without a Grammar by Conversational Exercises: For Housekeepers, Farmers, Overseers, Storekeepers, Doctors, Police and All Such as Come into Frequent Contact with Natives* (Pietermaritzburg, South Africa: Davis, 1909); Franz Mayr, *Zulu Simplified: Being an English-Zulu Exercise-Book with Key for Colonists and Natives* (Pietermaritzburg, South Africa: P. Davis, 1911). In his classic study of Swahili phrase books, grammars, and glossaries in the Belgian Congo, Johannes Fabian cautions us against assuming that the language was actually spoken in the way that the books describe and prescribe. Produced and published in a colonial context, they may, Fabian suggests, more reliably be seen as an expression of symbolic power, exerted through systematic description and taxonomy. Fabian, *Language and Colonial Power*, 136–42. This may well be true too of the South African Zulu manuals, and also of the Fanagalo handbooks, especially those, as mentioned above, which were printed for use outside of the mining sector. They probably also symbolize the seldom-realized *wish* to learn Zulu that runs through the secret history. One suspects, in other words, that, although purchased and owned, and perhaps given a cursory perusal, the majority of copies sold may never have been used.
88. "The negative attitudes towards isiZulu being taken as an additional language at schools in KZN is a result of the perception that isiZulu and other African languages are exceptionally difficult. This perception is, to a large degree, the result of the extremely difficult examination papers for genuine non-mother-tongue speakers that are set at Grade 12 level both for the IEB and the government's provincial examina-

tions." Turner, "Status of isiZulu Second-Language Learning," 104–5. The phrase "genuine non-mother-tongue speakers" is there to acknowledge that, for mother tongue speakers who take Zulu as a second language at English-medium schools at which they take English as a first language, and who in fact appear to be the majority of those taking Zulu as a second language at those schools, this difficulty might not exist. Although I do not think that Turner is saying that different (let alone easier) examination papers are being set for mother tongue Zulu speakers, her peculiar phrasing vividly shows how the doxa of "difficulty" can masquerade as fact. At the same time, it should be noted that, historically, pass rates for students taking Zulu as a *first* language in Grade 12 have been low—in 1992, below 50%. This is ascribed to divergence between the language as spoken by students as their mother tongue and that taught at schools: "[M]any African students do not understand the variety of Zulu that they are being taught." Zungu, "Status of Zulu," 41.
89. See the addresses of the Reverend Msimang and Archdeacon Roach, cited above. Stuart, ed. *Zulu Orthography*, 10, 13, 27.
90. C.L.S. Nyembezi, *Learn More Zulu* (Pietermaritzburg, South Africa: Shuter & Shooter, 1970), 1.
91. Ibid.
92. Ibid.
93. Bold, *Dictionary*, 6.
94. Nyembezi, *Learn More Zulu*, 1.
95. For a defining statement of this position, see J. M. Coetzee, "Apartheid Thinking," in *Giving Offense: Essays on Censorship* (Chicago: University of Chicago Press, 1996), 163–84.
96. Sigmund Freud, *The Interpretation of Dreams*, 1900, in *The Standard Edition of the Complete Psychological Works of Sigmund Freud*, ed. James Strachey (London: Hogarth Press, 1953–1974), vol. 4, 480.
97. Sigmund Freud, "Mourning and Melancholia," 1917, in *Standard Edition*, vol. 14, 250–52; see also Klein, "Mourning and Its Relation to Manic-Depressive States."
98. Nyembezi, *Learn More Zulu*, 82–83, 85.
99. C.L.S. Nyembezi, *Learn Zulu*, 5th ed. (Pietermaritzburg, South Africa: Shuter & Shooter, 1990), 4.
100. Nyembezi, *Learn More Zulu*, 194–95, 201, 199.
101. Ibid., 199.
102. Ibid., 199–200.
103. *Kalahari Surfers: Vol. 1. The Eighties*, Compact disc with insert (London: ReR, n.d.).
104. William Cobbett and Brian Nakedi, "The Flight of the Herschelites: Ethnic Nationalism and Land Dispossession," in *Popular Struggles in South Africa*, ed. William Cobbett and Robin Cohen (Trenton, NJ: Africa World Press, 1988), 77–89.
105. K. Hopkin-Jenkins, *Basic Bantu* (Pietermaritzburg, South Africa: Shuter & Shooter, [1948]), n.p.
106. Cole, "Fanagalo and the Bantu Languages," 1.
107. "Obituary: Cyril Nyembezi," *Natal Witness* [2003].
108. S. E. Aitken-Cade, *So! You Want to Learn the Language! An Amusing and Instructive Kitchen Kaffir Dictionary* (Salisbury, Southern Rhodesia: Centafrican Press, 1951), 8, quoted by Cole, "Fanagalo and the Bantu Languages," 8.
109. Aitken-Cade, *So! You Want to Learn the Language!*, 3.

110. Ibid., 8.
111. Adendorff, "Fanakalo," 195–96.
112. Julie Frederikse, *None but Ourselves: Masses vs. Media in the Making of Zimbabwe* (Johannesburg: Ravan Press, 1982), 20–21.
113. Nyembezi, *Learn More Zulu*, 162.
114. David Attwell, *Rewriting Modernity: Studies in Black South African Literary History* (Pietermaritzburg, South Africa: University of KwaZulu-Natal Press, 2005), 77–110.
115. See Georg Scriba and Gunnar Lislerud, "Lutheran Missions and Churches in South Africa," in *Christianity in South Africa: A Political, Social and Cultural History*, ed. Richard Elphick and Rodney Davenport (Berkeley: University of California Press, 1997), 182–83.
116. Vanessa Lourens, "Vertaling van die Bybel Duitse vrou se roeping" [Translation of the Bible German woman's calling], *Die Burger* [Cape Town], June 7, 1996: 8, http://152.111.1.87/argief/berigte/dieburger/1996/06/07/8/10.html.
117. Ibid.
118. Nyembezi, *Learn More Zulu*, 320–28.
119. C.L.S. Nyembezi, *Zulu Proverbs* (Johannesburg: Witwatersrand University Press, 1954).
120. C. L. Sibusiso Nyembezi, *Inkinsela yaseMgungundlovu* (Pietermaritzburg, South Africa: Shuter & Shooter, 1961), translated by Sandile Ngidi as *The Rich Man of Pietermaritzburg* (Laverstock, UK: Aflame Books, 2008).
121. Nyembezi, *Learn More Zulu*, 284–85.
122. W. P. Steenkamp, *Is the South-West African Herero Committing Race Suicide?* (Cape Town: Unie-Volkspers, 1944).
123. Nyembezi, *Learn More Zulu*, 112, 122–24.
124. Ibid., 75, 78.
125. Ibid., 64.
126. Ibid., 94.
127. Ibid., 1.
128. Ibid., 257.
129. Ibid., 94.
130. Brown, "Rise and Fall of Fanakalo," 313.
131. *On Safari with the Petersen Brothers*, sound disc ([South Africa]: Columbia, 1958). See http://soulsafari.wordpress.com/2009/10/31/the-bleached-zulu/.
132. *African Jazz and Variety*, sound disc (Johannesburg: Record Industries, 1952). See http://electricjive.blogspot.com/2011/01/change-through-african-jazz-and-variety.html.
133. Nyembezi, *Learn More Zulu*, 232–35.
134. Ibid., 233.
135. Ibid., 51–52.
136. Ibid., 51.
137. Ibid., 51–52.
138. Nyembezi, *Learn Zulu*, 239–41.
139. Nyembezi, *Learn More Zulu*, 52.
140. Phuzekhemisi noKhethani, "Imbizo," *Imbizo*, CDTIG 456, compact disc (South Africa: RPM Records, 1994).

141. Nyembezi, *Learn More Zulu*, 434.
142. Ibid., 291.
143. Ibid., 292.
144. Ibid., 149, cf. 236.
145. See also Nyembezi, *Learn More Zulu*, 379.
146. Alan Paton, *Lafa elihle kakhulu*, trans. Sibusiso Nyembezi, 3rd ed. (Pietermaritzburg, South Africa: Shuter & Shooter, 1995), 131.
147. Pierre de la Rey, "'Speak Up' Advice Given to Africans," *Star* [Johannesburg], May 18, 1974: 5.
148. Mzala, *Gatsha Buthelezi*, 11. See also Maré and Hamilton, *An Appetite for Power*, 156.
149. Nyembezi, *Learn More Zulu*, 292.
150. Ibid., 350.
151. Ibid., 414.
152. Ibid., 30–31.
153. See, for example, Marks, *Ambiguities of Dependence*, 81.
154. Nyembezi, *Learn More Zulu*, 1.
155. Gayatri Chakravorty Spivak, "Righting Wrongs," *South Atlantic Quarterly* 103.2–3 (2004): 532; see also "Interview with Gayatri Chakravorty Spivak," in Mark Sanders, *Gayatri Chakravorty Spivak: Live Theory* (London: Continuum, 2006), 119–20.
156. Nyembezi, *Learn More Zulu*, 1.
157. Ibid., 334–35, 367–69.
158. Ibid., 394–95; D.B.Z. Ntuli, *Isipho sikaKhisimuzi*, in *Woza nendlebe* (Pietermaritzburg, South Africa: Shuter & Shooter, 1988), 81–94.
159. Nyembezi, *Learn More Zulu*, 253.
160. Ibid., 327.
161. Ibid., 144.
162. Ibid., 399, 421.
163. Ibid., 39.
164. C.L.S. Nyembezi, *A Review of Zulu Literature* (Pietermaritzburg, South Africa: University of Natal Press, 1961), 5.
165. *A Survey of Race Relations in South Africa*, ed. Muriel Horrell (Johannesburg: South African Institute of Race Relations, 1971), 178–79.
166. Nyembezi, *Learn More Zulu*, 279.
167. Ibid., 266.
168. Tiyo Soga, "Mission People and Red People," 1864, in *The Journal and Collected Writings of the Reverend Tiyo Soga*, ed. Donovan Williams (Cape Town: A. A. Balkema, 1983), 175–77.
169. Nyembezi, *Learn More Zulu*, 123.
170. "Obituary: Cyril Nyembezi."
171. Nyembezi, *Learn More Zulu*, 253.
172. Mieke Bal, *Narratology: Introduction to the Theory of Narrative*, 3rd ed. (Toronto: University of Toronto Press, 2009), 163–64.
173. Nyembezi, *Learn More Zulu*, 451.
174. Bloke Modisane, *Blame Me on History* (London: Thames & Hudson, 1963), 18.
175. Italo Svevo, *The Nice Old Man and the Pretty Girl*, 1929, trans. L. Collison-Morley (New York: Melville House, 2010), 83, 93.

Chapter 2: A Teacher's Novels

1. Sibusiso Nyembezi, *Mntanami! Mntanami!* (Johannesburg: Afrikaanse Pers-Boekhandel, 1950), 74.
2. For a discussion of the novel and its translation, see Mark Sanders, "Undone by Laughter," *Safundi* 10.3 (2009): 353–59.
3. Nyembezi, *Learn More Zulu*, 451.
4. Nyembezi, *Mntanami!*, 171–72, 211–12.
5. Ibid., 94.
6. Ibid., 65, 159, 190, 214.
7. Ibid., 158–59.
8. Ibid., 150.
9. Ibid., 147.
10. Ibid., 51, cf. 94.
11. I have not been able to research the textual history of *Mntanami! Mntanami!* exhaustively, but have discovered that chapter 12 is missing from the third edition of the novel published in 1975 and issued in a ninth impression by Educum publishers in Johannesburg in 1985. The frequency of the novel's reprinting suggests that it was a prescribed book for schools during that time.
12. Nyembezi, *Mntanami!*, 21–22, 24–25.
13. Ibid., 81–82, 84.
14. Ibid., 93.
15. Ibid., 96–97.
16. Ibid., 208.
17. Ibid., 106.
18. Ibid., 137–38, 148.
19. Ibid., 214.
20. Ibid.
21. Ibid., 75–76.
22. Ibid., 74.
23. Alan Paton, *Cry, the Beloved Country*, 1948 (New York: Scribner, 1987), 268.
24. Ibid., 111.
25. Tony Morphet, "Alan Paton: The Honour of Meditation," *English in Africa* 10.2 (1983): 1–10.
26. Paton, *Cry, the Beloved Country*, 261.
27. B.G. Lloyd, *Kitchen-Kafir Grammar and Vocabulary*, 6th ed. (n.p., South Africa: Central News Agency, Ltd., 1944), 3.
28. Sibusiso Nyembezi, *Ubudoda abukhulelwa*, 1953 (Johannesburg: Afrikaanse Pers-Boekhandel, n.d.), 8.
29. Paton, *Cry, the Beloved Country*, 213, 215.
30. J. M. Coetzee, *White Writing: On the Culture of Letters in South Africa* (New Haven, CT: Yale University Press, 1988), 129.
31. Paton, *Cry, the Beloved Country*, 46.
32. Coetzee, *White Writing*, 127.
33. Paton, *Cry, the Beloved Country*, 33.
34. Nyembezi, *Ubudoda*, 104.
35. Paton, *Lafa elihle*, 167.

36. Nyembezi, *Mntanami!*, 59.
37. Paton, *Cry, the Beloved Country*, 45.
38. Nyembezi, *Mntanami!*, 72.
39. Paton, *Cry, the Beloved Country*, 47.
40. Paton, *Lafa elihle*, 13.
41. Paton, *Cry, the Beloved Country*, 269.
42. Ibid., 316.
43. Colenso, *Ten Weeks in Natal*, 75, 198.
44. Colenso, *First Steps in Zulu*, 25.
45. Paton, *Cry, the Beloved Country*, 315.
46. Colenso, *Ten Weeks in Natal*, 56–61, 115, 160, 215, 240.
47. Ibid., 57.
48. Paton, *Lafa elihle*, 213.
49. Paton, *Lafa elihle*, 214.
50. Paton, *Cry, the Beloved Country*, 282–83.
51. Melanie Klein, "Envy and Gratitude," 1957, in *Envy and Gratitude and Other Works, 1946–1963* (London: Hogarth Press, 1975), 176–235.
52. Paton, *Lafa elihle*, 224.
53. Ibid., 225.
54. Paton, *Cry, the Beloved Country*, 283.
55. This could be a misprint, as here a British edition reads "the only words that he knows." Paton, *Cry, the Beloved Country: A Story of Comfort in Desolation*, 1948 (Harmondsworth, UK: Penguin, 1988), 212.
56. Paton, *Lafa elihle*, 225.
57. Ludwig Wittgenstein, *Philosophical Investigations*, trans. G.E.M. Anscombe, 1953, 3rd ed. (Oxford: Blackwell, 2001), ¶ 151.
58. Paton, *Cry, the Beloved Country*, 282–83.
59. Ibid., 310.
60. Ibid., 103.
61. Paton, *Lafa elihle*, 68.
62. Ibid., 224.
63. By a strange coincidence, J. W. Colenso used a similar expression in lamenting the loss of Theophilus Shepstone's friendship over the trial of Langalibalele: "The light had all gone out from his life in Natal." Letter from Harriette Colenso to Theophilus Shepstone, quoted in Guy, *The Heretic*, 219.
64. S.E.K. Mqhayi, "The Prince of Britain," trans. Robert Kavanagh and Z. S. Qangule, in *The New Century of South African Poetry*, ed. Michael Chapman (Johannesburg: Ad Donker, 2002), 67. Xhosa original in S.E.K. Mqhayi, *Inzuzo*, rev. ed. (Johannesburg: Witwatersrand University Press, 1974), 73.
65. Paton, *Cry, the Beloved Country*, 284.
66. Paton, *Lafa elihle*, 225.
67. Paton *Cry, the Beloved Country*, 211; *Lafa elihle*, 162.
68. Nyembezi, *Ubudoda*, 8–9, 51, 53, 104. In trade union poetry, Fanagalo has on occasion been used to distinguish a traitor from his comrades: "Fast ran the impimpis [traitors, or sellouts] / And reported to their bosses and said: / 'Baas, Baas, thina bukile lomvukuzane buya losayidi / Kalofethri kathina' [Boss, boss, we saw the mole (i.e., the trade union, FOSATU) arrive at our factory]." Alfred Temba Qabula, "Praise

Poem to FOSATU," in *Black Mamba Rising: South African Worker Poets in Struggle*, ed. Ari Sitas (Durban, South Africa: Worker Resistance and Culture Publications, 1986), 11. I thank Kelwyn Sole for directing me to Qabula's poem.
69. Nyembezi, *Mntanami!*, 71, 73–74.
70. Ibid., 73, 79.
71. Modisane, *Blame Me on History*, 57.
72. Ibid., 80.
73. Ibid., 82.
74. Nyembezi, *Learn More Zulu*, 1.
75. See Nyembezi, *Mntanami!*, 28, 55–56.
76. Union of South Africa, *Report of the Commission of Enquiry in Regard to Undesirable Publications*, UG 42 (Pretoria: Government Printer, 1957), 8, 21.
77. Modisane, *Blame Me on History*, 5.
78. See Mark Sanders, *Ambiguities of Witnessing: Law and Literature in the Time of a Truth Commission* (Stanford, CA: Stanford University Press, 2007), 26–27.
79. J. W. Colenso, *First Steps in Zulu*, 1.

CHAPTER 3: *IPI TOMBI*

1. Fula Paxinos, "Rocking with Laughter at Cinderella," *Sea Point Magazine* 1975: 64.
2. Jacques Derrida and Safaa Fathy, *Tourner les mots: Au bord d'un film* (Paris: Galilée, 2000), 96.
3. Paxinos, "Rocking with Laughter."
4. W. S. Kaplan, "Alive and Vital African Revue," *Argus*, November 28, 1974: 23; Tom Lambert, "Rousing Tribal Musical Cracks South Africa's Racial Barriers," *Los Angeles Times*, December 31, 1974: B11–12.
5. W.S. Kaplan, "Tribal Rock Musical," *Argus*, May 27, 1975: 24.
6. Stanley Uys, "Theatre's Racial Face," *Guardian*, February 22, 1975: 1; "Cape Town Theater Shifts Policy on Integration Again," *New York Times*, Feburary 22, 1975: 9.
7. Assiatou Diallo, "L'immense success des ballets Sud-Africains Ipi Tombi," *Bingo*, November 1975: 70–71.
8. "Ipi Tombi Means Dance, Dance, Dance!," *Drum* [Lagos], October 1976: 16–17.
9. Naiwu Osahon, "Who Let in Vorster's Ipi-Tombi?," *Newbreed*, end-November 1976: 15; Bosun Adewunmi, "Ipi-Tombi Dancers Confess: 'We're Financed by Apartheid,'" *Newbreed*, end-Februrary 1977: 42.
10. Andrew Horn, "South African Theatre: Ideology and Rebellion," in *Readings in African Popular Culture*, ed. Karin Barber (Bloomington: Indiana University Press / Oxford: James Currey, 1997), 74.
11. See Andrew Apter, *The Pan-African Nation: Oil and the Spectacle of Culture in Nigeria* (Chicago: University of Chicago Press, 2005).
12. John Darnton, "Nigeria Is Preparing for Arts Festival," *New York Times*, October 30, 1976: 17.
13. Peter Niesewand, "Enter Slaves Left," *Guardian*, November 29, 1976: 1; "Demo Stops Black Show," *Guardian*, November 30, 1976: 1.
14. C. Gerald Fraser, "Black Committee Urges Boycott of 'Ipi Tombi,' from South Africa," *New York Times*, December 28, 1976; Lyndonn Prince, "500 Protest Ipi Tombi Open-

ing," *New York Amsterdam News,* January 1, 1977: C1; Clive Barnes, "Furor Surrounds Tedious 'Ipi-Tombi,'" *New York Times,* January 13, 1977; Lynn Hudson, "It's Curtains for 'Ipi Tombi,'" *New York Amsterdam News,* February 12, 1977: A1.
15. Billy Pierce, Jr., "Marchers Protesting the Opening of Ipi Tombi" (photograph), *New York Amsterdam News,* January 8, 1977: D7.
16. Prince, "500 Protest Ipi Tombi"; see also (Black) Rabbi Judah Anderson, Letter to the Editor, *New York Amsterdam News,* January 1, 1977: A4.
17. Prince, "500 Protest Ipi Tombi."
18. Dan Sullivan, "'Ipi Tombi' Opens at Hartford," *Los Angeles Times,* June 6, 1980: H1, 13; Dan Sullivan, "Protestors vs. 'Ipi Tombi'—Who Won?," *Los Angeles Times,* July 6, 1980: O1.
19. Associated Press, "South Africans Apply for Extended Visas," September 4, 1980; "Former Cast of African Musical Given Contracts, Visa Extensions," September 25, 1980.
20. "The History of Ipi-Tombi—Its Travels and Triumphs." *Ipi-Tombi* Publicity Material, University of Nevada, Las Vegas, Library Special Collections.
21. Hudson, "It's Curtains for 'Ipi Tombi.'"
22. Mel Tapley, "Death of 'Ipi Tombi' Spawns 'Soweto Sounds,'" *New York Amsterdam News,* January 7, 1978: D9.
23. Russell Vandenbroucke, "South African Blacksploitation," *Yale / Theatre* 8 (1976): 71.
24. On Louw and *bestaansreg,* see Mark Sanders, *Complicities: The Intellectual and Apartheid* (Durham, NC: Duke University Press, 2002), 77.
25. Sigmund Freud, *From the History of an Infantile Neurosis,* 1918, *Standard Edition,* vol. 17, 37–38, 44–45.
26. It is thus sadly ironic that David Evans, as I learned while making final revisions to my book, was lost at sea with nobody at hand to rescue him, in February 2013, when his little boat was washed out from the mouth of the Duiwenhoks River, near Vermaaklikheid in the South-Eastern Cape. He had closed his practice in Cape Town many years previously, moving to the village of Stanford, home to many artists, where he was a potter, and is fondly remembered for his active involvement in the life of the community. "In Memoriam: Dr. David Evans 7 August 1939–9 February 2013," *Stanford River Talk* 92 (April 2013): 6; "Man Feared Drowned off Witsand," *News24,* February 10, 2013, http://www.news24.com/SouthAfrica/News/Man-feared-drowned-off-Witsand-20130210.
27. See, for example, Jacques Lacan, "The Mirror Stage as Formative of the *I* Function as Revealed in Psychoanalytic Experience," 1949, in *Écrits: The First Complete Edition in English,* trans. Bruce Fink (New York: Norton, 2006), 75–81.
28. Program for *Ipi-Tombi,* Don Hughes Productions [1980]. *Ipi-Tombi* Publicity Material, University of Nevada, Las Vegas, Library Special Collections.
29. Sullivan, "'Ipi Tombi' Opens," H1.
30. (Black) Rabbi Judah Anderson, Letter to the Editor.
31. Sullivan, "'Ipi Tombi' Opens," H13
32. Mshengu is evidently Robert Mshengu Kavanagh, whose actual name was Robert McLaren, who, as a lecturer in drama at the University of the Witwatersrand, helped to found the Workshop '71 theatre group, and directed its play, *Survival* (1976). It is worth noting, however, that, in that milieu, at least on stage, linguistic purism seems

not to have applied: "Tsotsitaal [urban and township patois] .... was used by Workshop '71 ... as a more popular alternative to English as a lingua franca. It could easily be understood by all blacks, including Coloureds and Indians, in the urban areas of the Reef and by those whites who spoke Afrikaans as well." Robert Mshengu Kavanagh, *South African People's Plays: Ons Phola Hi: Plays by Gibson Kente, Credo Mutwa, Mthuli Shezi and Workshop '71* (London: Heinemann, 1981), xxxi.

33. Mshengu, "Where Are the Girls? (or Iph' intombi?)," *S'ketsh*, Summer 1974/75: 10.
34. Program for *Ipi-Tombi*, Don Hughes Productions [1980]. *Ipi-Tombi* Publicity Material, University of Nevada, Las Vegas, Library Special Collections.
35. Mshengu, "Where Are the Girls?" 10
36. Mshengu, "Where Are the Girls?" 10. For further details, see David Coplan, *In Township Tonight! South Africa's Black City Music and Theatre*, 2nd ed. (Chicago: University of Chicago Press, 2008), 280–82. For useful discussions of Gibson Kente and *Sikalo* (1966), see Robert Mshengu Kavanagh, *Theatre and Cultural Struggle in South Africa* (London: Zed Books, 1985), 115–23; Loren Kruger, *The Drama of South Africa: Plays, Pageants and Publics since 1910* (New York: Routledge, 1999), 139.
37. Vandenbroucke, "South African Blacksploitation," 68.
38. Alan Rich, "Rave Revue," *New York Magazine*, January 31, 1977: 68.
39. Kruger, *Drama of South Africa*, 141.
40. These men included Henry Francis Fynn. Benedict Carton, "Faithful Anthropologists: Christianity, Ethnography and the Making of 'Zulu Religion' in Early Colonial Natal," in *Zulu Identities*, ed. Carton et al., 158.
41. Dunn was, by all accounts, fluent in Zulu. After the battle of Ndondakusuka in 1856, in which Cetshwayo defeated Mbuyazi, his brother and rival heir to the kingship, Dunn was given land by Cetshwayo in the Ungoye district of Zululand. He also became the king's adviser and intermediary with the colony. After the battle of Isandlwana in 1879, however, Dunn abandoned Cetshwayo and joined forces with the British. In the postwar "settlement," he was given one of the thirteen chiefdoms, which greatly enlarged the territory under his control, until the settlement collapsed and Dunn became a relatively minor figure. Charles Ballard, *John Dunn: The White Chief of Zululand* (Johannesburg: Ad Donker, 1985), 25, 65, 134–36, 152–53, 218–19. Bishop Colenso, who will have encountered a countertype in Dunn of the white man who, like Shepstone, despite speaking Zulu, does great ill, is known to have railed against him in his last years, both in print and in his letters. He wrote thus to Frank Chesson, Secretary for the Aborigines Protection Society: "And this double-dyed traitor"—Dunn is alleged by Colenso to have given intelligence to Cetshwayo just after Isandlwana—"has been just appointed by Sir G[arnet] Wolseley to be ruler of the largest of his thirteen provinces, where, with his native wives and concubines, to whom he may add at his pleasure, he will set a splendid example of morality," quoted in Ballard, *John Dunn*, 181. Zulu writers have emphasized Dunn's treachery. Herbert Dhlomo's play, *Cetshwayo* (1936), represents Dunn as a conniving turncoat and symbol of white supremacy; he actually shoots and kills the king in the final scene (a departure from historical fact). *H.I.E. Dhlomo: Collected Works*, ed. Nick Visser and Tim Couzens (Johannesburg: Ravan, 1985), 176. In his life of Cetshwayo, published in 1952, R.R.R. Dhlomo succinctly describes what the king discovered on returning from exile: "John Dunn, the great enemy he had adopted after the battle of Ndondakusuka, was given a large territory, a richly fertile tract neighboring his."

R.R.R. Dhlomo, *uCetshwayo*, 3rd ed. (Pietermaritzburg, South Africa: Shuter & Shooter, 1961; originally published 1952), 118. Later testimony by one of Dunn's sons indicates that, at least in the days of the "settlement," Dunn's children were encouraged by their father to think of themselves not as Zulu but as coloured—an identity that would complicate the position of Dunn's descendants during the eras of segregation and apartheid, causing them a great deal of misery. Ballard, *John Dunn*, 225, 243–61.

42. Perhaps the same could be said of lesser-known contemporary "white Zulus" such as Barry Leitch and Kingsley Holgate, who have made names for themselves in cultural tourism. Benedict Carton and Malcolm Draper, "Bulls in the Boardroom: The Zulu Warrior Ethic and the Spirit of South African Capitalism," in *Zulu Identities*, ed. Carton et al., 591–605.
43. David B. Coplan, "A Terrible Commitment: Balancing the Tribes in South African National Culture," in *Perilous States: Conversations on Culture, Politics, and Nation*, ed. George E. Marcus (Chicago: University of Chicago Press, 1993), 317–18.
44. Philippe Conrath, *Johnny Clegg: La passion zoulou* (Paris: Seghers, 1988), 77.
45. Samuel G. Freedman, "Johnny Clegg's War on Apartheid," *Rolling Stone*, March 22, 1990: 60.
46. Freedman, "Johnny Clegg's War on Apartheid," 62. See also Conrath, *Johnny Clegg*, 65, 94.
47. Conrath, *Johnny Clegg*, 57.
48. Ibid., 41.
49. In a 1995 interview, Clegg once again elaborates on the theme:

> I had the sense that the universe was winking at me saying, there's a very big secret here, and it can be yours if you want it. As I watched, I saw these people so given to what they were doing, so committed and so enjoying it. And these body positions and movements were so different from my culture. For the first time in my life, this strong awareness came to me, that these people did not need my culture. They did not need me, they did not need what I stood for. They did not need my motor-cars, and didn't need my rockets to the moon. They were completely self-sufficient in their own cultural identity. It was an overwhelming realisation, and I was jealous. And, at the same time, there was another level there, in that they were so intensely celebrating their maleness. I responded to that, because I was a young adolescent male with lots of conflicts. My stepfather had run off. As a husband he was totally a failure. My own father never communicated with me, and here were these men celebrating their maleness in a way which was just so complete.
>
> "Johnny Clegg," in *Cutting through the Mountain: Interviews with South African Jewish Activists*, ed. Immanuel Suttner (Sandton, South Africa: Penguin, 1997), 88.

50. Coplan, "Terrible Commitment," 312.
51. Ibid., 319.
52. Conrath, *Johnny Clegg*, 42, 46.
53. Ibid., 51–56.
54. Coplan, "Terrible Commitment," 333, Coplan's interpolation.
55. Conrath, *Johnny Clegg*, 55, 42. See also Suttner, *Cutting through the Mountain*, 80–81.

56. Quoted in Christopher Connelly, "Juluka: The Other Side of the Boycott," *Rolling Stone,* December 3, 1983: 51.
57. Freedman, "Johnny Clegg's War on Apartheid," 63.
58. Coplan, "Terrible Commitment," 318.
59. Coplan, "Terrible Commitment," 317; Conrath, *Johnny Clegg,* 66–67.
60. Coplan, "Terrible Commitment," 312; Conrath, *Johnny Clegg,* 43, 52.
61. Conrath, *Johnny Clegg,* 99.
62. Freedman, "Johnny Clegg's War on Apartheid," 64.
63. Coplan, "Terrible Commitment," 321.
64. Ibid., 325. See also Freedman, "Johnny Clegg's War on Apartheid," 64.
65. On "Woza Friday," see Conrath, *Johnny Clegg,* 120.
66. Freedman, "Johnny Clegg's War on Apartheid," 64.
67. Conrath, *Johnny Clegg,* 124. The wedding took place in 1973, whereas Clegg gives the year as 1977.
68. Coplan, "A Terrible Commitment," 324.
69. Conrath, *Johnny Clegg,* 127.
70. Ibid., 150–51.
71. Bhungani kaMzolo, "Kuzomele izikhulu zokhozi zibabhekele abasakazi abasha" [The bosses of Ukhozi will need to look after young broadcasters], *Isolezwe,* November 19, 2012: 16.
72. On the reception of "Impi," also see Coplan, "A Terrible Commitment," 326–27.
73. Conrath, *Johnny Clegg,* 133.
74. An excellent example is Clegg's history of "faction fighting" in the Msinga and Mpofana locations in rural Natal, which shows how, faced with chronic land shortage, people took sides on the basis of their place of residence rather than kinship alone. Jonathan Clegg, "Ukubuyisa isidumbu—'Bringing Back the Body': An Examination into the Ideology of Vengeance in the Msinga and Mpofana Rural Locations, 1882–1944," in *Working Papers in Southern African Studies,* vol. 2, ed. Philip Bonner (Johannesburg: Ravan Press, 1981), 164–98.
75. *Truth and Reconciliation Commission of South Africa Report,* vol. 2, 134–44, 233–34.
76. Freedman, "Johnny Clegg's War on Apartheid," 120–22.
77. See also Julie Frederikse, *David Webster* (Cape Town: Maskew Miller Longman, 1998), 57–58.
78. For details, see Deborah James, "David Webster: An Activist Anthropologist Twenty Years on," *African Studies* 68.2 (2009): 287–97.
79. Quoted in Frederikse, *David Webster,* 41.
80. Bertha Slosberg, *Pagan Tapestry* (London: Rich & Cowan, 1940), 213. Slosberg (1910–1998) later lived in the United States, where she wrote fiction, as well as for the screen, under the name Froma Sand. The motif of the Zulu female as "girl" becomes canonical with Roy Campbell's poem "The Zulu Girl" (1926). See Michael Chapman, ed., *The New Century of South African Poetry* (Johannesburg: Ad Donker, 2002), 83. An interesting exception to this is *Zulu Woman,* American feminist author Rebecca Hourwich Reyher's account, based on a series of interviews, of the marriage of Christina Sibiya to King Solomon kaDinuzulu, whom she eventually left. Reyher's preface clearly declares how her book was motivated by identification: "In the spring of 1934 I was in Reno for the usual reason, indulging in the usual Reno pastime of introspection and personal stocktaking . . . . One casual day I realized how much

the Reno Hills looked like those of Zululand [she had been there in 1924], and how much nicer it would be there, where there were no problems of divorce, no civilized memories that legal decisions could not dissemble. What did Zulu women do? How did they manage lifelong marriage? Were they happy? Was polygamy, as my sophisticated friends assured me, the natural state of man? . . . Suddenly it seemed urgent to get the answers to these questions of what Zulu women felt, and did, and talked about." Rebecca Hourwich Reyher, *Zulu Woman: The Life Story of Christina Sibiya*, 1948 (New York: Feminist Press, 1999), 8. In the opening paragraph to the first draft of *Zulu Woman*, quoted by Marcia Wright in her introduction to the 1999 Feminist Press edition, Reyher's identification with Sibiya is more emphatic: "I have tried to write Christina's story as she told it to me, but her story is mine also." Reyher, *Zulu Woman*, xiv.
81. Slosberg, *Pagan Tapestry*, 79.
82. Ibid., 312–13.
83. See Kruger, *Drama of South Africa*, 31–34, 43.
84. Mshengu, "Where Are the Girls?" 9.
85. J. M. Coetzee, *Giving Offense: Essays on Censorship*, 176.
86. Zoë Wicomb, "Translations in the Yard of Africa," *Journal of Literary Studies* 18.3-4 (2002): 220.
87. "Lashon' Ilanga," *Ipi Ntombi—Original Cast Recording*, compact disc (Gallo South Africa, 2002).
88. Malcolm Lombard, Liner Notes to *Ipi Ntombi—Original Cast Recording*, 22.
89. Ibid., 3–4.
90. "The Warrior," *Ipi Ntombi—Original Cast Recording*.
91. Ibid.
92. Ibid.
93. Nelson Mandela, *Long Walk to Freedom* (Boston: Little, Brown, 1994), 248–49.
94. For some Africans, the defeat at Blood River has signified eschatologically. In an undated "Prayer for Dingana's Day December 16," Isaiah Shembe, who founded the Ibandla lamaNazaretha (Nazareth Church) in 1910, exclaims: "So! There it is! Our blood is upon us as retribution for our sins." *The Man of Heaven and the Beautiful Ones of God: Isaiah Shembe and the Nazareth Church / Umuntu wasezulwini nabantu abahle bakaNkulunkulu: Isiah Shembe neBandla lamaNazaretha*, ed. and trans. Liz Gunner (Pietermaritzburg, South Africa: University of KwaZulu-Natal Press, 2004), 69.
95. Phehello Mofokeng, "The Power of the Zulu Brand," *Sawubona*, July 2007: 122.
96. Kaplan, "Alive and Vital African Revue."
97. For more on the meaning of weddings, see Mark Sanders, "Modisane's Weddings," *Social Dynamics* 36.3 (2010): 479–82.
98. Linda Christmas, "Rhapsody in Black," *Guardian*, December 10, 1975: 11.
99. See also Mshengu, "Where Are the Girls?"; Vandenbroucke, "South African Blacksploitation."
100. Vandenbroucke, "South African Blacksploitation," 70.
101. See http://electricjive.blogspot.com/2011/01/change-through-african-jazz-and-variety.html.
102. Sullivan, "'Ipi Tombi' Opens," H1.
103. Percy Baneshik, "'Ipi-Tombi' a Hybrid Stunner," *Star*, March 26, 1974: 23.
104. Sigmund Freud, "Fetishism," 1927, *Standard Edition*, vol. 21, 152–53.

105. Percy Mtwa, Mbongeni Ngema and Barney Simon, *Woza Albert!* (London: Methuen, 1983), 42.
106. Mshengu, "Where Are the Girls?" 9.
107. Christmas, "Rhapsody in Black," 11.
108. "Ipi Ntombi," *Ipi Ntombi—Original Cast Recording*.
109. McKenzie Porter, "Ipi Tombi Electrifies," [*Toronto Sun*, n.d.]. *Ipi Tombi* Publicity Material, University of Nevada, Las Vegas, Library Special Collections.
110. For biographical details on Bertha Egnos (1912–2003) and Gail Lakier (1942–2010), see "Eureka! Tribute to Bertha Egnos." *Soul Safari*, June 10, 2013, http://soulsafari.wordpress.com/2013/06/10/eureka-tribute-to-bertha-egnos/.
111. See Veit Erlmann, "'Spectatorial Lust': The African Choir in England, 1891–1893," in *Africans on Stage: Studies in Ethnological Show Business*, ed. Bernth Lindfors (Bloomington: Indiana University Press, 1999), 107–34. The tendency, also apparent in colonial South African photography, has had a long afterlife; see Helen Bradford, "Framing African Women: Visionaries in Southern Africa and Their Photographic Afterlife, 1850–2004," *Kronos* 30 (2004): 70–93. The codes of representation in question complicate contemporary politics and aesthetics of visibility; see Andrew van der Vlies, "Queer Knowledge and the Politics of the Gaze in Contemporary South African Photography: Zanele Muholi and Others," *Journal of African Cultural Studies* 24.2 (2012): 140–56.
112. It has, however, been argued that Baartman was "a figure of the anti-erotic." Z. S. Strother, "Display of the Body Hottentot," in *Africans on Stage*, ed. Lindfors, 1–61.
113. Loren Kruger, "So What's New? Women and Theater in the 'New South Africa,'" *Theater* 25.3 (1995): 47–48.
114. Thembi Mtshali-Jones and Yael Farber, *A Woman in Waiting*, in Yael Farber, *Theatre as Witness: Three Testimonial Plays from South Africa: In Collaboration with and Based on the Lives of the Original Performers* (London: Oberon, 2008), 76–77.
115. Ibid., 77–78.
116. Ibid., 78.
117. Ibid., 79.
118. Ibid.
119. See Kruger, *Drama of South Africa*, 154–84, for a critical overview.
120. Mtshali-Jones and Farber, *A Woman in Waiting*, 80.
121. Ibid., 74.
122. Ibid., 80.
123. Ibid.
124. Ibid., 66, 78.
125. Ibid., 65.
126. "The Warrior," *Ipi Ntombi—Original Cast Recording*.
127. Anita Chaudhuri, "Waiting in the Wings," *Guardian*, June 6, 2001, http://www.theguardian.com/world/2001/jun/07/gender.uk2.
128. For more on guilty white sons and daughters, and their remembered relations to African caregivers, see Derek Hook, *(Post)apartheid Conditions: Psychoanalysis and Social Formation* (Basingstoke, UK: Palgrave Macmillan, 2013), 126–29, 136–46, 157–67.
129. Mxolisi Mchunu, "A Modern Coming of Age: Zulu Manhood, Domestic Work and the 'Kitchen Suit,'" in *Zulu Identities*, ed. Carton et al., 578. Mchunu points to the irony that "madam-servant relations, imposed by colonial segregationists," became

an element, for many, of their initiation into Zulu manhood: "Certainly the most striking similarity between traditional male initiation and the trials of the *Abaqulusi* is the emphasis on male separation (seclusion) from all things female, from the amputation warning of the red piping on the kitchen suit [worn by the "house boy"] to the (breast) milk taboo, symbolising the (forced) severance of young men from their mothers—in this instance their figurative 'maternal' missus." Mchunu, 579.

Chapter 4: 100% Zulu Boy

1. Now called the South Gauteng High Court.
2. Michael Wines, "A Highly Charged Rape Trial Tests South Africa's Ideals," *New York Times*, April 10, 2006.
3. Antjie Krog, *Begging to Be Black* (Cape Town: Random House Struik, 2009).
4. See Sigmund Freud, "On the Sexual Theories of Children," 1908, *Standard Edition*, vol. 9, 213–14.
5. Wines, "Highly Charged Rape Trial."
6. Ahmadou Kourouma, *Allah Is Not Obliged*, 2000, trans. Frank Wynne (New York: Anchor, 2007).
7. Aubrey Matshiqi, *Undamaged Reputations? Implications for the Criminal Justice System of the Allegations against and the Prosecution of Jacob Zuma* (Braamfontein, South Africa: Centre for the Study of Violence and Reconciliation, 2007), 8.
8. Fraser Mtshali, "Umzuzu nomzuzu elawini likaZuma" [Minute-by-minute in Zuma's guest room], *UmAfrika,* March 10–16, 2006: 4.
9. Fraser Mtshali, "Akakukhumbuli okuningi umama" [Mother does not remember much], *UmAfrika*, March 17–23, 2006: 6.
10. Evidence of Accused, *State v. Jacob Gedleyihlekisa Zuma* 2006, High Court of South Africa (Witwatersrand Local Division), SS321/05, Record of the Court, 917, 1022.
11. W.J. van der Merwe, Judgment in *State v. Jacob Gedleyihlekisa Zuma*, High Court of South Africa (Witwatersrand Local Division), May 8, 2006, 22–37, 164, http://www.saflii.org/za/cases/ZAGPHC/2006/.
12. Gill Gifford, "The Woman Who Took on Zuma," *IOL News*, May 10, 2006, http://www.iol.co.za/news/south-africa/the-woman-who-took-on-zuma-1.277146#.UAmPjkSIevI.
13. Van der Merwe, Judgment, 167–70.
14. Raymond Suttner, "The Jacob Zuma Rape Trial: Power and African National Congress (ANC) Masculinities," *NORA—Nordic Journal of Feminist and Gender Research* 17.3 (2009): 227.
15. Mmatshilo Motsei, *The Kanga and the Kangaroo Court: Reflections on the Rape Trial of Jacob Zuma* (Auckland Park, South Africa: Jacana, 2007), 181–82.
16. Lisa Vetten, "Violence against Women in South Africa," in *State of the Nation. South Africa 2007*, ed. Sakhela Buhlungu et al. (Cape Town: HSRC Press, 2007), 439.
17. Vetten, "Violence against Women," 439–40. For an excellent history of "Umshini wami" (My Machine Gun) in the context of South African liberation songs, see Liz Gunner, "Jacob Zuma, the Social Body, and the Unruly Power of Song," *African Affairs* 108/430 (2008): 27–48.

18. Fraser Mtshali, "Alindwe ngengoma amazwi amnandi" [Sweet words awaited by song], *UmAfrika*, May 12–18, 2006: 9.
19. Karyn Maughan, "Poetic Judge Paints the True Picture," *Star*, May 9, 2006: 4.
20. Motsei, *The Kanga and the Kangaroo Court*, 181.
21. Jeremy Gordin, *Zuma: A Biography* (Johannesburg: Jonathan Ball, 2008), 154.
22. Motsei, *The Kanga and the Kangaroo Court*, 181.
23. Suttner, "Jacob Zuma Rape Trial," 227.
24. Steven Robins, "Sexual Politics and the Zuma Rape Trial," *Journal of Southern African Studies* 34:2 (2008): 426.
25. Mtshali, "Alindwe ngengoma."
26. The name of the group comes from the finding of a 2002 study that only one in nine women raped makes a report to the police. See http://www.oneinnine.org.za/22.page.
27. "'I Was Raped and I Am Sane,'" interview with "Khwezi" by Dawn Cavanagh and Prudence Mabele, *City Press*, May 14, 2006: 4, http://152.111.1.87/argief/berigte/citypress/2006/05/14/C1/4/02.html.
28. Ibid.
29. Ibid.
30. Ibid. The sentence in square brackets appears in the Zulu-language version of the interview published in *UmAfrika*, Cavanagh and Mabele, "Ukhipha okumudla ngaphakathi obophe uMsholozi" [The one who had Umsholozi arrested draws out what is eating her inside], *UmAfrika*, May 19–25, 2006: 4.
31. Cavanagh and Mabele, "Ukhipha," 4.
32. Van der Merwe, Judgment, 108. See also Evidence of Complainant, *State v. Zuma*, Record of the Court, 222.
33. Michel Foucault, *The History of Sexuality*, vol. 1, trans. Robert Hurley (New York: Pantheon, 1978), 69-70.
34. Van der Merwe, Judgment, 23.
35. Presumably she refers to Van der Merwe's summary of her mother's testimony, and that of Dr. Olivier, the psychologist who testified as expert witness for the defense, as well as to parts of the judge's concluding summation. Van der Merwe, Judgment, 62, 138ff, 161, 172.
36. "'I Was Raped and I am Sane.'"
37. Ibid.
38. Mtshali, "Akakukhumbuli."
39. H. J. Simons, *African Women: Their Legal Status in South Africa* (Evanston, IL: Northwestern University Press, 1968), 117–18, see also 228ff on "seduction."
40. Elizabeth Thornberry, "Defining Crime through Punishment: Sexual Assault in the Eastern Cape, c.1835–1900," *Journal of Southern African Studies* 37.3 (2011): 429–30.
41. According to Anne Mager, in Ciskei during the 1940s and '50s, "[f]ew rapists were subjected to the full weight of criminal law." *Gender and the Making of a South African Bantustan: A Social History of the Ciskei, 1945–1959* (Portsmouth, NH: Heinemann, 1999), 184.
42. Mark Hunter, *Love in the Time of AIDS: Inequality, Gender, and Rights in South Africa* (Bloomington: Indiana University Press, 2010), 2–3.
43. Evidence of Complainant's mother, *State v. Zuma*, 315, ellipses in the original.

44. For an account of the significance of cattle more generally, see Marguerite Poland, David Hammond-Tooke, and Leigh Voigt, *The Abundant Herds: A Celebration of the Cattle of the Zulu People* (Simon's Town, South Africa: Fernwood Press, 2003). See also W. D. Hammond-Tooke, "Cattle Symbolism in Zulu Culture," in *Zulu Identities*, ed. Carton et al., 62–68.
45. Mtshali, "Akakukhumbuli."
46. The record of the court has it as follows: "[Advocate Brauns:] Was this the type of concept that was being discussed with Dr Mkhize?–[Witness:] Well I do not know, you see people can see one thing differently and as we were talking, or in our discussions, I discovered that he was also including this issue of compensation because he had to pay some reparation." Evidence of Complainant's mother, *State v. Zuma*, 315.
47. Fraser Mtshali, "Kuqala eyokugwema ibhokisi kuZuma" [It begins, the matter with Zuma avoiding the witness box], *UmAfrika*, March 24–30, 2006: 5.
48. Mtshali, "Akakukhumbuli."
49. Evidence of Accused, *State v. Zuma*, 1019–22.
50. Fraser Mtshali, "UZuma uchaza okwenzeka ngesingaye" [Zuma explains what happened according to him], *UmAfrika*, April 7–13, 2006: 6.
51. The *Star*'s reporting on negotiations about "compensation" displays no inkling that an alternative legal mechanism might have been in play; see Karyn Maughan, Jeremy Gordin, and Gill Gifford, "Zuma Tried to Buy My Silence, Says Complainant," *Star*, March 7, 2006: 3.
52. Mpume Zamisa and SAPA, "Wavakashela ishawa uMsholozi" [Umsholozi visited the shower], *Ilanga*, April 6–8, 2006: 1; "Ngangingenankinga ngelobolo: JZ" [I did not have a problem with *ilobolo*: JZ], *Isolezwe*, April 6, 2006.
53. Fraser Mtshali, "Isiyolala ibonene kwelikaMsholozi" [Judge is now going to sleep and be face-to-face with the case of Umsholozi], *UmAfrika*, May 5–11, 2006: 5. The judge, however, reminds the court that Zuma denied having mentioned *ilobolo* when the complainant visited his house on November 2, 2005. Van der Merwe, Judgment, 99. See also Evidence of Accused, *State v. Zuma*, 894.
54. Fraser Mtshali, "Umzuzu." See also Evidence of Complainant, *State v. Zuma*, 14.
55. Mtshali, "Akakukhumbuli."
56. Evidence of Complainant, *State v. Zuma*, 42, cf. 210.
57. Hunter, *Love in the Time of AIDS*, esp. 130–77.
58. Van der Merwe, Judgment, 117. See also Evidence of Complainant, *State v. Zuma*, 234ff.
59. "'I Was Raped and I Am Sane.'"
60. See Thornberry, "Defining Crime," 429.
61. Evidence of Complainant, *State v. Zuma*, 236.
62. Evidence of Accused, *State v. Zuma*, 1020.
63. Wines, "Highly Charged Rape Trial."
64. Gill Gifford and Karyn Maughan, "I Couldn't Stop, Zuma Testifies in Rape Trial," *Star*, April 4, 2006: 1.
65. Vetten, "Violence against Women," 438.
66. Van der Merwe, Judgment, 102.
67. Robins, "Sexual Politics," 423.
68. Mtshali, "UZuma uchaza," 6.

69. "'Babungekho ubungozi bengculazi'" [There was no risk of AIDS], *Isolezwe*, April 4, 2006.
70. Evidence of Accused, *State v. Zuma*, 907.
71. Thembisa Waetjen and Gerhard Maré, "Tradition's Desire: The Politics of Culture in the Rape Trial of Jacob Zuma," *Concerned Africa Scholars Bulletin* 84 (2010): 57–60.
72. Evidence of Accused, *State v. Zuma*, 1006.
73. Volovolo Memela, "Esikubona njengoba kuqulwa elikaMsholozi siyokuxoxela amagwababa echobana" [What we see just as Umsholozi's case is being tried we are going to tell it to the crows while looking for lice on one another (i.e., we will have something interesting to tell)], *Isolezwe*, April 19, 2006: 8.
74. Mpume Zamisa and SAPA, "Bafuna ukuchitha icala abameli baJacob Zuma" [Jacob Zuma's lawyers seek dismissal of case], *Ilanga*, March 27–29, 2006: 3.
75. Gordin, *Zuma*, 188, Gordin's interpolation.
76. Ibid.
77. See Van der Merwe, Judgment, 152.
78. Obituary for Judson Khuzwayo, *Sechaba*, July 1985, http://www.sacp.org.za/docs/biography/2006/jdkhuzwayo.html.
79. Gordin, *Zuma*, 5.
80. Motsei, *The Kanga and the Kangaroo Court*, 166.
81. Bhabha Madlala, "'Babukise ngami ko-TV abezindaba'" ["They made a spectacle about me on TV, the newsmedia people"], *UmAfrika*, May 12–18, 2006: 16.
82. Benedict Carton, "Why Is the '100% Zulu Boy' So Popular?," *Concerned Africa Scholars Bulletin* 84 (2010): 37.
83. I wrote this sentence before the furor that erupted over Brett Murray's painting, *The Spear* (2012), which, parodying Viktor Ivanov's famous poster of Lenin, *Lenin Lived, Lenin Is Alive, Lenin Will Live* (1967), depicts Jacob Zuma with a set of male genitalia hanging from his trousers. I let the sentence stand to underline the stakes involved in disinvesting from the symbolic surplus that makes a penis a phallus. It nevertheless remains likely that it is this phallic investment that, for those who objected to it, litigated against it, and defaced it, made Murray's painting an insult to Zuma—as national leader, father, and middle-aged man—and a slur against black men in general. Notable responses to the events in question include Njabulo Ndebele, "The Emperor Is Naked," *City Press*, June 16, 2012, http://www.citypress.co.za/Columnists/The-Emperor-is-naked-20120616; Achille Mbembe, "The Spear That Divided the Nation," *Cape Times*, June 5, 2012: 11; Kendall Geers, "Respect the Plumed Serpent," *Mail & Guardian*, July 20, 2012, http://mg.co.za/article/2012-07-19-respect-the-plumed-serpent. For an interesting meditation on *The Spear* in the context of iconoclasm in the history of art, see David Freedberg, "The Case of the Spear," *Art South Africa* 11.1 (2012): 36–41.

Chapter 5: 2008

1. *Mail & Guardian*, May 24, 2008, parenthetical gloss in original.
2. Nonhlanhla Jele, "Ushenge ukhale izinyembezi ngezifiki" [Shenge wept for immigrants], *Ilanga*, May 26–28, 2008: 1.

3. Annelene Moses, "'Meer slegte Suid-Afrikaners in townships'" ["More bad South Africans in townships"], *Beeld*, May 23, 2008: 4, first parenthetical gloss in original.
4. Judges 12:6. On this point, see Gqola, "Brutal Inheritances," 214–15.
5. Aldi Schoeman and Adeline de Lange, "Selfs Sjangaans nou onwelkom" [Even Shangaans unwelcome now], *Beeld*, May 20, 2008: 5, parenthetical gloss in original.
6. Media 24 Africa Office, "Meer as 20 000 is ontwortel" [More than 20,000 are uprooted], *Beeld*, May 22, 2008: 4.
7. When I visited South Africa in April 2015, there were again outbreaks of xenophobic violence in KwaZulu-Natal and Gauteng. A speech the previous month by the Zulu king, Goodwill Zwelithini, in which he had called upon foreigners to leave the country, was widely seen as having contributed to the climate of hatred—so much so that the king was prompted to hold a mass *imbizo* (official gathering) in Durban at which, although he stood by what he had said in his earlier speech, he also called for an end to violence. See, for example, Celani Sikhakhane, "'Ngeke ngiyihoxise inkulumo'" ["I will never retract the speech"], *Isolezwe*, March 25, 2015: 10; Beauregard Tromp, Nathi Olifant, and Matthew Savides, "Kill Thy Neighbour: Alex Attack Brings Home SA's Shame," *Times Live*, April 19, 2015, http://www.timeslive.co.za/local/2015/04/19/kill-thy-neighbour-alex-attack-brings-home-sa-s-shame1; David Smith, "Zulu Leader Suggests Media to Blame for South Africa's Xenophobic Violence," *Guardian*, April 20, 2015, http://www.theguardian.com/world/2015/apr/20/south-africa-xenophobic-violence-zulu-king-goodwill-zwelithini. A repudiation of xenophobia and gentle criticism of the king was voiced by Volovolo Memela, "Izinja sezaba nobuntu sezidlula nabanye bethu" [Dogs now have ubuntu (i.e., humanity), surpassing even some of our people], *Isolezwe*, April 22, 2015: 10.
8. See Gqola, "Brutal Inheritances," 214–15.
9. Cobus Claassen, "'SA moenie dié reputasie kry'" ["SA mustn't get *this* reputation"], *Beeld*, May 19, 2008: 4; Alex Eliseev and Shaun Smillie, "Voetsek! The Message from These Thugs as They Rampage through Alex on a Door-to-Door Purge," *Star*, May 14, 2008: 1.
10. See Alison Gillwald and Cyril Madlala, "'A Black Coup'—Inkatha and the Sale of *Ilanga*," *Transformation* 7 (1988): 27–36.
11. For reflections in the aftermath, see Anton Harber, *Diepsloot* (Johannesburg: Jonathan Ball, 2011), 120–35.
12. See Bonner and Nieftagodien, *Alexandra: A History*, 416–21, as well as Noor Nieftagodien, "Xenophobia's Local Genesis: Historical Constructions of Insiders and the Politics of Exclusion in Alexandra Township," in *Exorcising the Demons within: Xenophobia, Violence and Statecraft in Contemporary South Africa*, ed. Loren B. Landau (Johannesburg: Wits University Press, 2011), 109–34.
13. For a comprehensive chronology for 1994–2008, see *The Perfect Storm: The Realities of Xenophobia in Contemporary South Africa* (Cape Town: Southern African Migration Project, 2008), 44–54.
14. See Patrick Harries, *Work, Culture, and Identity: Migrant Laborers in Mozambique and South Africa, c. 1860–1910* (Portsmouth, NH: Heinemann / Johannesburg: Witwatersrand University Press / London: James Currey, 1994), 121–24.
15. For an absorbing account of how one Somali man experienced the events of those

months, see Jonny Steinberg, *A Man of Good Hope* (New York: Knopf, 2014), 221–55.
16. Zama Mkhize, "Kuqiniswa ezokuphepha eKZN" [Security affairs are strengthened in KZN], *UmAfrika*, May 23–29, 2008: 16.
17. Quoted in Eric Worby, Shireen Hassim, and Tawana Kupe, "Introduction: Facing the Other at the Gates of Democracy," in Hassim et al., *Go Home or Die Here*, 4. See also "'Sisazobemukela kakhulu abokuhamba kuleli'" ["We are still going to admit in high numbers immigrants in this country"], *UmAfrika*, May 23–29, 2008: 16.
18. Adam Habib, "Explosion of a Dream Deferred," *Star*, June 17, 2008, Never Again Supplement: 2. See also Stephen Gelb, "Behind Xenophobia in South Africa: Poverty or Inequality?," in Hassim et al., *Go Home or Die Here*, esp. 79–80; Devan Pillay, "Relative Deprivation, Social Instability and Cultures of Entitlement," in Hassim et al., 93–103.
19. Michael Neocosmos, *From "Foreign Natives" to "Native Foreigners": Explaining Xenophobia in Post-Apartheid South Africa: Citizenship and Nationalism, Identity and Politics*, 2nd ed. (Dakar, Senegal: CODESRIA, 2010).
20. Daniel Bell, "The Dispossessed," in *The Radical Right: The New American Right*, ed. Daniel Bell (Garden City, NY: Anchor, 1964), 42.
21. Summarizing the history of the concept in social psychology, W. G. Runciman emphasizes that "[r]elative deprivation should always be understood to mean a *sense* of deprivation; a person who is 'relatively deprived' need not be 'objectively' deprived in the more usual sense that he is demonstrably lacking something. In addition, relative deprivation means that the sense of deprivation is such as to involve a comparison with the imagined situation of some other person or group." W. G. Runciman, *Relative Deprivation and Social Justice: A Study of Attitudes to Social Inequality in Twentieth-Century England* (Berkeley: University of California Press, 1966), 10–11.
22. Runciman, however, observes that "relative deprivation retains the merit of being value-neutral as between a feeling of envy and a perception of injustice. To establish what resentment of inequality can be vindicated by an appeal to social justice will require that this distinction should somehow be made. But in determining first of all what is the empirical relation between inequality and grievance, it is important to use a term which in no way begs the distinction between 'legitimate' and 'illegitimate' grievances." *Relative Deprivation*, 10.
23. Mamphela Ramphele, "A Mirror Image of Our Society," *Star*, May 22, 2008: 17.
24. See Maré and Hamilton, *An Appetite for Power*, 55.
25. My translation of the title of Nxumalo's trilogy of articles calls for explanation. Grammatically, the word "esiyingcwenga" is a relative adjective, made up of the relative prefix "esi-," which agrees with "isiZulu," the copula "yi-," and the noun "ingcwenga." This gives "isiZulu" the qualities of "ingcwenga," yielding: Zulu that is *ingcwenga*, or *ingcwenga* Zulu. Translating the word "ingcwenga" is tricky. It is possible to take it as being a variant spelling of *incwenga*, which is a hlonipha word for *umlaza* (whey), and is a noun derived from the verb *cwenga*, which means to sift, refine, and so forth, for instance the whey from the curds (*amasi*), and can be used metaphorically to describe a careful choosing of words; see Doke et al., *English-Zulu, Zulu-English Dictionary*, entries for *cwenga* and *-cwenga*. In other words, *incwenga* or *ingcwenga*, or what was *ingcwenga*, would be the product of a sifting or refining

process. Doke et al.'s dictionary was compiled more than fifty years ago. In contemporary usage, the word *ingcwenga* is employed quite loosely to refer to something that is excellent or outstanding. We have the expression *ingcwenga yebhola*, for example, frequently found in the sports pages of *Isolezwe*, which, in context, appears to mean something like "great soccer" or "top-class soccer" when referring to the play of an individual star or to a specific match. A multilingual lexicon of soccer terminology, prepared by the South African Department of Arts and Culture for use during the 2010 World Cup, defines *ingcwenga yebhola* as "spectacular game," when the term refers to a particular match. *Multilingual Soccer Terminology List* ([Pretoria]: Department of Arts and Culture, [2010]), 202. Basing one's choice on Doke et al., one could translate Nxumalo's title as "Challenges of Pure Zulu" or "Challenges of Purified Zulu." As we shall see, however, Nxumalo's purism is a qualified one. I therefore opt for "Challenges of Refined Zulu," to preserve the idea of refining, specifically through care exercised in speech and writing, but also to convey the connotations in English of the word "refined," which, in a certain idiom, is a general term of approbation for manners, tastes, or modes of speech that are thought, from the point of view of the speaker, not to be vulgar. I opt for this translation over "Challenges of Standard Zulu," an alternative translation that has been proposed to me, and which does indeed represent one strand in Nxumalo's argument, because, in English, "standard" means good, but, typically, does not mean the best.
26. O.E.H.M. Nxumalo, "Izinselelo zesiZulu esiyingcwengwa [*sic*]" [Challenges of refined Zulu], *Ilanga*, April 14–16, 2008: 5.
27. Ibid.
28. Ibid.
29. O.E.H.M. Nxumalo, "Izinselelo zesiZulu esiyingcwenga (Isigaba sesibili)" [Challenges of refined Zulu (Part two)], *Ilanga*, April 28–30, 2008: 5.
30. Nxumalo, "Izinselelo zesiZulu esiyingcwengwa [*sic*]."
31. Ibid.
32. Nxumalo, "Izinselelo (Isigaba sesibili)."
33. Nxumalo, "Izinselelo zesiZulu esiyingcwengwa [*sic*]."
34. Nxumalo, "Izinselelo (Isigaba sesibili)."
35. Hamilton and Wright, "The Making of the AmaLala," 19. See also Gilmour, *Grammars of Colonialism*, 120–22.
36. O.E.H.M. Nxumalo, "Izinselelo zesiZulu esiyingcwenga (Isiqephu sesithathu)" [Challenges of refined Zulu (Part three)], *Ilanga*, May 5–7, 2008: 5.
37. See Jacques Derrida, *Schibboleth: pour Paul Celan* (Paris: Galilée, 1986), 44; "Shibboleth: For Paul Celan," in *Sovereignties in Question: The Poetics of Paul Celan*, ed. Thomas Dutoit and Outi Pasanen (New York: Fordham University Press, 2005), 22.
38. Nxumalo, "Izinselelo (Isiqephu sesithathu)."
39. Nyembezi, *Lafa elihle kakhulu*, 225.
40. Nxumalo also cites the mixing of languages in the title of Ukhozi FM's popular iVuka Breakfast Show (now called Vuka Mzansi), and in phrases used by the radio station's announcers. Nxumalo, "Izinselelo (Isiqephu sesithathu)."
41. Formed in response to the imposition of English as the official language at the Cape by the British in 1812, which, by making Dutch optional as a school subject, "equated it with Kaffir-language [*Kaffertaal*]," the Genootskap van Regte Afrikaanders (Fellowship of True Afrikaners) declared in the first issue of its newspaper: "And the

worst is, they deprive us of what they can never give us again. Because there is but one mother-language [*moedertaal*], the language of our heart. The language in which at mother's breast we learned to say *pa* and *ma*,—the language in which we received our first impressions,—the language in which our pious mother taught us as children to pronounce the dear name of our Lord Jesus." *Die Afrikaanse Patriot 1876: 'n Faksimilee-weergawe van die eerste jaargang* (Cape Town: Tafelberg, 1974), 8–9.
42. Klein, "Envy and Gratitude."
43. Doke et al., *English-Zulu, Zulu-English Dictionary*, entry for *cwenga*.
44. Nxumalo, "Izinselelo zesiZulu esiyingcwengwa [*sic*]."
45. O.E.H.M. Nxumalo, "Ukuqhubukusha abantu bokufika," *Ilanga*, May 26–28, 2008: 5
46. The word is used, for example, in a headline from the same edition of *Ilanga* in which Nxumalo's column appears. Jele, "Ushenge ukhale izinyembezi ngezifiki."
47. Nxumalo, "Ukuqhubukusha abantu bokufika."
48. Neliswe Ntshang[a]se, "Uma kuxoshwa abezizwe kukhethelwani abamnyama?" [When foreign people are driven out why are black people singled out?], *UmAfrika*, May 23–29, 2008: 18–19.
49. *Ilanga*, May 22–24, 2008: 4.
50. Nxumalo, "Ukuqhubukusha abantu bokufika."
51. Ibid.
52. Ibid.
53. Ibid.
54. Gqola, "Brutal Inheritances," 219.
55. Siyabonga Mkhwanazi, "Mbeki Slams 'Shameful Actions of a Few,'" *Star*, May 26, 2008: 3; see also Thabo Mbeki, "Radio and Television Address to the Nation by President Thabo Mbeki, on the Occasion of Africa Day," May 25, 2008, http://www.anc.org.za/show.php?id=4172; Claassen, "'SA moenie.'"
56. Nxumalo, "Ukuqhubukusha abantu bokufika."
57. "Bayekeleni bagoduke abafuna ukubuyela emakhaya" [Let them go those who want to return home], *Ilanga* June 9–11, 2008: 4.
58. O.E.H.M. Nxumalo, "Ukuqhubukusha abantu bokufika (Isigaba sesibili)" [Elbowing out immigrants (Part two)], *Ilanga*, June 9–11, 2008: 5
59. Ibid.
60. Ibid.
61. Ibid.
62. In an official report on the "Durban Riots" of January 1949, which began after an Indian shopkeeper assaulted an African youth, with whom his shop assistant had had an altercation, we read the following: "[The Native's—i.e., Africans in Natal generally] complaint . . . is that when he enters an Indian shop in which there are a number of Indians and he himself is unattended by friends or witnesses, he is apt to be overcharged, given the wrong change or no change at all, or subjected to conditional buying in order to obtain what he wants. If he protests he is liable to be assaulted; if he complains to the Police a prosecution rarely materializes because there is not proof of his allegations." The Commissioners add that "[w]e believe that there is much truth to this allegation. A number of credible witnesses have appeared before us and recounted their personal experiences. Indians not connected with trade complained to us that they had received similar treatment at the hands of Indian shop-

keepers, but they were loth to give evidence for fear of reprisals." Union of South Africa, *Report of the Commission of Enquiry into Riots in Durban* (Cape Town: Cape Times, 1949), 16.
63. Ntshang[a]se, "Uma kuxoshwa."
64. As Minister of Education from 1999–2004, Asmal presided over a massive and contentious restructuring of South African higher education, including the shuttering of several teacher-training colleges in KwaZulu-Natal, a decision for which he was criticized by many, including O.E.H.M. Nxumalo. Nxumalo, "Ayevalelwani amak[h]olishi nje nempela?" [Why were the colleges even shut at all?] *Ilanga*, October 6–8, 2008: 5; "Ayevalelwani amakholishi othis[h]a? (Isigaba sesibili)" [Why were the teachers' colleges shut? (Second part)] *Ilanga*, October 13–15, 2008: 5. Among Nxumalo's bitter *ad hominem* remarks against Asmal in the latter column is the charge that, as for "Zulu, that in which is being written here, he does not know it." For Asmal's own account of the restructuring, see Kader Asmal, Adrian Hadland, and Moira Levy, *Kader Asmal: Politics in My Blood: A Memoir* (Auckland Park, South Africa: Jacana, 2011), 273–83.
65. The Nhlapo Commission's report states that Soshangane was a cousin of Zwide. *Report of the Commission on Traditional Leadership Disputes and Claims* (Pretoria: Republic of South Africa, 2010), 544.
66. Nxumalo, "Ukuqhubukusha (Isigaba sesibili)."
67. *Perfect Storm*, 16–17.
68. Jele, "UShenge ukhale."
69. Dries Liebenberg, "'Aanval op ons almal'" ["Attack on all of us"], *Beeld*, May 24, 2008: 2, parenthetical gloss is *Beeld*'s.
70. Nxumalo, "Ukuqhubukusha [Part one]."
71. See J. D. Omer-Cooper, *The Zulu Aftermath: A Nineteenth-Century Revolution in Bantu Africa* (Evanston, IL: Northwestern University Press, 1966), 57–63; *Report of the Commission on Traditional Leadership Disputes and Claims*, 548.
72. Omer-Cooper, *Zulu Aftermath*, 63
73. Ibid., 33.
74. *Report of the Commission on Traditional Leadership Disputes and Claims*, 544. Drawing on Ndwandwe oral history recorded in the 1980s, recent historiography has revised the received "Zuluist" account on which both the *Report* and O.E.H.M. Nxumalo rely. It tells us that the migration of the Ndwandwe under Soshangane may not have been a direct result of a defeat or quarrel with Shaka but "was due mainly to internal political tensions." It likewise tells us that the migration of the Khumalo under Mzilikazi may have been to escape subjugation by the Ndwandwe as much as by the Zulu. Wright, "Rediscovering the Ndwandwe Kingdom," 230–31.
75. Wright, "Rediscovering the Ndwandwe Kingdom," 232–33.
76. On the uBumbano lwamaZwide (Unity Association of the Zwides), which was formed in 2006, see Mbongiseni Buthelezi, *"Sifuna umlando wethu" (We Are Looking for Our History): Oral Literature and the Meanings of the Past in Post-Apartheid South Africa*, PhD. diss., Columbia University, 2012, esp. 24, 83–84, 98–99, 117.
77. *Report of the Commission on Traditional Leadership Disputes and Claims*, 534–63. After being contested, the ruling of the Commission was upheld in 2014 by the Constitutional Court of South Africa. *Nxumalo v. President of the Republic of South*

Africa and Others, 2014 ZACC 27, http://www.saflii.org/za/cases/ZACC/2014/27.pdf.
78. Henri A. Junod, *The Life of a South African Tribe*, 1912 (New Hyde Park, NY: University Books Inc., 1962), vol. 1, 28.
79. Niren Tolsi, "Bling Fit for a King," *Mail & Guardian*, April 18, 2008, http://mg.co.za/article/2008-04-18-bling-fit-for-a-king.
80. Buthelezi, "*Sifuna umlando wethu*," 12.
81. The risks include being perceived as challenging the legitimacy of the Zulu royal establishment. Buthelezi, "*Sifuna umlando wethu*," 62–63.
82. N. P. van Wyk Louw, *Versamelde prosa 2* (Cape Town: Human & Rousseau, 1986), 623. The poetry of Adam Small, which can be read as a sustained interrogation of such assumptions, relentlessly insists on speech as a marker of racial difference. In 1963, for example, Small published a poem entitled "Sê Sjibbolet," which ends, in an imprecation that radically changes the tone of the Biblical verses it translates, "nai? / ôrait, / ma sê net, / sê net / Sjibbolet!" (nay? / orright / g'on jus say / jus say / Shibboleth!). Adam Small, *Sê Sjibbolet* (Johannesburg: Afrikaanse Pers-Boekhandel, 1963), 53.
83. Nxumalo, "Ukuqhubukusha abantu bokufika (Isigaba sesibili)."
84. See Nxumalo, "Ayevalelwani amak[h]olishi nje nempela?"; "Ayevalelwani amakholishi othis[h]a? (Isigaba sesibili)."
85. Mokoena, *Magema Fuze*; Khumalo, "Class of 1856."
86. Nxumalo, "Ayevalelwani amakholishi othis[h]a? (Isigaba sesibili)."
87. Volovolo Memela, "AmaNu kade ngawatshela ukuthi akunikelwa esontweni ngemali yokuqwayiza" [For a long time I have been telling the Babies that prostitution money is not contributed in church], *Isolezwe*, May 19, 2010, 10, http://www.isolezwe.co.za/index.php?fArticleId=5475216.
88. Ibid. For the earlier column, see Volovolo Memela, "Abaqwayizi bangaphandle abahambe bayoqwayiza ngakubo" [Let the foreign prostitutes go and prostitute themselves in their own countries], *Isolezwe*, March 17, 2010, 10.
89. "Bayekeleni bagoduke abafuna ukubuyela emakhaya" [Let them go those who want to return home], *Ilanga*, June 9–11, 2008: 4.
90. This influx never materialized. See Wim Delva et al., "Sex Work during the 2010 FIFA World Cup: Results from a Three-Wave Cross-Sectional Survey," *PLoS ONE* 6.12 (2011), www.plos.org: e2836. doi:10.1371/journal.pone.0028363.
91. See, for instance, "Ngezobani izingane ezizothengisa ngemizimba?" [Whose children will be selling their bodies?], *Ilanga*, July 10–12, 2008: 4.
92. Memela, "AmaNu kade ngawatshela."
93. Ibid.
94. See Eddie Cottle, ed. *South Africa's World Cup: A Legacy for Whom?* (Pietermaritzburg, South Africa: University of KwaZulu-Natal Press, 2011); Zapiro, "Self-Satisfied Sepp Blatter Hands Over R680 Million to SAFA as a Reward for a Successful World Cup," *Times*, December 21, 2010, http://www.zapiro.com/cartoon/208845-101221tt#.UAb9R3Drxdo.
95. See Sibusiso Nyembezi and O.E.H.M. Nxumalo, *Inqolobane yesizwe*, 4th ed. (Pietermaritzburg, South Africa: Shuter & Shooter, 1996), 172; Doke et al., entry for *-iso*.
96. Volovolo Memela, "Bhejane ungaphumi esiqiwini esiyinhliziyo yami. Bayede, wena weNdlovu!" [Rhinoceros do not leave the enclosure that is my heart. Bayede, wena weNdlovu!], *Isolezwe*, October 20, 2004: 8.

97. Volovolo Memela, "Nginenkinga ngokuthi abantu baqanjwe amagama aphambana nabo" [I have a problem with people being given names at cross purposes with them], *Isolezwe*, August 2, 2006: 8.
98. Volovolo Memela, "Kuyadabukisa ukubona owesifazane ezipende ngeruji kodwa angaqatshulwa" [It is saddening to see a woman painting herself with lipstick but not getting kissed], *Isolezwe*, September 22, 2004: 8
99. Volovolo Memela, "UJabu Pule ugeqa amagula ngezintombi, utshwala nezidakamizwa" [Jabu Pule reveals all about girls, beer, and drugs], *Isolezwe*, January 22, 2003: 9.
100. Quoted in Niren Tolsi, "The All New Zulu," *Mail & Guardian*, May 28, 2008, parenthetical gloss in *Mail & Guardian*.
101. I thank Sally-Ann Murray for sharing with me her knowledge and thoughts about The Point.
102. See Volovolo Memela, "Amadlingozi kaKhisimusi ayingozi, enza abantu benze imisangano" [Christmas festivities are a danger, making people do muddled things], *Isolezwe*, December 19, 2007: 8.
103. See Volovolo Memela, "Ngifuna ubukhosi basePhoyinti bube nesihlalo eNdlini yabaHoli boMdabu" [I want the chieftainship of The Point to have a seat at the House of Traditional Leaders], *Isolezwe*, May 27, 2009.
104. See, for instance, Volovolo Memela, "UMkhandlu ungakhuluma kanjani ngezindaba ezithinta omahosha ungayithintanga inkosi yabo?" [How can the city council speak about matters affecting prostitutes without having contacted their chief?], *Isolezwe*, July 16, 2008; "Kuyaxaka ukuthi ngithi ngiyinkosi yasePhoyinti kodwa ngingathintwa uma kukhulunywa ngabantu bami" [It is confusing that I am Chief of The Point but I am not contacted when my people are spoken about], *Isolezwe*, June 3, 2009.
105. See, for example, Volovolo Memela, "Ingxoxo ekhethekile kaBhavaneselula noMntwana wakwaPhindangene" [Exclusive interview by He-Who-Baths-with-a-Cellphone with Mntwana wakwaPhindangene (i.e., Chief Mangosuthu Buthelezi)], *Isolezwe*, September 9, 2009; "ULekota uthi isikhundla sokuhola iCOPE ngesakhe futhi sisazohlala kuye" [Lekota says that the leadership of COPE is his and will continue to remain with him], *Isolezwe*, June 2, 2010.
106. *iSilo samabandla*, Lion of the Assemblies, is one of the main praise names (*izibongo*) of King Zwelithini.
107. *uBhejane phuma esiqiwini kade babekuvalele* is another of the king's praises. A slightly different version of this praise is given by Liz Gunner and Mafika Gwala: "UBhejane odl' abakayise ph-u-um' esiqiwini kade bekuvalele" (Rhinoceros who subdued his brothers, br-e-e-ak out of this game reserve where they've locked you up!). *Musho! Zulu Popular Praises*, translated and edited by Liz Gunner and Mafika Gwala (East Lansing: Michigan State University Press, 1991), 56–57. Nxumalo and his co-authors give the context for the praise as Zwelithini's return to Nongoma from KwaNdebele, where he had been taken by his sister, who feared that rivals were planning to kill him, and his assertion of his claim to the Zulu kingship, which he attained in 1968, being officially crowned in 1971. O.E.H.M. Nxumalo, C. T. Msimang, and I. S. Cooke, *King of Goodwill: The Authorised Biography of King Goodwill Zwelithini kaBhekuzulu* (Cape Town: Nasou Via Afrika, 2003), 52. Volovolo parodies this praise on occasion, hailing the king: Memela, "Bhejane ungaphumi esiqiwini

esiyinhliziyo yami" [Rhinoceros do not leave the enclosure that is my heart]; also "Ugogo mumbe ungifanise nembuzi yomxokozelo wendodana yakhe" [Another granny compared me to her son's clamorous goat], *Isolezwe*, June 7, 2006: 8.
108. *uHlanga Lwezwe*, Reed of the Nation, is also a praise name of the king.
109. Volovolo Memela, "Ukuba kuya ngezifiso zenkosi yasePhoyinti ngabe uKhozi neGagasi kuyahlanganiswa" [If it were according to the wishes of the Chief of The Point, Ukhozi and Gagasi would be merged], *Isolezwe*, April 2, 2008.
110. A catalyst for my thoughts on irreducible ambiguity in praise genres was a discussion involving Magalí Armillas-Tiseyra and Lily Saint in my African novel seminar at New York University in Fall 2006 on Ahmadou Kourouma's novel, *Waiting for the Wild Animals to Vote*.
111. Archie Mafeje, "The Role of the Bard in a Contemporary African Community," *Journal of African Languages* 6.3 (1967): 197.
112. Where I have translated it as "private royal enclosure," Volos uses the word *isigodlo*, which refers to the "[u]pper part of the royal kraal, reserved as the King's private enclosure, and consisting of the huts of the King's wives and children"; Doke et al., entry for *isigodlo*. The implication is thus that, if things turn out as he wishes, the Chief of The Point will be surrounded solely by revering women—namely, his "people" or the *amaNu*.
113. *iMbube*, Lion, another praise name of the king.
114. Memela, "Ukuba kuya ngezifiso zenkosi yasePhoyinti ngabe uKhozi neGagasi kuyahlanganiswa."
115. Mafeje, "Role of the Bard," 196.
116. Mikhail Bakhtin, *Rabelais and His World* (1965), trans. Helene Iswolsky (Cambridge, MA: MIT Press, 1968), 5.
117. Memela, "UJabu Pule ugeqa amagula."
118. Memela, "Nginenkinga."
119. See Volovolo Memela, "Amakhansela kumele athengele uVolos unyanyavu lwemoto" [The councilors should buy Volos a fancy car], *Isolezwe*, February 6, 2008.
120. Volovolo Memela, "Abantu abafunde ukubekezela abanye njengokuthanda kwabo amaselula" [Let people learn to be patient with others, just as they love their cellphones], *Isolezwe*, July 14, 2010.
121. Volovolo Memela, "Ngeso likaVolovolo," *Isolezwe*, September 10, 2008.
122. Memela, "AmaNu kade ngawatshela."
123. Memela, "UMkhandlu ungakhuluma kanjani?"
124. See Delva et al., "Sex Work during the 2010 FIFA World Cup."
125. Volovolo Memela, "Ludinga ukuxoxwa udaba lokulandwa kwabantu abafele ezindaweni ezithile" [The matter of fetching people who die in certain places needs to be discussed], *Isolezwe*, August 5, 2009.
126. See Ndlovu, "21st-Century Pencil Test."
127. Memela, "AmaNu kade ngawatshela."
128. Volovolo Memela, "Inkosi yasePhoyinti isinenduna ezinze eNew York, kwelaseMelika" [The Chief of The Point now has an induna who is settled in New York, in America], *Isolezwe*, February 2, 2011: 10.
129. Volovolo Memela, "Kufanele ludingidwe udaba lwamadoda nabesifazane" [It must be investigated, the matter of men and women], *Isolezwe*, June 14, 2006: 10.

Select Bibliography

Achebe, Chinua. "The African Writer and the English Language." In *Morning Yet on Creation Day*, 74–84. Garden City, NY: Anchor, 1976.
Adendorff, Ralph. "Fanakalo: A Pidgin in South Africa." In *Language in South Africa*, edited by Rajend Mesthrie, 179–98. Cambridge, UK: Cambridge University Press, 2002.
Aitken-Cade, S. E. *So! You Want to Learn the Language! An Amusing and Instructive Kitchen Kaffir Dictionary*. Salisbury, Southern Rhodesia: Centafrican Press, 1951.
Attwell, David. *Rewriting Modernity: Studies in Black South African Literary History*. Pietermaritzburg, South Africa: University of KwaZulu-Natal Press, 2005.
Ballard, Charles. *John Dunn: The White Chief of Zululand*. Johannesburg: Ad Donker, 1985.
Bleek, Wilhelm. *The Natal Diaries of Dr. W.H.I. Bleek, 1855–1856*. Translated by O. H. Spohr. Cape Town: A. A. Balkema, 1965.
———. "On the Languages of Western and Southern Africa." *Transactions of the Philological Society* 4 (1855): 40–50.
Bold, J. D. *Dictionary, Grammar and Phrase-Book of Fanagalo (Kitchen Kafir): The Lingua Franca of Southern Africa as Spoken in the Union of South Africa, the Rhodesias, Portuguese East Africa, Nyasaland, Belgian Congo, Etc.* 5th ed. N.p., South Africa: Central News Agency, 1958.
Bonner, Philip, and Noor Nieftagodien. *Alexandra: A History*. Johannesburg: Wits University Press, 2008.
Brown, David. "The Basements of Babylon: Language and Literacy on the South African Gold Mines." *Social Dynamics* 14.1 (1988): 46–56.
———. "The Rise and Fall of Fanakalo: Language and Literacy Policies of the South African Gold Mines." In *Language in South Africa: An Input into Language Planning for a Post-Apartheid South Africa*, edited by Victor N. Webb, 309–27. Pretoria: LiCCA Research and Development Programme, 1995.
Buthelezi, Mbongiseni. "The Empire Talks Back: Re-Examining the Legacies of Shaka and Zulu Power in Post-Apartheid South Africa." In *Zulu Identities*, edited by Carton et al., 23–34.
———. "*Sifuna umlando wethu*" (We Are Looking for Our History): Oral Literature and the Meanings of the Past in Post-Apartheid South Africa. PhD. diss., Columbia University, 2012.
Carton, Benedict. "Why Is the '100% Zulu Boy' So Popular?" *Concerned Africa Scholars Bulletin* 84 (2010): 34–38.
Carton, Benedict, John Laband, and Jabulani Sithole, eds. *Zulu Identities: Being Zulu, Past and Present*. Pietermaritzburg, South Africa: University of KwaZulu-Natal Press, 2008.

Cavanagh, Dawn, and Prudence Mabele. "'I Was Raped and I Am Sane.'" Interview with "Khwezi." *City Press*, May 14, 2006: 4. http://152.111.1.87/argief/berigte/citypress/2006/05/14/C1/4/02.html.

———. "Ukhipha okumudla ngaphakathi obophe uMsholozi" [The one who had Umsholozi arrested draws out what is eating her inside]. *UmAfrika*, May 19–25, 2006: 4–5.

Cobbett, William, and Brian Nakedi. "The Flight of the Herschelites: Ethnic Nationalism and Land Dispossession." In *Popular Struggles in South Africa*, edited by William Cobbett and Robin Cohen, 77–89. Trenton, NJ: Africa World Press, 1988.

Coetzee, Carli. *Accented Futures: Language Activism and the Ending of Apartheid*. Johannesburg: Wits University Press, 2013.

Coetzee, J. M. "Apartheid Thinking." In *Giving Offense: Essays on Censorship*, 163–84. Chicago: University of Chicago Press, 1996.

———. *White Writing: On the Culture of Letters in South Africa*. New Haven, CT: Yale University Press, 1988.

Cole, D. T. "Fanagalo and the Bantu Languages in South Africa." *African Studies* 12.1 (1953): 1–9.

Colenso, Harriette Emily. Preface to J. W. Colenso, *Zulu-English Dictionary*, 4th ed., v–vii. N.p., Natal, South Africa: Vause & Slatter, 1905.

Colenso, J. W. *Bringing Forth Light: Five Tracts on Bishop Colenso's Zulu Mission*. Edited by Ruth Edgecombe. Pietermaritzburg, South Africa: University of Natal Press / Durban, South Africa: Killie Campbell Africana Library, 1982.

———. *Church Missions: To the Members of the Church of England, The Earnest Appeal of the Bishop of Natal on Behalf of the Heathen Tribes within and on the Borders of the Diocese*. [1854]. In Colenso, *Bringing Forth Light*, 1–28.

———. *First Steps in Zulu: Being an Elementary Grammar of the Zulu Language*. 5th ed. Pietermaritzburg and Durban, South Africa: P. Davis & Sons, 1904.

———. *First Steps of the Zulu Mission (Oct. 1859)*. 1860. In *Bringing Forth Light*, 43–161.

———. *Langalibalele and the amaHlubi Tribe: Being Remarks upon the Official Record of the Trials of the Chief, His Sons and Induna, and Other Members of the amaHlubi Tribe*. London: William Clowes & Sons, 1875. Reprinted in *Accounts and Papers of the House of Commons: 1875*, Vol. 12 (C. 1141). London: British House of Commons, 1875.

———. *Ten Weeks in Natal: A Journal of a First Tour of Visitation among the Colonists and Zulu Kafirs of Natal*. Cambridge, UK: Macmillan, 1855.

———. *Three Native Accounts of the Visit of the Bishop of Natal in September and October, 1859, to Umpande, King of the Zulus: With Explanatory Notes and a Literal Translation and a Glossary of All the Zulu Words Employed in the Same: Designed for the Use of Students of the Zulu Language*. 3rd ed. Pietermaritzburg, South Africa: Vause & Slatter, 1901.

———. "William, the Kafir Teacher." *The Mission Field* 2 (1857): 150–53.

———. Preface to the Second Edition. 1878. In *Zulu-English Dictionary*, 4th ed., viii–xiii.

———. *Zulu-English Dictionary*. 4th ed. N.p., Natal: Vause & Slatter, 1905.

Comaroff, Jean, and John Comaroff. *Of Revelation and Revolution: Christianity, Colonialism, and Consciousness in South Africa*. Vol. 1. Chicago: University of Chicago Press, 1991.

Conrath, Philippe. *Johnny Clegg: La passion zoulou*. Paris: Seghers, 1988.
Coplan, David B. *In Township Tonight! South Africa's Black City Music and Theatre*. 2nd ed. Chicago: University of Chicago Press, 2008.
———. "A Terrible Commitment: Balancing the Tribes in South African National Culture." In *Perilous States: Conversations on Culture, Politics, and Nation*, edited by George E. Marcus, 305–58. Chicago: University of Chicago Press, 1993.
Derrida, Jacques. "Force of Law: The 'Mystical Foundation of Authority.'" Translated by Mary Quaintance. *Cardozo Law Review* 11.5/6 (1990): 921–1045.
———. *Monolingualism of the Other; or, The Prosthesis of Origin*. Translated by Patrick Mensah. Stanford, CA: Stanford University Press, 1998.
———. "Shibboleth: For Paul Celan." In *Sovereignties in Question: The Poetics of Paul Celan*, edited by Thomas Dutoit and Outi Pasanen, 1–64. New York: Fordham University Press, 2005.
Derrida, Jacques, and Safaa Fathy. *Tourner les mots: Au bord d'un film*. Paris: Galilée, 2000.
Dlamini, Jacob. *Native Nostalgia*. Auckland Park, South Africa: Jacana, 2009.
Doke, C. M., and D. T. Cole. *Contributions to the History of Bantu Linguistics*. Johannesburg: Witwatersrand University Press, 1961.
Doke, C. M., D.M. Malcolm, J.M.A. Sikakana, and B.W. Vilakazi. *English-Zulu, Zulu-English Dictionary*. 1953, 1958. Combined ed. Johannesburg: Witwatersrand University Press, 1990.
Dubow, Saul. *Scientific Racism in Modern South Africa*. Cambridge, UK: Cambridge University Press, 1995.
Fabian, Johannes. *Language and Colonial Power: The Appropriation of Swahili in the Former Belgian Congo, 1880–1938*. Cambridge, UK: Cambridge University Press, 1986.
Frederikse, Julie. *David Webster*. Cape Town: Maskew Miller Longman, 1998.
———. *None but Ourselves: Masses vs. Media in the Making of Zimbabwe*. Johannesburg: Ravan Press, 1982.
Freud, Sigmund. *The Standard Edition of the Complete Psychological Works of Sigmund Freud*. Edited by James Strachey. London: Hogarth Press, 1953–1974. 24 vols.
Fuze, Magema M. *Abantu abamnyama lapa bavela ngakona*. Pietermaritzburg, South Africa: City Printing Works, 1922.
———. *The Black People and Whence They Came: A Zulu View*. Translated by H. C. Lugg. Edited by A. T. Cope. Pietermaritzburg, South Africa: University of Natal Press / Durban, South Africa: Killie Campbell Africana Library, 1979.
Gilmour, Rachael. *Grammars of Colonialism: Representing Languages in Colonial South Africa*. Basingstoke, UK: Palgrave Macmillan, 2006.
———. "'A Nice Derangement of Epitaphs': Missionary Language-Learning in Mid-Nineteenth Century Natal." *Journal of Southern African Studies* 33.3 (2007): 521–38.
Gordin, Jeremy. *Zuma: A Biography*. Johannesburg: Jonathan Ball, 2008.
Gqola, Pumla Dineo. "Brutal Inheritances: Echoes, Negrophobia and Masculinist Violence." In *Go Home or Die Here*, edited by Hassim et al., 209–22.
Gunner, Liz, "Jacob Zuma, the Social Body, and the Unruly Power of Song." *African Affairs* 108/430 (2008): 27–48.
———. ed. and trans. *The Man of Heaven and the Beautiful Ones of God: Isaiah Shembe and the Nazareth Church / Umuntu wasezulwini nabantu abahle bakaNkulunkulu:*

Isiah Shembe neBandla lamaNazaretha. Pietermaritzburg, South Africa: University of KwaZulu-Natal Press, 2004.

Gunner, Liz, and Mafika Gwala, ed. and trans. *Musho! Zulu Popular Praises*. East Lansing: Michigan State University Press, 1991.

Guy, Jeff. "Class, Imperialism and Literary Criticism: William Ngidi, John Colenso and Matthew Arnold." *Journal of Southern African Studies* 23. 2 (1997): 219–41.

———. "The Colenso Daughters: Three Women Confront Imperialism." In *The Eye of the Storm: Bishop John William Colenso and the Crisis of Biblical Inspiration*, edited by Jonathan Draper, 345–63. New York: T & T Clark International, 2003.

———. *The Destruction of the Zulu Kingdom: The Civil War in Zululand, 1879–1884*. London: Longman, 1979.

———. *The Heretic: A Study of the Life of John William Colenso, 1814–1883*. Johannesburg: Ravan Press / Pietermaritzburg, South Africa: University of Natal Press, 1983.

———. *Theophilus Shepstone and the Forging of Natal: African Autonomy and Settler Colonialism in the Making of Traditional Authority*. Pietermaritzburg, South Africa: University of KwaZulu-Natal Press, 2013.

———. *The View across the River: Harriette Colenso and the Zulu Struggle against Imperialism*. Cape Town: David Philip, 2001.

Hamilton, Carolyn. *Terrific Majesty: The Powers of Shaka Zulu and the Limits of Historical Invention*. Cambridge, MA: Harvard University Press, 1998.

Hamilton, Carolyn, and John Wright. "The Making of the AmaLala: Ethnicity, Ideology and Relations of Subordination in a Precolonial Context." *South African Historical Journal* 22.1 (1990): 3–23.

Harries, Patrick. "Imagery, Symbolism and Tradition in a South African Bantustan: Mangosuthu Buthelezi, Inkatha, and Zulu History." *History and Theory* 32.4 (1993): 105–25.

———. "The Roots of Ethnicity: Discourse and the Politics of Language Construction in South-East Africa." *African Affairs* 87/347 (1988): 25–52.

———. *Work, Culture, and Identity: Migrant Laborers in Mozambique and South Africa, c. 1860–1910*. Portsmouth, NH: Heinemann / Johannesburg: Witwatersrand University Press / London: James Currey, 1994.

Hassim, Shireen, Tawana Kupe, and Eric Worby, eds. *Go Home or Die Here: Violence, Xenophobia and the Reinvention of Difference in South Africa*. Johannesburg: Wits University Press, 2008.

Hook, Derek. *(Post)apartheid Conditions: Psychoanalysis and Social Formation*. Basingstoke, UK: Palgrave Macmillan, 2013.

Hopkin-Jenkins, K. *Basic Bantu*. Pietermaritzburg, South Africa: Shuter & Shooter, [1948].

Hunter, Mark. *Love in the Time of AIDS: Inequality, Gender, and Rights in South Africa*. Bloomington: Indiana University Press, 2010.

Ipi Ntombi—Original Cast Recording. Compact disc with insert. Gallo: South Africa, 2002.

Jeater, Diana. "Speaking like a Native: Vernacular Languages and the State in Southern Rhodesia, 1890–1935." *Journal of African History* 42.3 (2001): 449–68.

Kalahari Surfers: Vol. 1. The Eighties. Compact disc with insert. London: ReR, n.d.

Kavanagh, Robert Mshengu. *South African People's Plays: Ons Phola Hi: Plays by Gibson Kente, Credo Mutwa, Mthuli Shezi and Workshop '71*. London: Heinemann, 1981.

———. *Theatre and Cultural Struggle in South Africa*. London: Zed Books, 1985.
Khumalo, Vukile. "The Class of 1856 and the Politics of Cultural Production(s) in the Emergence of Ekukhanyeni, 1855–1910." In *The Eye of the Storm: Bishop John William Colenso and the Crisis of Biblical Inspiration*, edited by Jonathan Draper, 207–41. New York: T & T Clark International, 2003.
Klein, Melanie. *Envy and Gratitude and Other Works, 1946–1963*. London: Hogarth Press, 1975.
———. *Love, Guilt and Reparation, and Other Works, 1921–1945*. London: Hogarth Press, 1975.
Kozain, Rustum. "Moedertang." *LitNet Seminar Room*. October 19, 2005. http://www.oulitnet.co.za/seminarroom/kozain_moedertang.asp.
Krog, Antjie. *Begging to Be Black*. Cape Town: Random House Struik, 2009.
Krog, Antjie, Nosisi Mpolweni, and Kopano Ratele. *There Was This Goat: Investigating the Truth Commission Testimony of Notrose Nobomvu Konile*. Pietermaritzburg, South Africa: University of KwaZulu-Natal Press, 2009.
Kruger, Loren. *The Drama of South Africa: Plays, Pageants and Publics since 1910*. New York: Routledge, 1999.
Lazar, John. "Verwoerd Versus the 'Visionaries': The South African Bureau of Racial Affairs (SABRA) and Apartheid, 1948–1961." In *Apartheid's Genesis, 1935–1962*, edited by Philip Bonner, Peter Delius, and Deborah Posel, 362–92. Johannesburg: Ravan Press and Witwatersrand University Press, 1993.
Lindfors, Bernth, ed. *Africans on Stage: Studies in Ethnological Show Business*. Bloomington: Indiana University Press, 1999.
Lloyd, B. G. *Kitchen-Kafir Grammar and Vocabulary*. 6th ed. N.p., South Africa: Central News Agency, 1944.
Mafeje, Archie. "The Role of the Bard in a Contemporary African Community." *Journal of African Languages* 6.3 (1967): 193–223.
Mager, Anne Kelk. *Gender and the Making of a South African Bantustan: A Social History of the Ciskei, 1945–1959*. Portsmouth, NH: Heinemann, 1999.
Mahoney, Michael R. *The Other Zulus: The Spread of Zulu Ethnicity in Colonial South Africa*. Durham, NC: Duke University Press, 2012.
Mandela, Nelson. *Long Walk to Freedom*. Boston: Little, Brown, 1994.
Maré, Gerhard, and Georgina Hamilton. *An Appetite for Power: Buthelezi's Inkatha and South Africa*. Johannesburg: Ravan Press / Bloomington: Indiana University Press, 1987.
Marks, Shula. *The Ambiguities of Dependence in South Africa: Class, Nationalism, and the State in Twentieth-Century Natal*. Baltimore: Johns Hopkins University Press, 1986.
———. "Harriette Colenso and the Zulus, 1874–1913." *Journal of African History* 4.3 (1963): 403–11.
———. *Reluctant Rebellion: The 1906–1908 Disturbances in Natal*. Oxford: Clarendon Press, 1970.
Mchunu, Mxolisi. "A Modern Coming of Age: Zulu Manhood, Domestic Work and the 'Kitchen Suit.'" In *Zulu Identities*, edited by Carton et al., 573–82.
Memela, Volovolo. "Abantu abafunde ukubekezela abanye njengokuthanda kwabo amaselula" [Let people learn to be patient with others, just as they love their cellphones]. *Isolezwe*, July 14, 2010: 10.

———. "Amakhansela kumele athengele uVolos unyanyavu lwemoto" [The councilors should buy Volos a fancy car]. *Isolezwe*, February 6, 2008: 8.

———. "AmaNu kade ngawatshela ukuthi akunikelwa esontweni ngemali yokuqwayiza" [For a long time I have been telling the Babies that prostitution money is not contributed in church]. *Isolezwe*, May 19, 2010: 10.

———. "Inkosi yasePhoyinti isinenduna ezinze eNew York, kwelaseMelika" [The Chief of The Point now has an induna who is settled in New York, in America]. *Isolezwe*, February 2, 2011: 10.

———. "Kuyaxaka ukuthi ngithi ngiyinkosi yasePhoyinti kodwa ngingathintwa uma kukhulunywa ngabantu bami" [It is confusing that I am Chief of The Point but I am not contacted when my people are spoken about]. *Isolezwe*, June 3, 2009.

———. "UJabu Pule ugeqa amagula ngezintombi, utshwala nezidakamizwa" [Jabu Pule reveals all about girls, beer, and drugs]. *Isolezwe*, January 22, 2003: 9.

———. "Ukuba kuya ngezifiso zenkosi yasePhoyinti ngabe uKhozi neGagasi kuyahlanganiswa" [If it were according to the wishes of the Chief of The Point, Ukhozi and Gagasi would be merged]. *Isolezwe*, April 2, 2008: 10.

———. "UMkhandlu ungakhuluma kanjani ngezindaba ezithinta omahosha ungayithintanga inkosi yabo?" [How can the city council speak about matters affecting prostitutes without having contacted their chief?]. *Isolezwe*, July 16, 2008: 8.

Mesthrie, Rajend. "The Origins of Fanagalo." *Journal of Pidgin and Creole Languages* 4.2 (1989): 211–40.

Miners' Companion in Zulu: For the Use of Miners on the Witwatersrand Gold Mines: Issued by the Prevention of Accidents Committee of the Rand Mutual Assurance Co., Ltd. Johannesburg: Argus, 1920.

Miners' Dictionary English—Fanakalo / Woordeboek vir Mynwerkers Afrikaans—Fanakalo. N.p., South Africa: Mine Safety Division of the Chamber of Mines of South Africa, 1985.

Modisane, Bloke. *Blame Me on History*. London: Thames & Hudson, 1963.

Mokoena, Hlonipha. *Magema Fuze: The Making of a Kholwa Intellectual*. Pietermaritzburg, South Africa: University of KwaZulu-Natal Press, 2011.

Morphet, Tony. "Alan Paton: The Honour of Meditation." *English in Africa* 10.2 (1983): 1–10.

Motsei, Mmatshilo. *The Kanga and the Kangaroo Court: Reflections on the Rape Trial of Jacob Zuma*. Auckland Park, South Africa: Jacana, 2007.

Mshengu, "Where Are the Girls? (or Iph' intombi?)." *S'ketsh*, Summer 1974/75: 9–11.

Mtshali, Fraser. "Akakukhumbuli okuningi umama" [Mother does not remember much]. *UmAfrika*, March 17–23, 2006: 6.

———. "Alindwe ngengoma amazwi amnandi" [Sweet words awaited by song]. *UmAfrika*, May 12–18, 2006: 9, 14.

———. "Isiyolala ibonene kwelikaMsholozi" [Judge is now going to sleep and be face-to-face with the case of Umsholozi]. *UmAfrika*, May 5–11, 2006: 5.

———. "Kuqala eyokugwema ibhokisi kuZuma" [It begins, the matter with Zuma avoiding the witness box]. *UmAfrika*, March 24–30, 2006: 5.

———. "Umzuzu nomzuzu elawini likaZuma" [Minute-by-minute in Zuma's guest room]. *UmAfrika*, March 10–16, 2006: 4–5.

———. "UZuma uchaza okwenzeka ngesingaye" [Zuma explains what happened according to him]. *UmAfrika*, April 7–13, 2006: 4–6.

Mtshali-Jones, Thembi, and Yael Farber. *A Woman in Waiting*. In Yael Farber, *Theatre as Witness: Three Testimonial Plays from South Africa: In Collaboration with and Based on the Lives of the Original Performers*, 30–85. London: Oberon, 2008.

Mzala. *Gatsha Buthelezi: Chief with a Double Agenda*. London: Zed Books, 1988.

Ndebele, Njabulo. "The English Language and Social Change in South Africa." In *South African Literature and Culture: Rediscovery of the Ordinary*, 98–116. Manchester: Manchester University Press, 1994.

Ndlovu, Nosimilo, "The 21st-Century Pencil Test." *Mail & Guardian*, May 24, 2008.

Neocosmos, Michael. *From "Foreign Natives" to "Native Foreigners": Explaining Xenophobia in Post-Apartheid South Africa: Citizenship and Nationalism, Identity and Politics*. 2nd ed. Dakar, Senegal: CODESRIA, 2010.

Ngũgĩ wa Thiong'o, "The Language of African Literature." In *Decolonising the Mind: The Politics of Language in African Literature*, 4–33. London: James Currey, 1986.

Ngwane, Nkosinathi I. *Ngicela uxolo*. 2nd ed. Pietermaritzburg, South Africa: New Dawn Publishers, 2006.

Nhlapo, Jacob. *Bantu Babel: Will the Bantu Languages Live?* Cape Town: African Bookman, 1944.

Nieftagodien, Noor. "Xenophobia's Local Genesis: Historical Constructions of Insiders and the Politics of Exclusion in Alexandra Township." In *Exorcising the Demons within: Xenophobia, Violence and Statecraft in Contemporary South Africa*, edited by Loren B. Landau, 109–34. Johannesburg: Wits University Press, 2011.

Norval, Aletta J. *Deconstructing Apartheid Discourse*. New York: Verso, 1996.

Ntuli, D.B.Z. *Woza nendlebe*. Pietermaritzburg, South Africa: Shuter & Shooter, 1988.

Nxumalo, O.E.H.M. "Izinselelo zesiZulu esiyingcwengwa [sic]" [Challenges of refined Zulu]. *Ilanga*, April 14–16, 2008: 5.

———. "Izinselelo zesiZulu esiyingcwenga (Isigaba sesibili)" [Challenges of refined Zulu (Part two)]. *Ilanga*, April 28–30, 2008: 5.

———. "Izinselelo zesiZulu esiyingcwenga (Isiqephu sesithathu)" [Challenges of refined Zulu (Part three)]. *Ilanga*, May 5–7, 2008: 5.

———. "Ukuqhubukusha abantu bokufika" [Elbowing out immigrants]. *Ilanga*, May 26–28, 2008: 5

———. "Ukuqhubukusha abantu bokufika (Isigaba sesibili)" [Elbowing out immigrants (Part two)]. *Ilanga*, June 9–11, 2008: 5

Nyembezi, C. L. Sibusiso. *Inkinsela yaseMgungundlovu*. Pietermaritzburg, South Africa: Shuter & Shooter, 1961.

———. *Learn More Zulu*. Pietermaritzburg, South Africa: Shuter & Shooter, 1970.

———. *Learn Zulu*. Pietermaritzburg, South Africa: Shuter & Shooter, 1957.

———. *Mntanami! Mntanami!* Johannesburg: Afrikaanse Pers-Boekhandel, 1950.

———. *My Child! My Child!* Translated by Daniel P. Kunene. Cape Town: Maskew Miller Longman, 2010.

———. *A Review of Zulu Literature*. Pietermaritzburg, South Africa: University of Natal Press, 1961.

———. *The Rich Man of Pietermaritzburg*. Translated by Sandile Ngidi. Laverstock, UK: Aflame Books, 2008.

———. *Ubudoda abukhulelwa*. 1953. Johannesburg: Afrikaanse Pers-Boekhandel, n.d.

———. *Zulu Proverbs*. Johannesburg: Witwatersrand University Press, 1954.

Omer-Cooper, J. D. *The Zulu Aftermath: A Nineteenth-Century Revolution in Bantu Africa*. Evanston, IL: Northwestern University Press, 1966.

Paton, Alan. *Cry, the Beloved Country*. 1948. New York: Scribner, 1987.

———. *Lafa elihle kakhulu*. Translated by Sibusiso Nyembezi. 1957. 3rd ed. Pietermaritzburg, South Africa: Shuter & Shooter, 1995.

The Perfect Storm: The Realities of Xenophobia in Contemporary South Africa. Cape Town: Southern African Migration Project, 2008.

Phuzekhemisi noKhethani. *Imbizo*. CDTIG 456, compact disc. South Africa: RPM Records, 1994.

Procopius, *Secret History*. Translated by Richard Atwater. 1927. Ann Arbor: University of Michigan Press, 1961.

Ramphele, Mamphela. "A Mirror Image of Our Society." *Star*, May 22, 2008: 17.

Rees, Wyn, ed. *Colenso Letters from Natal*. Pietermaritzburg, South Africa: Shuter & Shooter, 1958.

Report of the Commission on Traditional Leadership Disputes and Claims. Pretoria: Republic of South Africa, 2010.

Report of Proceedings of Zulu Orthography Conference Held at Durban, Natal, South Africa, May 29, 30, 31, 1907. Pietermaritzburg, South Africa: P. Davis & Sons, [1911].

Reyher, Rebecca Hourwich. *Zulu Woman: The Life Story of Christina Sibiya*. 1948. New York: Feminist Press, 1999.

Robins, Steven. "Sexual Politics and the Zuma Rape Trial." *Journal of Southern African Studies* 34:2 (2008): 411–27.

Runciman, W. G. *Relative Deprivation and Social Justice: A Study of Attitudes to Social Inequality in Twentieth-Century England*. Berkeley: University of California Press, 1966.

Samuelson, R.C.A. *Long, Long Ago*. Durban, South Africa: Knox, 1929.

Sanders, Mark. *Ambiguities of Witnessing: Law and Literature in the Time of a Truth Commission*. Stanford, CA: Stanford University Press, 2007.

———. *Complicities: The Intellectual and Apartheid*. Durham, NC: Duke University Press, 2002.

———. "Modisane's Weddings." *Social Dynamics* 36.3 (2010): 479–82.

———. "Undone by Laughter." *Safundi* 10.3 (2009): 353–59.

Simons, H. J. *African Women: Their Legal Status in South Africa*. Evanston, IL: Northwestern University Press, 1968.

Sithole, Jabulani. "Preface: Zuluness in South Africa: From 'Struggle' Debate to Democratic Transformation." In *Zulu Identities*, edited by Carton et al., xv-xxvi.

Slosberg, Bertha. *Pagan Tapestry*. London: Rich & Cowan, 1940.

Small, Adam. *Sê Sjibbolet*. Johannesburg: Afrikaanse Pers-Boekhandel, 1963.

Soga, Tiyo. "Mission People and Red People." 1864. In *The Journal and Collected Writings of the Reverend Tiyo Soga*, edited by Donovan Williams, 175–77. Cape Town: A. A. Balkema, 1983.

Spivak, Gayatri Chakravorty. "Interview with Gayatri Chakravorty Spivak." In Mark Sanders, *Gayatri Chakravorty Spivak: Live Theory*, 104–24. London: Continuum, 2006.

———. "Righting Wrongs." *South Atlantic Quarterly* 103.2–3 (2004): 523–81.

Steenkamp, W. P. *Is the South-West African Herero Committing Race Suicide?* Cape Town: Unie-Volkspers, 1944.

Steinberg, Jonny. *A Man of Good Hope*. New York: Knopf, 2014.
Stuart, J., ed. *Zulu Orthography: Being Some Account of the Proceedings of the Zulu Orthography Conference Held in Pietermaritzburg in 1906, Especially in Regard to Speeches Delivered, Rules Submitted, Etc., to Which Is Added the Set of Rules Recently Passed (March, 1907) by the Zulu Orthography Committee*. Durban, South Africa, 1907.
Suttner, Raymond. "The Jacob Zuma Rape Trial: Power and African National Congress (ANC) Masculinities." *NORA—Nordic Journal of Feminist and Gender Research* 17.3 (2009): 222–36.
Thornberry, Elizabeth. "Defining Crime through Punishment: Sexual Assault in the Eastern Cape, c.1835–1900." *Journal of Southern African Studies* 37.3 (2011): 415–30.
Truth and Reconciliation Commission of South Africa Report. 7 vols. Cape Town: Truth and Reconciliation Commission, 1998–2003.
Vandenbroucke, Russell. "South African Blacksploitation." *Yale/Theatre* 8 (1976): 68–71.
Vetten, Lisa. "Violence against Women in South Africa." In *State of the Nation: South Africa 2007*, edited by Sakhela Buhlungu, John Daniel, Roger Southall, and Jessica Lutchman, 425–47. Cape Town: HSRC Press, 2007.
Vinson, Robert, and Robert Edgar, "Zulus, African Americans and the African Diaspora." In *Zulu Identities*, edited by Carton et al., 240–49.
Waetjen, Thembisa, and Gerhard Maré. "Tradition's Desire: The Politics of Culture in the Rape Trial of Jacob Zuma." *Concerned Africa Scholars Bulletin* 84 (2010): 52–61.
Wright, John. "A. T. Bryant and the 'Lala.'" *Journal of Southern African Studies* 38.2 (2012): 355–68.
———. "Politics, Ideology, and the Invention of the 'Nguni.'" In *Resistance and Ideology in Settler Societies*, edited by Tom Lodge, 96–118. Johannesburg: Ravan Press, 1986.
———. "Rediscovering the Ndwandwe Kingdom." In *500 Years Rediscovered: Southern African Precedents and Prospects*, edited by Natalie Swanepoel, Amanda Esterhuysen, and Philip Bonner, 217–38. Johannesburg: Wits University Press, 2008.
———. "Reflections on the Politics of Being 'Zulu.'" In *Zulu Identities*, edited by Carton et al., 35–43.
———. "Turbulent Times: Political Transformations in the North and East, 1760s–1830s." In *The Cambridge History of South Africa*. Vol. 1, *From Early Times to 1885*, edited by Carolyn Hamilton, Bernard K. Mbenga, and Robert Ross, 211–52. Cambridge, UK: Cambridge University Press, 2010.
Wright, John, and Carolyn Hamilton, "Traditions and Transformations: The Phongolo-Mzimkhulu Region in the Late Eighteenth and Early Nineteenth Centuries." In *Natal and Zululand: From Earliest Times to 1910*, edited by Andrew Duminy and Bill Guest, 49–82. Pietermaritzburg, South Africa: University of Natal Press / Shuter & Shooter, 1989.
Zungu, Phyllis Jane. "The Status of Zulu in KwaZulu-Natal." In *Multilingualism in a Multicultural Context: Case Studies on South Africa and Western Europe*, edited by Guus Extra and Jeanne Maartens, 37–49. Tilburg, Netherlands: Tilburg University Press, 1998.

Index

abaqulusi, 95, 171n129
Abrahams, Peter, 66
Adendorff, Ralph, 25, 34
African National Congress (ANC), 21, 72, 88, 98–99, 109–10, 114, 117, 119, 129; Youth League of, 99, 119
Afrikaans, 9, 23–28, 61, 69–70, 119, 123–24, 126, 135, 166n32, 178n41, 180n82
Afrikaner nationalism, 8, 20, 126, 134
Aitken-Cade, S.E., *So! You Want to Learn the Language!*, 34–35
Alexandra, 115–19
Amakwerekwere, 12, 116
Amaqongqo, 5, 136
apartheid, 8–10, 16, 21, 23, 26–30, 32, 38, 43, 46, 76–77, 84–87, 109, 116, 128–29
appropriation, 9, 12, 22, 66, 81. *See also* property
Asmal, Kader, 131, 136, 179n64

Baartman, Sara, 92
Bakhtin, Mikhail, 140
Bantu Education, 26–28, 34
Bantu languages, 22–28, 32
Benjamin, Walter, 7, 57
Bhaca, 81–83, 151n20
Bhambatha Rebellion, 20
Bhudu, Golden Miles, 112
Black Consciousness, 76
Blatter, Sepp, 137
Bleek, Wilhelm, 151n21, 155n63
Blood River, battle of, 8, 19, 88–89, 169n94
bobbemeises, 4, 97
Bold, J.D., *Dictionary, Grammar and Phrase-Book of Fanagalo (Kitchen Kafir)*, 23–24, 27, 29, 158n87
Botha, P.W., 33
breast, 3, 65–66, 127; as fetish, 140; as source of language, 3, 92–93, 114, 123, 126, 178n41; as sexual object, 93; as spectacle, 79, 92
breastfeeding, 93–94
breast milk, 94–95, 171n129
Brooke of Borneo, 16
Brown, David, 24, 40
Brusciotto, Giacinto, 23, 155n63
Bryant, A.T., 19
Buthelezi, Mangosuthu, 8, 21, 114, 132–33

Campbell, Roy, 168n80
Cape Town, 29, 32–33, 36, 42, 76, 115, 119
carnivalesque, 114, 140
castration, 89, 91, 98, 113
cattle, 35, 38, 43, 50, 54, 67–68, 105–6, 108–9
censorship, 44, 54, 71, 89
Cetshwayo, 8, 15–16, 19–20, 82, 89, 149n5, 152n25, 166n41
Chief of The Point. *See* Memela, Volovolo
Chilapalapa, 35. *See also* Fanagalo, Kitchen Kafir
Chinese, people, 72, 131, 134
Clegg, Johnny, 11, 81–86, 95
Coetzee, J.M., 47, 57–60, 66, 87
Cole, D.T., 25–26, 34
Colenso, Harriette Emily, 14–18, 26–28, 151n21, 152nn25 and 28, 157n77
Colenso, John William, Bishop, 9, 14–19, 22, 25, 27–28, 62–63, 72, 123, 155n63, 163n63, 166n41
colonialism, 8–9, 18–20, 28, 51, 56, 89, 91, 106, 121–22, 152n28
coloureds, 25, 116, 134, 148n24, 167n41
Columbia University, 2, 30, 61, 136
Come Back, Africa (Rogosin), 61, 71
Congo, Belgian, 23, 155n65, 158n87
Congo, Democratic Republic of, 116–17
Congress of South African Trade Unions (COSATU), 99, 117, 119
corruption, 41–42, 98–99, 110, 119–21, 129
crime, 38, 51, 54–55, 69–71, 102, 105–6, 110, 127
criminal law, 106–7, 109–10

Cronjé, Geoffrey, 71, 87
Cronjé, Ina, 125–27, 136, 143
customary law, 16, 20, 105, 107–8, 152n28
Cyprian Bhekuzulu, 20–21

Daily Sun, 11
dance, 11, 75–76, 79, 81–90
De Beer, Charin, 100, 107–8, 110–12
deprivation, 46, 54, 68, 126, 129; of patrimony, 56; relative, 12, 120, 127
Derrida, Jacques, 7, 12, 75, 124
Dhlomo, H.I.E., 5, 35, 166n41
Dhlomo, R.R.R., 5, 166n41
Diepsloot, 118–19
difficulty, supposed, of Zulu, 27, 29–30, 62, 158n88
Dingane, 8, 19, 27, 89, 169n94
Dinuzulu, 16, 20, 152n21
dipping, of cattle, 43–44
District 9 (Blomkamp), 141–42
Doke, C.M., 36, 57
Drum, 60–61, 69, 71, 76
Dube, John, 21, 118, 152n21
Dunn, John, 81–82, 166n41
Durban, 5–6, 43, 45, 128–29, 138–40
Durban Point, 128–29, 138

Egnos, Bertha, 80, 89–91
Ekukhanyeni, 15–17
E'Lollipop (film), 76
Engelbrecht, J.A., 26–27
English, 4–5, 9, 14, 16–18, 23–27, 29, 38, 56–59, 63–68, 70, 80, 84–85, 92, 101–2, 105, 112, 121–25, 141–42, 155n65, 159n88, 166n32, 177n41
envy, 6, 65–66, 120, 126–27, 131, 135, 143–44
Eschen, Hedwig, 35–42, 44, 54
Evans, David, 78, 165n26
exile, political, 20, 98–99, 108, 114, 128–30, 132, 134

Fabian, Johannes, 158n87
Fanagalo, 9–11, 14–15, 22–29, 31, 34–35, 38–40, 46, 58, 64, 66, 68–70, 72, 84, 86–87, 90–91, 97, 114, 117, 125, 141. *See also* Chilapalapa, Kitchen Kafir
"Fanagalo" (song), 40, 90–91, 142
Farber, Yael, 93
feminism, 101
FESTAC (Second World Black and African Festival of Arts and Culture), 76

fetish, 73, 89, 91, 97–98, 140
fossilization, of language, 25–26, 36, 135
Freud, Sigmund, 3, 7, 30, 78, 91
Fuze, Magema, 16–17, 135, 151n20; *Abantu abamnyama lapa bavela ngakona*, 155n63
Fyn, Henry Francis, 166n40

Gauteng, 8, 115, 119
Gaza Kingdom, 132
Gazankulu, 131
Goodwill Zwelithini kaBhekuzulu, 21, 85, 121, 133, 138–39, 175n7
Gqola, Pumla, 129
gratitude, 39, 143
Grout, Lewis, Reverend, 17, 21, 150n14, 151n21
guilt, 2–3, 6–7, 11–12, 30, 51–56, 66, 70–71, 89, 94, 96, 99, 109–10
Gungunyama, 132
Guy, Jeff, 17

Haggard, H. Rider, 8, 22
Hamilton, Carolyn, 153n34
Harlem, 79
Harry the Strandloper, 19
Hawthorne, Nathaniel, 43
Herero, 38
heterosexuality, as norm, 103–4, 109, 129
HIV-AIDS, 99–100, 111
Hlubi, 16, 33
Hlubi, Makumalo, 86
Hopkin-Jenkins, K., *Basic Bantu*, 26, 34
Holgate, Kingsley, 167n42
hospitality, 5, 12, 114, 128–30, 134
houseboys, 40, 90

identification, 101; with girl, 94, 96–98; with migrant, 117–18; with "Zulu" as name of language, 97, 102, 110, 113–14; of "Zulu" and African, 9; of "Zulu" and masculinity, 11; as Zulu Boy, 72, 78, 87, 96, 102; as Zulu girl, 86–87, 168n80
Ilanga, 116, 118, 121, 127–28, 130, 132, 134, 136, 152n21
ilobolo (bridewealth), 100, 106–9
Imbali, 136
immigration policy, 116, 121, 129
"Impi" (song), 85
Indians, 9, 25, 34, 46, 69–70, 72, 95, 119, 131, 141, 148n24, 178n62
indirect rule, 16

Index • 195

Industrial and Commercial Workers' Union (ICU), 21
inhlawulo (forfeit, fine), 100, 105–10
Inkatha, 8, 20–21, 43, 118, 121
Inkatha Freedom Party, 8, 21, 72, 99, 120, 138
Ipi Tombi, 8, 11, 74–81, 86–94, 96, 113
"Ipi Tombi?" (song), 80, 91–92
Isandlwana, battle of, 8, 20, 22, 89, 166n41
isiKula, 25, 34
isiZulu, 3, 9, 11, 27, 72–73, 111, 114, 148n20, 151n20
IsiZulu soqobo, 37
Isolezwe, 47, 85, 111, 118, 136–44
izibongo, 98, 139–40, 143–44

jealousy, 11–12, 49, 65–67, 72, 83, 97, 116, 126, 135, 152n22, 167n49
Jews, 75, 82–84, 86, 92
Jim Comes to Joburg (Swanson), 40, 80, 90
Johannesburg, 2–3, 38, 40, 51–52, 55–56, 64, 67, 69–71, 75, 79–80, 82–83, 90–93, 96, 99, 115–19, 121, 124, 136
Jozini, 2, 85, 118, 121, 136
Juluka, 84–86
Justinian, 19

Kafka, Franz, 75
Kalahari Surfers, 33
Kemp, Kemp J., 100, 105, 108, 110–11
Kente, Gibson, 80–81
Kentridge, William, 66
Khumalo, people, 116
Khuzwayo, Judson, 174n78
Khwezi, 101–10, 113
Kitchen Kafir, 9, 14–15, 18, 23, 34, 57, 72, 155n65, 158n87. *See also* Chilapalapa, Fanagalo
Klein, Melanie, 3, 39, 57, 61, 65–66, 68, 94, 120, 126, 143
Kourouma, Ahmadou, 98, 182n110
Krog, Antjie, 96
Kunene, Daniel P., 52–54
KwaZulu, 8, 21
KwaZulu-Natal, 8, 21, 27, 85, 114, 118, 122–23, 132–34

Lacan, Jacques, 78
Lakier, Gail, 80
Langalibalele, 16–18
laughter, 14, 31, 39–40 , 50, 60–61, 65, 137, 140

learning, generalization of, 12, 114
Leitch, Barry, 167n42
lesbian, as sexual identity, 99, 103–4, 109–10
Limpopo, 117, 131, 133
Lloyd, B.G., *Kitchen-Kafir Grammar & Vocabulary*, 14, 29, 57, 72
load shedding, electrical, 3, 119
loan words, 18, 31, 124
Louw, N.P. van Wyk, 26, 78, 134
Luthuli, Albert, 21

Mafeje, Archie, 139–40
Mahoyiza, 16
making good. *See* reparation
Malawi, 116, 119
"Mama Tembu's Wedding" (song), 80, 89
Mandela, Nelson, 88, 97, 142
Market Theatre, 93
masculinism, 114, 129, 140
masculinity, 11, 83, 86, 98, 167n49
Matanzima, Kaiser, 33
Mbatha, Thulani, 138, 142
Mbeki, Thabo, 98–99, 114, 119–20, 129–30, 134
Mchunu, Sipho, 84–85
Memela, Volovolo, 47, 118, 136–44
Mesthrie, Rajend, 25
Mfeka, Raymond, 84
migrants, 5, 8, 11–12, 19, 22, 34–35, 40, 46, 84–85, 114–19, 124–37, 140–43
mimesis, 78, 84, 86, 89
mimicry, 12, 31, 40, 82, 91, 142
Miners' Dictionary English—Fanakalo/Woordeboek vir Mynwerkers Afrikaans—Fanakalo, 25, 72
Miners' Companion in Zulu, 23–24, 29, 72
mines, 8, 23–25, 58–60, 65–66, 80–81, 92, 132
missionaries, 9–10, 15, 17, 25–28, 36, 62–63, 72, 80, 151n21, 152n23, 157n77
Mkhize, Zweli, 99, 107–8
Mngadi, Qap's, 137, 143
Modisane, Bloke, 48, 69, 71
Moloi, Charles, 102, 106
Motsei, Mmatshilo, 101, 114
Mozambique, 46, 85–86, 118, 129, 131–34
Mpande, 17, 19, 27, 149n5, 157n83
Mpumalanga, 8, 117, 132–33
Mqhayi, S.E.K., 32, 68
Msimang, C.T., 5
Msimang, Sebastian, Reverend, 151–52n21
Mtimkulu, Abner, Reverend, 152n21

mourning, 30, 53, 71
Mshengu (aka Robert Mshengu Kavanagh, Robert McLaren), 80, 87, 90–91
Mthethwa, 123
Mthethwa Lucky Stars, 86
Mtshali, Fraser, 105–7, 111
Mtshali-Jones, Thembi, 93–94
Murray, Brett, 174n83
music, 11, 79–81, 83–86, 89–90, 131
Mzila, Charlie, 82–83
Mzilikazi, 116, 133

Nachträglichkeit, 78, 113
Natal, 8, 15–17, 19–21, 24–25, 27, 36, 42, 45, 50–51, 55, 62, 70, 122, 131
Ncome River, battle of. *See* Blood River
Ndebele, language, 22, 116, 121; people, 24, 132–33
Ndebele, Njabulo, 24, 37, 148n22
Ndwandwe, 19, 114, 132–36, 179n74
Nel, de Wet, 139, 143
New York Times, 96–97, 110, 112
"Ngeso likaVolovolo". *See* Memela, Volovolo
"Ngisika elijikayo". *See* Nxumalo, O.E.H.M.
Ngoza, 16, 62
Nguni, language group, 5, 22–24, 36; Standard 27
Ngwane, Nkosinathi I., *Ngicela uxolo*, 1, 4–7, 56
Nhlapo, Jacob, 26–27
Nhlapo Commission (Commission on Traditional Leadership Disputes and Claims), 132–33
Nico Malan Opera House, 76–77
Nietzsche, Friedrich, 43
Nkosi, Lewis, 61
noun-class system, 23–24, 28, 42, 57, 61–62, 91, 155n63
Ntuli, D.B.Z., *Ngicela uxolo*, 1, 3–4, 5, 7, 30; *Isipho sikaKhisimuzi*, 44
Nxamalala, 114
Nxumalo, Mpisane, 132
Nxumalo, Mpisane Eric, 133
Nxumalo, O.E.H.M., 11, 118, 121–36, 143, 176n25
Nyembezi, Sibusiso, 5; *Inqolobane yesizwe*, 121; *Lafa elihle kakhulu*, 10, 42, 59–70, 72, 125; *Learn More Zulu*, 10, 28–48, 49–50, 53–56, 61, 68–70, 72, 114; *Learn Zulu*, 28, 30–31, 34, 37, 39, 41; *Mntanami! Mntanami!* (My Child! My Child!), 50–56, 59, 64, 69–71, 131, 135, 162n11; *A Review of Zulu Literature*, 45; *Inkinsela yaseMgungundlovu* (The Rich Man of Pietermaritzburg), 37–38, 43, 45–46, 50; *Ubudoda abukhulelwa*, 57–58, 64, 69–71, 131; *Zulu Proverbs*, 37

One in Nine Campaign, 102
orthography, Zulu, 17, 72, 125; conferences, 28, 151n21, 152n23
ownership. *See* property

Pan-Africanism, 76, 134
paranoia, 4, 7, 10, 12, 30, 53–54, 64, 68, 83, 89, 97, 112–14, 118, 120, 125–26, 129, 135–36, 143
parody, 40, 47, 90, 116, 140–41, 174n83, 181n107
pass laws, 43–44, 51, 55
Paton, Alan, *Cry, the Beloved Country*, 10, 41–42, 51, 54–57, 59–61, 64, 67–68, 72, 83, 87. *See also,* Nyembezi, Sibusiso, *Lafa elihle kakhulu*
persecution complex, 86–87
phallus, 98, 112, 114, 174n83
Phuzekhemisi, 41
pidginization, of Zulu, 9, 15, 18, 22, 24–25, 27, 34, 46, 67, 92
Pietermaritzburg, 5, 15–16, 28, 43, 85
Plan 9 from Outer Space (Wood), 91
poverty, 38, 45–46
praise names. *See izibongo*
primal scene, 10–11, 83, 97
Procopius, 9, 19
property, 8, 12, 106, 116, 121, 129. *See also* appropriation
protest writing, 42–44, 89
proverbs, 37, 42, 137
psychoanalysis, 3, 6, 10, 83, 89, 112, 140, 143
psychopolitics, 10–11, 22, 30, 120, 127, 142
Pule, Jabu, 140
Purim, 75
purism, linguistic and cultural, 9–10, 12, 26, 28, 46, 56, 70, 72, 84, 87, 114, 121, 123–25, 128, 135, 151n20, 165n32, 177n25

Qabula, Alfred Temba, 163n68
Qwabe, 20, 123

Rabelais, François, 140
racism, 34, 134; scientific, 27

Ramphele, Mamphela, 121
rape, 11, 72, 96–114, 118, 144
Reconstruction and Development Programme (RDP), 119–20, 129
reparation, 3–4, 7, 9, 10, 12–13, 15, 17–18, 22–23, 26–30, 33, 57, 60, 63–68, 70, 83, 89, 93–94, 96–98, 101, 144; manic, 3, 67, 87, 90–91
respect (*inhlonipho, ukuhlonipha*), 38–39, 130–31, 134–35
retribution, 3, 87, 89, 169n94
Reyher, Rebecca Hourwich, 168n80
Rhodesia, 24, 35, 78, 84; Southern, 34; Northern, 155n65
rights, 12, 100, 102, 105, 112, 120, 127, 142
Roach, Archdeacon, 152n21
Robben Island, 97, 99, 112–13
Robinson Crusoe (Defoe), 24
Royal Household, Zulu, 123, 126, 134

sadism, 71
Samuelson, R.C.A., 157n77
Sand, Froma. *See* Slosberg, Bertha
satire, 11, 118, 137–38, 140, 142
Savuka, 85–86
Sea Point, 32, 35, 97
second-language acquisition, 25, 27, 61, 114, 122, 157n77, 158n88
secret, 65, 75, 82–84, 94, 101–2, 167n49
Segal, Hanna, 3
sex, 52, 71, 79, 87, 89, 93, 96–114, 129, 138, 140
sex workers, 136–42
Shaik, Schabir, 98
Shaka, 19–21, 27, 114, 116, 131–33
Shakespeare, William, 109
Shangaan, language, 117, 133; people, 119, 131–34, 152n23
Shembe, Isaiah, 169n94
Shepstone, Theophilus, 16–17, 27, 163n63, 166n41
shibboleth, 8, 11–13, 72, 115–17, 124, 143
"Shosholoza" (song), 74–75, 78, 80, 84
Shuter and Shooter, 34
Sibiya, Christina, 168n80
Sinethezekile Combined School, 2, 10, 40, 85, 141
Singana, Margaret, 80, 91
S'ketsh, 80, 91
Slosberg, Bertha, 86–87
Small, Adam, 180n82
Smith, Wilbur, 65–66

Soetwater, 119
Soga, Tiyo, Reverend, 46
Solomon kaDinuzulu, 20, 168n80
Sophiatown, 51, 54, 69, 71
Soshangane, 131–33, 179n74
Sotho, 9, 22, 27, 58, 69–70, 80, 87, 117, 123, 135
South African Broadcasting Corporation (SABC), 32, 88
South African Bureau of Racial Affairs (SABRA), 26–27
South African Communist Party (SACP), 99
South African Institute of Race Relations, 45, 90
South African Library, 29–30, 36
South African Native National Congress (SANNC), 21
Soweto uprising, 76–78, 94
Spielrein, Sabina, 147n3
Spivak, Gayatri Chakravorty, 44
Springbok Radio, 40
standardization, linguistic, 17, 22, 27–28, 123–24, 151n20, 152n23
Star, 101, 110–12, 118
stone throwing, 47–48, 50, 54–56, 69
strangers, 46, 48, 50, 55, 67, 127–28
Stuart, James, 153n34
Svevo, Italo, 48
Swahili, 155n65, 158n87
Swati, 22, 36, 123

Tarr, Wrex, 35
tekeza, 27, 72, 123
Temple Israel, 78
thefula, 27, 72, 123, 157n83
Thonga, 85, 114, 133–34
townships, 37–38, 77, 80, 118, 130, 134, 141
traders, 81, 119–20, 129, 137–38; unfair practices of, 120, 130–31, 178n62
transference, 1, 9, 49, 78, 113, 143; counter-, 49–50, 143
Transkei, 32–33, 77, 106, 139
translation, 2, 9–10, 15, 28, 44, 52, 54, 103–05, 108–09, 111–12, 121–23, 130–31, 136, 139, 176n25, 180n82; of Bible, 36; by court interpreter in *State v. Zuma*, 101–2, 105–6; of Paton's *Cry, the Beloved Country* by Nyembezi, 10, 59–68, 125; of title of *Ipi Tombi*, 11, 91–92; and "transfer," 57
Truth and Reconciliation Commission of South Africa, 93

Truth Commission Special Report, 48
Tsonga, 58, 133, 152n23
Tsotsitaal, 69, 166n32

uBumbano lwamaZwide (Unity Association of the Zwides), 133
ubuntu, 46, 72, 127, 130, 175n7
Ukhozi FM, 40, 138, 177n40
UmAfrika, 103–12, 127, 131
"Umshini wami" (song), 98, 101, 118, 171n17
United Democratic Front (UDF), 21, 117
University of Cape Town (UCT), 31, 33, 65, 117, 125
University of Fort Hare, 34, 71
University of Natal, 45
University of South Africa (UNISA), 36, 43
University of the Witwatersrand, 3, 26, 37, 85

Van der Merwe, Willem, Judge, 100–103, 111
Venda, 117
Verryn, Paul, Bishop, 117
Verwoerd, H.F., 21, 26, 32
Vilakazi, B.W., 5, 35
Visser, Nick, 65
Vladislavić, Ivan, 30
Von Trotha, Lothar, 38

"The Warrior" (song), 80, 88
Webster, David, 85–86

weddings, 80, 85, 89
Wertham, Fredric, 71
Wittgenstein, Ludwig, 67
Witwatersrand, 8, 22, 24
Woltemade, Wolraad, 19, 78
Workshop '71, 165n32
World Cup, soccer, 136–38, 141–42, 177n25
Wright, John, 134, 153n34

xenophobia, 8, 11–12, 114, 115–21, 127–37, 140–43, 175n7
Xhosa, 9, 16, 22, 24, 27–28, 31–33, 36, 62, 80–81, 87, 91, 121, 123–24, 139, 151n20

Zambia, 84, 155n65
Zapiro, 100, 137
Ziervogel, D., 26–27
Zimbabwe, 99, 109–10, 115–16, 118, 129, 132, 134
Zola (Bonginkosi Dlamini), 46
"Zulu," as cultural identity, 19; as fetish, 73; as privileged or phallic signifier, 8–9, 11, 21, 72, 83–84, 87, 92, 98, 109, 112, 114
Zulu Dawn, 45
Zulu Kingdom, 17, 19–21, 123, 133; as promotional brand, 21, 89
Zululand, 8, 17, 19–21, 40, 58, 87, 114
Zuma, Jacob, 11, 72, 96–114, 117–19, 129, 134, 137, 144

Translation / Transnation
Series Editor Emily Apter

Writing Outside the Nation by Azade Seyhan

The Literary Channel: The Inter-National Invention of the Novel edited by Margaret Cohen and Carolyn Dever

Ambassadors of Culture: The Transamerican Origins of Latino Writing by Kirsten Silva Gruesz

Experimental Nations: Or, the Invention of the Maghreb by Réda Bensmaïa

What Is World Literature? by David Damrosch

The Portable Bunyan: A Transnational History of "The Pilgrim's Progress" by Isabel Hofmeyr

We the People of Europe? Reflections on Transnational Citizenship by Étienne Balibar

Nation, Language, and the Ethics of Translation edited by Sandra Bermann and Michael Wood

Utopian Generations: The Political Horizon of Twentieth-Century Literature by Nicholas Brown

Guru English: South Asian Religion in a Cosmopolitan Language by Srinivas Aravamudan

Poetry of the Revolution: Marx, Manifestos, and the Avant-Gardes by Martin Puchner

The Translation Zone: A New Comparative Literature by Emily Apter

In Spite of Partition: Jews, Arabs, and the Limits of Separatist Imagination by Gil Z. Hochberg

The Princeton Sourcebook in Comparative Literature: From the European Enlightenment to the Global Present edited by David Damrosch, Natalie Melas, and Mbongiseni Buthelezi

The Spread of Novels: Translation and Prose Fiction in the Eighteenth Century by Mary Helen McMurran

The Event of Postcolonial Shame by Timothy Bewes

The Novel and the Sea by Margaret Cohen

Hamlet's Arab Journey: Shakespeare's Prince and Nasser's Ghost
by Margaret Litvin

Archives of Authority by Andrew N. Rubin

Security: Politics, Humanity, and the Philology of Care
by John T. Hamilton

Dictionary of Untranslatables: A Philosophical Lexicon edited
by Barbara Cassin

Learning Zulu: A Secret History of Language in South Africa
by Mark Sanders

In the Shadow of World Literature: Sites of Reading in Colonial Egypt,
by Michael Allan

GPSR Authorized Representative: Easy Access System Europe - Mustamäe tee
50, 10621 Tallinn, Estonia, gpsr.requests@easproject.com

www.ingramcontent.com/pod-product-compliance
Lightning Source LLC
Chambersburg PA
CBHW020839160426
43192CB00007B/712